Carrying the Banner

Carrying the Banner
Women, Leadership and Activism in Australia

Joan Eveline and Lorraine Hayden (eds)

University of Western Australia Press

First published in 1999 by
University of Western Australia Press
Nedlands, Western Australia, 6907

This book is copyright. Apart from any fair dealing for the purposes of private study, research, criticism, or review, as permitted under the Copyright Act 1968, no part may be reproduced by any process without written permission. Enquiries should be made to the publisher.

Copyright © Contributors 1999

National Library of Australia
Cataloguing-in-Publication entry:

Carrying the banner: women, leadership and activism in Australia.

Bibliography.
ISBN 1 876268 30 1.

1. Feminism — Australia. 2. Leadership in women – Australia. 3. Women — Australia — Social conditions. I. Eveline, Joan, 1940– . II. Hayden, Lorraine.

305.420994

Produced by Benchmark Publications Management, Melbourne
Consultant editor: Deborah Taylor, Perth
Series design by
Robyn Mundy Design, Perth
Cover design and typesetting by
Derrick I Stone Design, Lilydale
Typeset in Garamond
Printed by Frank Daniels, Perth

COVER: Details of banners created for the Women's Electoral Lobby Centenary of Suffrage Banner Project by; Yanchep Senior High School; Nardine Women's Refuge; Fitzroy Crossing Senior High School; the Mid West Domestic Violence Action Group; Ishar Multicultural Centre for Women's Health; the Salt Lakes Ottey Family and Neighborhood Centre; the New Opportunities for Women Class, West Coast College of Tafe, Carine Campus; the Community and Public Sector Union; Mercedes College; Ballajura Community College; and the Latin American Women's Group from Women's Health Care House.

CONTENTS

Acknowledgements ix

Introduction 1
JOAN EVELINE

Regenerating Politics 15
JOAN WILLIAMS	Women Carrying Banners	16
PATRICIA GILES	One Generation after Another	32
DAME RACHEL CLELAND	Across the Decades	45
CARMEN LAWRENCE	In Labor: An Interview	56
JO VALLENTINE	A Tapestry of Passion and Peace	69

My Place, My Work 81
JOSIE BOYLE	The Colour of Stories	82
SHIRLEY DE LA HUNTY	Making Strides	91
HELEN CREED	Keeping the Flame Burning	101
MARY PATETSOS	An Outsider on the Inside	111
LYN SHERWOOD	Industrious Women	119
DEBRA SHORTER	Reinventing Leadership	127

CONTENTS

Professing Difference   **135**
FAY GALE	Taking on the Academy	136
ANTOINETTE KENNEDY	A Virus in the Priesthood	145
DONELLA CASPERSZ	Juggling Activism and Leadership	153
ANN GHISALBERTI	Science, Books and Me	160
PATRICIA CRAWFORD	Not an Ivory Tower: Learning and Teaching in a University	168
VAL MARSDEN	Doing It Differently	177

Heart Dreaming   **187**
JOAN WINCH	A Letter to Lillian	188
BARBARA BUICK	Public Bisnis, Private Bisnis	197
MALI VALAMANESH	Freedom and Loss: An Iranian Story	207
VERONICA BRADY	It's All in the Unfolding	217
ANNIE GOLDFLAM	Transformative Moments	224

Suggestions for Further Reading   233

ACKNOWLEDGEMENTS

This book was prompted by intellectual discussions about West Australian women's citizenship in the History Department at The University of Western Australia (UWA). At the time the question of whether women's contributions to academic life warranted special support was being widely debated throughout the university and in the History Department in particular. Whenever those discussions seemed to disregard the gender dynamics of citizenship and leadership we were reinforced in our belief that an anthology of, and by, West Australian women leaders was long overdue.

There were many people at UWA who encouraged this project. In particular, we thank the Deputy Vice-Chancellor Alan Robson who saw the book as a significant contribution to West Australian women's recent history and gave generous support with publication costs. Fay Gale and Trish Crawford helped with ideas for potential contributors in the early planning, while Linda Key gave valuable legal advice on some of the chapters.

Generous support came too from sources outside UWA. Our thanks to the Centre for Research for Women, an inter-university body, for their publication grant, and to Val Marsden and Annie

ACKNOWLEDGEMENTS

Goldflam who helped compile the first list of potential contributors. Harry Phillips of Edith Cowan University found some essential Hansard material at very short notice while Susan Magarey of the University of Adelaide gave emotional support and valuable advice on content. The Women's Electoral Lobby championed the theme of the book by organizing the Suffrage Banner Project, which celebrates women's contributions to West Australian life, for the centenary of women's suffrage in 1999.

A very special thank you to the women who contributed to this book, some by writing their own chapters and others by being willing to be interviewed. All gave generously of their time, their advice and their friendship, while demonstrating through their stories the spectrum of passion and vision that shapes women's lives.

We are grateful to the anonymous reader whose excellent advice on the manuscript we have followed to the best of our ability. Our thanks to Jenny Gregory and Anthea Wu for their faith in the project, and to Deborah Taylor for copyediting.

We particularly wish to thank each other for the generosity and spirit which lies at the heart of this book, for enriching each other's lives, and for inspiring a continued belief in a feminist way of working. Last but not least we wish to thank members of our fami-lies — Michael Booth, Terri Hogan, Jen de Ness, Helmut Engelhard and Pam Hayden — for being our sounding-boards, for taking an interest and for sharing this experience with us. Finally, a special thankyou to Shannon whose struggle with Lorraine's feminist engagement is tempered by his desire for her ongoing happiness.

INTRODUCTION

Above our heads fireworks jewel the sky, launching another Festival of Perth. Chair of the Festival Committee, Fay Gale, opens the celebrations. A slim figure against the Supreme Court Gardens' stage, she laughs and tells an anecdote or two, swinging the crowd of evening picnickers into celebratory mood. As Western Australia's first female vice-chancellor, and the first woman to head the Australian Vice-Chancellors' Committee, Gale's working life has itself been a cause for celebration among feminists and their supporters. Yet as her chapter in this book shows, her performance as a public figure has not been without personal cost and heartache. Like many women leaders of her time, and certainly like those in this collection, she has not found it easy to loosen men's grip on public and political power.

A century ago, West Australian suffragists compiled a mile of signatures in the pursuit of voting rights. If we were to make a list of women in Western Australia who have taken public action since then, on justice for themselves and their communities, it would stretch at least that symbolic mile. This book celebrates that long history of women's activism, in politics, communities and workplaces. For more than a century feminists have carried their banners and chanted their demands in countless marches and demonstrations. They have won some campaigns and lost others. Throughout, they have retained their sense of sisterhood and solidarity, the rich legacy of passionate commitment left by their activist foremothers.

To commemorate the suffrage centenary, West Australian women have stitched, painted, embroidered and shaped another lengthy banner, modelled on the suffragists' original mile of cloth. On International Women's Day 1999, their new artwork had its first public showing. A cavalcade of colour, the banner stretched for hundreds of metres as women of all ages, backgrounds and cultures paraded it through the streets of central Perth. With children and a sprinkling of men marching in the ranks, it was women, and women only, who took it in turns to lead.

Yet the woman who leads the corporation, the political party, the public service, the university or the legal profession remains the exception rather than the rule. The woman in the public eye remains a source of social anxiety and speculation — 'How long will she last?', 'What can she change?', 'What difference will she make?', 'What price will she pay?'

Soothing this social anxiety is a constant hurdle for the woman leader. Joan Kirner claims that her hardest lesson as Premier of Victoria was to learn how to turn the media depiction of her, as an overweight housewife in spotted shift and slippers, to her advantage. Have other women who chanced the straits of leadership similar stories to tell? What caused the women in this book to step off women's beaten paths? Why do they continue fighting the odds? What inspires them to climb over the barriers blocking their way in public life?

In *Carrying the Banner* we glimpse the achievements, joys and frustrations of twenty-two of the many women who have taken themselves into public office while seeking to make the world a better place. We encounter the reasons why they succeed, strive and sometimes fail, and we sense their reasonableness in fame and in defeat. These are passionate, committed women. They are also reasonable women, thinking things through in a clear-headed way and communicating their goals and visions to others. Among them are well-known leaders: Carmen Lawrence, Fay Gale, Veronica Brady, Jo Vallentine, Helen Creed, Pat Giles. Among them also are women who, while less renowned as public figures, have taken the lead in particular professions, communities and social issues.

Several have become prominent in international arenas. Joan Williams, Shirley de la Hunty, Rachel Cleland, Fay Gale, Jo Vallentine and Pat Giles have for the past half-century been active in national and international organizations, ranging from peace and environment to government policy, education, social justice and sport. Joan Winch and Josie Boyle share a legacy of powerful women stretching back into a distant Australian past. They reclaim and affirm that heritage while tapping the collective resources they find in both their traditional and neo-indigenous culture. Donella Caspersz, Mali Valamanesh and Mary Patetsos have negotiated hybrid lives born of migration to a new land. Different again to the stories of survival and triumph by Aboriginal women, they similarly take the lead in fostering an Australia rich in cultural diversity. The feminist critique of the family misses the mark for many immigrant women — it fails to recognize that husbands and extended families are often their only source of support.

Linking the contributors is their relationship to Western Australia at a time when the State is celebrating the centenary of female suffrage. Revealingly, even that achievement is impossible to claim in the name of all women. Until the 1960s West Australian suffrage was for non-Aboriginal women only. Moreover, although white women in Western Australia won the vote in 1899, the law made them ineligible to stand for parliament until 1920.

The suffragists, who worked for women's advancement, would certainly be gratified to find that their efforts, and the efforts of many more besides, have resulted in equal opportunity legislation, child care and parental leave provisions, health and community services and greater choices for women in education and employment. These gains have allowed women to enter the public sphere. But what about the struggles that still need to be fought? It is now obvious that the game is not simply about getting there. It is also about staying there. Have women's efforts altered the organization of public life?

INTRODUCTION

A century of energetic striving has produced many breakthroughs for women, but few memorials to celebrate them. We wanted this book to be a different kind of monument, not the sort erected to men's successes. In our collective mind's eye we saw a patchwork of chapters by and about women leaders, in which some little-known or unnamed achievements would be stitched to some more renowned emblems.

Through the winter and into the early summer of 1996, in a quiet room among the historians and grand old trees at The University of Western Australia, contributors gathered to workshop the book. They reminisced, plotted and planned, commiserated on the pitfalls of writing about oneself, and swapped ideas as to what their chapters would include.

The concept of leadership posed some immediate problems. For a start, many of the authors remain unconvinced that 'leader' is how they should be described. The pace of their lives, the pots they have on the boil, their passions, networks and visions leave no inclination to claim personal fame for what they tend to see as collective achievements.

Underlying their reluctance was a distaste for what the term 'leader' has come to mean in common use. This was often the case among those who described themselves as feminists. Yet even former sports star Shirley de la Hunty, who makes no bones about her non-feminist colours, expresses her aversion to the self-seeking leadership that she met at times in her male colleagues.

A further hurdle was the crafting of autobiography itself. The actions of our contributors are no historical relics of the past. Their stories are living slices of the present, intimately bound up with fleshy negotiations of their working and personal relationships. Several writers had to think hard about how to protect friends, families, colleagues and adversaries from public misunderstanding, while remaining true to the task with which we charged them: to record their contributions to, and frustrations with, West Australian landscapes of community, work, politics and culture. Could they be critical of other women, they wondered, or of feminism's divergent paths? Would this be tantamount to hanging out dirty washing in public? The result is an eclectic mix of disclosures, incorporating some very different takes on leadership, told by women still living their own intimate histories.

Regenerating Politics
The first section celebrates the many women who have embarked on party or local politics. Joan Williams unfurls the banners and recounts the activism of a lifetime spent pursuing peace and justice through diverse political means. Williams begins with the emblem that prompts our title, the mile-long suffrage banner. This was an innovative petition stitched over many hours, and bearing thousands of signatures. Joan uses it as a motif of women's political energy. She sees it encircling the women who have inspired and sustained her own actions and writing, and links their causes to her grand daughter, a plumber, who nonchalantly builds the kind of future that women could only dream about a century ago.

Pat Giles and Jo Vallentine continue the theme of generating a life-giving politics. Like Joan, each links her fight for a better world to a new generation of daughters. Dr Giles found her forte in the Australian Senate and a half-century of international activism. But it was her life as a union organizer, combined with the teasing of her four daughters, which launched her onto the parliamentary stage. Pat's chapter records some of the highlights of that political career, and of a life lived generously in the service of women and socialism.

Papua New Guinea features in the lives of several contributors, namely Annie Goldflam, Barbara Buick and Dame Rachel Cleland. Rachel was made a Dame of the British Empire for her services to the people of Papua New Guinea during pre-independence days when her husband was Administrator, and also afterwards, when she lived there until 1979. Growing up amongst a group of strong feminists, particularly her aunt, Bessie Rischbieth, and mother, Olive Evans, led Rachel Cleland into the terrain of party politics, and into her work championing various community causes. Dame Rachel describes a life of political involvement spanning most of the century since suffrage, with an emphasis on her links to the Liberal Party at both national and State levels. Her involvement in attempts to remove a well-known Liberal Party powerbroker makes riveting reading.

INTRODUCTION

When a woman reaches the zenith of political office her success is often seen as a sign that political equality is to hand. The first Australian woman to break through the deadlocked Premier's door, Western Australia's Carmen Lawrence, was feted and celebrated, while the media enjoyed a heyday of speculation. Even the circumspect Australian pollster, Rod Cameron, became so excited he made a premature prediction: that we had entered a new era in which female politicians were destined to triumph over males.[1] Dr Lawrence, by contrast, calls her achievement 'a footnote in history'. Since then, Lawrence has experienced not only heady success but also the hard labour of political adversity.

Her chapter begins with the aftermath of the 1995 Royal Commission into the Abuse of Executive Power. Many observers view the commission as the dirtiest of political point-scoring. As we go to press, the legal and political fallout has still not been determined. Facing a charge which carries the possibility of a gaol term, Carmen Lawrence provides a cautionary tale for the woman who dares venture into the big league of parliamentary politics. Despite the political mudslinging, her story reveals a woman who performs her work with efficiency and flair, whether solving a problem for her Fremantle constituents, dealing with loftier affairs of state, or facing the prospect of legal and political disaster. When we asked Carmen Lawrence to participate in this project she replied: 'I don't believe it's appropriate for sitting members of parliament to write their memoirs or autobiographies'. For that reason her chapter, unlike the others in this book, is presented in interview format.

The starting point for Jo Vallentine's entry into the Senate was her concern, as a young mother, to achieve a peaceful world. Unhappily, when her quest for peace and environmental justice took her to Canberra each week, it was the warmth of holding her daughters in her arms that she had to leave behind. Jo describes significant transitions in her life: the triumph as she goes into politics; the complexities of negotiation and resolution that beset her as she shifts from being a single-issue independent to the leader of The Greens (WA); and her reflections as she moves away from the realm of parliamentary politics.

My Place, My Work
For all the authors, the issues of geography, space and cherished, inspiring terrain, are a key source of identity. As residents of Australia's West all contributors know the beauty of the vast and colourful landscape. As citizens of the world's most remote city, they also know the tyranny of distance. All combat insularity and parochialism through extensive networks and regular travel. Metaphors of home, place and region combine with talk of contested spaces. Their stories show the portability of everything from campaigns to careers, from families to carpentry skills, from European, Asian and Iranian cultures to Aboriginal storytelling. For several the self and home are one, home becomes an easily transportable place. Those grouped in 'My Place, My Work' are women whose 'homes', roots and spirit are in more places than one.

The section begins with Josie Boyle whose lyrical recounting of the colours of 'her country' and the skills of her skinfolk are complemented by her joy in talking and singing about them. Josie's passion and life's work is the retelling of Aboriginal folklore of the Western Desert, and she sets many of her stories to music. She passes on her ancient knowledge through workshops, recordings and educational institutions, and replenishes her Wongi spirit in regular 'walkabouts' along songlines of central Australia. Mindful of her experience of growing up in both white and Aboriginal cultures, Josie offers all women the goanna story. A symbol of survival from the beginning of time, the goanna is the emblem of powerful and resilient womanhood.

Famed as an Olympic triple medallist, life in the 1950s for Shirley De la Hunty (nee Strickland) involved dedication, world competition and travel. Now well into her seventies Shirley writes about her lifetime service to sport and her 'love of the bush', the source of her outspoken environmental activism.

Union work, and its direct link to broader political agitation, is a feature in common between Joan Winch, Helen Creed, Pat Giles and Joan Williams. Dorothy Cobble, in her book *Women and Unions,* suggests that 'the potential for forging a creative, productive partnership between working women and unions is greater now than at any other historic moment'.[2] When Jennie George was announced as President-elect of the Australian Council of Trade Unions (ACTU), this partnership seemed even more viable, with tough-talking union men standing on stage singing Helen Reddy's 'I Am Woman'. Helen Creed, Secretary of one of Western Australia's largest unions, describes such episodes in her account of women and unions. The matriarchs in Helen's life, her mother and six aunts, inspired her to seek her truth on the other side of Australia, and to make the terrain of industrial relations her own. In her short history of women in the 'Missos', Creed shows what inspires workers to keep the flame of the labour movement burning.

Like Helen Creed, Mary Patetsos carries her leadership responsibilities with seeming ease. In similar style to Josie Boyle, Mary weaves between two cultures, in her case Greek and Australian. It was as child translator for her immigrant parents that Mary first experienced the contradictions of responsibility and power when one speaks on behalf of others. From her hybrid childhood she gained both a proficiency in speaking and a resolute determination to bridge the chasm between two diverse worlds, while using the resources of both to help other new arrivals to Australia.

In the field of workplace relations the women who take leading positions in the corporate world are of crucial importance. Building construction executive Lyn Sherwood, and advertising leader Debra Shorter, are two who have taken seats usually reserved for men. By their presence, these women throw down the gauntlet to masculinism and male-ordered workplace cultures. More significantly, they push for egalitarian policies in their workplaces and broader communities. For Lyn Sherwood, the Chief Executive Officer of the Building Industry Training Council, a key task is to achieve more places for women in construction, where they currently represent only 1 per cent of trained workers. A similar low percentage of women reach the top in professions and careers.

Those who believe that equality has been achieved would do well to remember the way the woman in the public eye stands out simply *as* a woman. As top advertising executive Debra

Shorter found, when she was named Australian Businesswoman of the Year, she became celebrated not on account of her business acumen but for how she managed her family and personal life. For the woman engaged in reinventing leadership, Shorter reveals, the secret is to create an individuality which short-circuits such sexist assumptions while retaining close alliances with other women. Her chapter provides a direct link to the next section, in which contributors reflect on the diversity and differences they draw upon and reshape whenever they take the lead.

Professing Difference
Inevitably, combining the pressures of work and family, and dealing with male-defined workplaces, have been central concerns for many if not all of our contributors. Based on their own experiences they have promoted and used woman-friendly practices for empowering women in their workplaces, institutions and communities. In most organizations, however, achieving a democratic, non-hierarchical appreciation of difference and diversity challenges the most determined advocate of change.

The women in this book reveal two crucial axes on which they differ from conventional approaches to 'leadership'. The usual image of the leader is of a towering figure exercising power over others. Yet the most frequent exercise of power for these women is their ability to give it away — their capacity to empower others. Secondly, their chapters suggest that coming to terms with one's own times of powerlessness is a key lesson if empowerment of others is the aim.

Empowering others, suggest the contributors in this section, involves seeing 'leadership' as a practice that nobody can forswear. Yet if the project is one of empowerment, how do we deal with those times when our own powerlessness seems irrefutable?

Analysts of leadership rarely address that question. Instead, as shown in Amanda Sinclair's study of male and female executives in Australia,[3] male-dominated institutions make invincibility emblematic of leadership. Senior executives, Sinclair indicates, invariably hold a particular view of the successful leader: it is a man bent on a heroic quest for success. Self-aggrandisement, self-absorption and no-holds-barred aggression are not only expected, but also highly valued; there is no recognition that the powers of *successful* leadership are limited and fragile.

When Professor Fay Gale became Vice-Chancellor of The University of Western Australia in 1990, the challenge was to promote democracy, diversity and excellence in the State's oldest, most prestigious and most male-populated university. At the time there were only two women professors among a total of 110. By 1997 Gale's policies had brought that figure to twelve. In 1995 she was elected President of the Australian Vice-Chancellors' Committee, when universities were facing their greatest threat to funding and intellectual autonomy. Fay Gale achieved some remarkable successes in her academic career, and survived a number of controversies. As we enter the new millennium, she reflects on her uneven path and provides a vision of women's empowerment in the future.

Today, many women are in the legal profession. In fact law schools generally have more women than men enrolled in undergraduate courses. In other professions, such as medicine and accountancy, women now roughly equal men as graduates. Have we now entered, as many seem to believe, a 'post-feminist' age where women hold all the advantages? One way to answer that question is to read Antoinette Kennedy's chapter, which shows the upper reaches of the profession are still dominated by men. Judge Kennedy, Western Australia's first woman to sit on the District Court Bench, describes how, despite formal equality, the notion of women as unequal has haunted her time in that role.

Donella Caspersz learned the lessons of what she defines as leadership — commitment, collectivism, individual effort and community activism — from her immigrant parents. But she also learned the humility that comes from acknowledging a complex powerlessness: she found that all her caring and energy could not save a dying friend from the racism and sexism some medical authorities meted out.

Ann Ghisalberti, who stepped into the male-defined domain of science as a young woman, takes a fresh, gender-sensitive approach to science in her role as Chief Executive Officer of the Scitech Discovery Centre in Perth. Neither Ghisalberti's early success as a scientist, nor the energy she finds in a collective feminism she discovered in midlife, prepared her for learning much about the nature of powerlessness. But, like Donella Caspersz, she meets that hard lesson through the loss of someone she loves. Ghisalberti retains her equilibrium as a scientist and her enthusiasm for creative community service by giving free rein to her legacy of childhood: her pleasure in books, literature and questioning,

Patricia Crawford, Professor of History at The University of Western Australia, shifts us away from the rapids of modern science to the calmer waters of Tudor history. In attempting to show women as historical agents, Crawford has encountered prolonged and bitter resistance. Like Donella Caspersz and Ann Ghisalberti, she learned that working collectively was not only a way to break through the forces ranged against women, it was also an essential survival tactic. Despite her own regular feelings of powerlessness, Crawford's work and example empowers a new generation of women, an acquired skill she shows is the essence of competent leadership.

Val Marsden, like Patricia Crawford, discovered the benefits of collective empowerment through her work with women who had similar goals. A key source of insight and political education for Val was the Women's Electoral Lobby, in which she found purpose, strength and support. When she won the task of coordinating a new government agency (the Women's Information and Referral Exchange), Marsden imported those values of non-hierarchical, democratic behaviour — which she holds dear — into the organization. She describes how, a few years later, party politics and the strictures of a male-defined bureaucracy destroyed this vital woman-centred space that women had laboured so hard to achieve. Her story conveys the crucial lesson, first espoused by women's liberationists: that any alliance between feminism and the state is brittle, unreliable, and can be a dangerous undertaking for women.

Heart Dreaming

Fortitude, brains and a generous spirit mark the lives of the women writing in this book. Some have been lucky enough to have those qualities fostered from an early age by mothers, fathers, aunts. Most also show an autonomous sense of self, nurtured

INTRODUCTION

through a reciprocal relationship with siblings, friends, life partners, or deeply felt cultural affinities. Those in the final section offer us inspiring lives in which service to their sisters and communities comprise models of joyous commitment. Despite this, all have felt the force of a masculinist culture. They have found men's interests may not necessarily be seen as opposed to women's — they are simply treated as the only ones which exist. The women contributing to the final section have challenged that male norm, but all recognize that gender is not the only source of inequality.

At the turn into the new century, Joan Winch no longer tries to convince non-Aboriginals of indigenous needs. Instead, she passes on her knowledge to the women who already stand in her shoes. Joan designs her chapter, therefore, as a letter to her daughter, Lillian. Winch's activist education began with union work and through winding paths lead to her founding the Marr Mooditj Aboriginal Health Centre. The centre is a model for those who seek Aboriginal empowerment.

The need for anti-discrimination legislation drew Barbara Buick to a decade of service on the Equal Opportunity Tribunal. Despite its importance, Buick's work in equal opportunities was, to borrow Carmen Lawrence's term, a 'footnote' in a life spent challenging discrimination against women in Papua New Guinea and Australia, and in rooting out sexist and racist discrimination in children's literature.

The juggling of two cultures, as we saw in the chapters by Josie Boyle and Mary Patetsos, is reiterated in the cultural blending that marks the experience of Mali Valamanesh. Mali brings the fight that was lost in Iran to the Australian context in a search for her culture and for her new self. However, she finds unexpected barriers and opportunities at both a personal and public level. Mali gives us an intimate view of the freedoms and losses that immigration can entail.

Like Josie Boyle, Veronica Brady embroiders her contribution with artistry, love of words, and a deep sense of the spiritual. Sister Veronica's formula for life has unfolded around her like a linen sheet, lovingly creased and smoothed with the help of others. Veronica weaves her chapter, like her life, with a rich tapestry of inspiring words and actions for social justice, including

Aboriginal land rights and a passion for liberal thought. She exhorts us to 'follow the dream, follow the dream, right to the end' so that we might recover in abundance the elusive but essential 'poetry of things'.

Annie Goldflam took her desires for a more equitable world to Papua New Guinea and places further afield. On her return to Western Australia, she worked for many causes in both paid and voluntary capacities. Then, amidst a generously full life, she faced her greatest challenge: to count her lesbianism among the causes she champions. Despite the urgings of second wave feminism, sexuality is still a topic that women find difficult to discuss among themselves. Annie breaches that near silence. Her recipe for leadership chimes with that of all the women in this book: to help others make decisions that will make this country, and this planet, a richer, more compassionate source of love, justice and hope.

West Australians rarely celebrate women's achievements. And when we do mark a woman's success, we often dress her up as eminently respectable, so that the challenges she posed can be safely forgotten. Many West Australians would recognize the Pioneer Women's Memorial fountain in King's Park. But how many would know that the clock tower at the park's entrance is a monument to Edith Cowan, Australia's first woman to gain a place on the parliamentary bench? Ironically, the city fathers who opposed the clock tower claimed it would 'catch every visitor's eye'.[4] For all that, the erection of the clock tower was touch and go in the 1930s. Supporters had to combat those who argued that this 'prime site' should be left for a 'thoroughly representative national' figure. Edith Cowan would have wondered whether her monument was worth the fuss and trouble.

This book is no silent, upstanding monument. Instead, it is brimming with reflections, issues, gossip, memories and forecasts that could well stretch a mile long. Rather than creating a typology of women leaders, it shows women courageously inventing what leadership can and cannot be.

---

1   Rod Cameron, 'Feminisation: The Major Emerging Trend Underlying Future Mass Audience Response'. Address to the 11th National Convention of Public Relations Institute of Australia, 19 October 1990.

INTRODUCTION

2 Dorothy S. Cobble, *Women and Unions: Forging a New Partnership*, ILR Press, Ithaca, New York, 1993.
3 Amanda Sinclair, *Doing Leadership Differently: Gender, Power and Sexuality in a Changing Business Culture*, Melbourne University Press, Carlton South, 1998.
4 King's Park Board correspondence, Accession Number 482A, Battye Library.

Regenerating Politics

WOMEN CARRYING BANNERS

JOAN (JUSTINA) WILLIAMS

Born in Kalgoorlie in 1916, Joan grew up in the Stirling Ranges near Albany in the south of Western Australia. Declining a scholarship to Albany High School, she opted for correspondence classes in order to remain with her family. Joan developed an early passion for writing and became a reporter for the *West Australian*. She also worked for the now defunct *Daily News*, and as a stringer for the London *News Chronicle*. Married with four children, Joan's participation in the postwar struggle for democratic rights, equality for women, child-care facilities, left-wing journalism and political activities put creative writing on hold for a couple of decades. Her feminist convictions prevailed and she entered the fray against ruling male editors who trivialized women's writing. Joan continues to work for her favourite causes: feminism, peace, Australian literature and history. When awarded the Order of Australia Medal, she accepted on behalf of all her unrecognized sisters who serve the community.

We are carrying banners sacred as childbirth,
words for women who demand liberation as women,
slogans that slip like new skin over wounds ...[1]

Yes, women have been carrying banners since the early petition in England in 1866 for women's enfranchisement, led by Emily Davies and Elizabeth Garrett and presented to parliament by John Stuart Mill.

It was in London that I carried my first banner, marching on May Day 1937, against fascism and war, chanting 'Down with Hitler, Tojo and Mussolini'. Now, at the age of eighty-three, I take a very personal look back down the years at the first and second waves of feminism and some of the women I have known at the forefront of the struggle for change in our status.

In our part of the world, the banners had been unfurled and voting rights won long before I was born: New Zealand in 1893, Australia in 1902, preceded by South Australia in 1894 and Western Australia in 1899. Today, we are learning more about the hidden lives of courageous women who have led the struggle for equality over the years. What brought them out in front? Why were they accepted? Why did they succeed or why did they fail?

In Western Australia back in 1894, the Women's Christian Temperance Union (WCTU) made an ingenious banner — a piece of cloth a mile long, with thousands of signatures demanding female suffrage. Rolling it up, they put it before the politically conservative Western Australian Legislative Council.[2] Wherever the idea came from, the WCTU leaders must have seen its potential, and organized action that would tap into the wider section of women in the community who were sick of being treated as second-class citizens. Most of the male legislators saw their own capitulation in 1899 as generosity, and useful to boot, and would have denied (as usual) that the petition influenced them.

The 1890s were a time of changing economic conditions for women in Australia and England. No amount of State-assisted propaganda for women's role as nurturers, homemakers and childbearers could stop the flood of women going to work in factories and white-collar trades. Widening education enabled knowledge of contraception to spread, though the devices were banned. The invention of the typewriter opened new doors outside the home. The looming Depression, in both countries, didn't stop the employment of women, although at cheaper rates than men. Many single women preferred going out to work to domesticity. Others, brought together in factories, were beginning to rebel against dreadful conditions. As inequalities became more obvious, a groundswell of anger was developing. In Australia, it was the women factory inspectors who came to the fore, exposing insanitary practices, poor pay and long hours. With some support from women workers and the public concern generated, they won changes which were written into Australian industrial law.

Because women in the factories had not at that stage found a collective voice, the suffragette leaders in English-speaking countries were mainly educated women, mostly middle-class, intellectually convinced of their cause. They could face gaol, force-feeding, scorn and ridicule bravely, but not always the slogging organizational work that could draw big numbers of working and house-bound women into action, carrying banners for their own demands. Without a clear goal, without strategy and tactics that would win wider allies, such leaders could easily succumb to the desire for individual glory, and many did. Membership of the suffragettes dropped off drastically when Emmeline Pankhurst headed a rush of patriotic fervour at the start of the First World War, though opposition to war had been one of the planks of the movement. However, the pacifist section, including Emmeline's daughter Adele Pankhurst Walsh, struggled on courageously for a peace settlement. Whatever their faults, the heroism of the suffragettes has inspired feminists, and their symbolic colours — white, green, and purple — have been celebrated in feminist banners ever since.

In Australia, the women who fought for the vote were called suffragists. Suffragist influences helped build our militant women's movement in Australia and the later struggle against conscription in the First World War. Katharine Susannah Prichard, who was working as a journalist in London around 1910, told me she was attracted to the suffragettes for a time, then repelled by their anti-male attitude; but in 1915, after they opposed wartime regulations being used against free speech and the trade unions, she saw the same developments in Australia and took part in the struggle against conscription. In 1911 Jessie Street, then a schoolgirl visiting London, carried a banner with the suffragettes, and in 1914 became more involved for a while. Vida Goldstein, 'the best-known suffragist in Australia', had spoken for the Women's Social and Political Union in London's Albert Hall in 1911 and addressed anti-conscription demonstrations in Victoria. Adele Pankhurst Walsh emigrated to Australia in March 1914 with her own ideas of the way ahead. Because women already had the vote here, she turned to a socialist program that included equality and peace. (Her sister Sylvia was following the same path in England.)

Pacifism and peace by negotiation, long expressed in the aims of the women's movement, were easily lost in time of war. But in Australia, three days after the First World War began, the Women's Peace Army was formed, with Vida Goldstein (by now editor of the *Woman Voter*) as President, and Adele Pankhurst as Secretary. Speaking of the 1916 and 1917 anti-conscription campaigns, Bertha Walker says, 'Women had never before participated in large numbers in any social movement', and that many of those who took part were inspired by the efforts of the suffragettes in England.[3] The Women's International League for Peace and Freedom and the Labor Women's Anti-conscription Committee were active. A week before the first referendum on conscription in 1916 a march and pageant of women defied an opposition countermarch. In Melbourne, before the 1917 referendum, several thousand women marched through city streets, and raided Parliament House in 'a war against food exploitation'.

Adele Pankhurst and Mrs A.K. Wallace were arrested and fined, but rabbits and butter were released from storage. My own grandmother took part in the West Australian campaign led by John Curtin — she was determined to save my father from the slaughter in the trenches and bitterly disappointed that the vote went the wrong way in Western Australia. (The poem 'The Blood Vote', written by W.R. Winspear and illustrated by Claude Marquet, was believed to have decided the 'No' vote of tens of thousands of women overall.) From a core of socialist and pacifist opposition to 'a rich man's war', the struggle against conscription took in Catholics, Protestants, trade unionists and Labor Party members, women across classes, and the soldiers at the front. Some fell by the wayside, including Adele Pankhurst Walsh, who quarrelled with Vida Goldstein on the issue, and was isolated by her own provocative and violent actions, and barely escaped deportation. As a leader, she eventually failed, like her mother Emmeline.[4]

In the Shell of the Old

During the first wave of feminism, strong individual leadership was commonly admired and thought desirable. But in the shell of the old, new attitudes were already developing, fostered by women writers putting new ideas between the covers of their books. Seamstress and poet Lesbia Harford was one of the first to put the dreams of Australian factory women into poetry:

> The foot of my machine
> Sails up and down
> Upon the blue of this fine lady's gown.
> Sail quickly, little boat,
> With gifts for me —
> Night and the goldy streets and liberty.[5]

Katharine Susannah Prichard showed her women characters striving for independence, doing whatever work they could get or, if they had talent, using it to the full. Though she believed that men and women should work together for a socialist society in which they would be equal, and made this clear when she spoke in public, her strong female characters dominated her novels. They weren't afraid to lead — they were good role models in a period when most women were expected to defer to men.

Identifying herself with the peace movement in word and deed, Katharine explained the causes of war from a Marxist viewpoint in her 1936 pamphlet, *Who Wants War?* I was soon attending the Modern Women's Club she had founded in Perth around the same time, to give working women and home-bound women a place to discuss their own needs and current affairs. She also hoped to draw in fringe-dwelling Aboriginal women that she and her friends had helped. Her deep convictions on the equality of women, white or black, took artistic shape in her novels. *Coonardoo* had caused a furore by challenging prevailing attitudes that sanctioned the sexual exploitation of Aboriginal women; her strong women characters challenged a society that denied them opportunity. She spoke at the first postwar International Women's Day in 1945 in Newcastle. With banners around her, she liked to appeal directly to her audience:

> As Mohammedan women threw off their veils on International Women's Day in Moscow many years ago, so let us throw off from our minds the veils of ignorance and apathy which for so long prevented us from seeing clearly that women must think and work strenuously if ever the

world of peace and security which we dream about is to become a reality.[6]

Katharine's play, *Women of Spain*, performed in the Perth Town Hall in 1937, exposed fascist aggression. I heard the public speeches of Mary Lowson and Ron Hurd, returning volunteers from the International Brigade, and was drawn into support of the elected government in the Spanish Civil War, and the Spanish Relief Fund. But the fiery speeches of 'La Passionara' — Communist Dolores Ibaruri, heroic leader of Spanish women — both inspired me and gave me food for thought. I learnt how fascism deliberately turned back the clock for women. I realized that women could lead both in ideas and in action; that they could be ordinary women who, in the march of events, saw the need to act, and express the common demands of the exploited and oppressed.

My own search for social justice, equality for women, and my opposition to fascism and war, drew me into the Communist Party. Rostered to help uphold the banner of free speech on the Perth Esplanade, my illusions about swaying the masses by my oratory were soon shattered by small and often hostile audiences.

In time, I found that many Australian women writers of different political convictions shared a compassionate view of our sex, white or black, and were a significant influence in changing societal attitudes. Mary Gilmore and Louisa Lawson had a simple approach that, in their time, drew working-class women to read their columns. Miles Franklin, in *My Brilliant Career* and other novels, challenged prevailing ideas on the place of women. (I did not know then of her enthusiastic but stressful work in the United States during the campaign for the vote.) Lyndall Hadow told me how her mother, Florence Stuart (organizer of the first Women's Labor League on the West Australian goldfields), had instituted an educative section for women in the *Westralian Worker*. I discovered how Ethel Hassell, in the last century, made friends with Aboriginal women on her husband's isolated property in Western Australia, and learnt and wrote down the words they taught her of their language. Later, Alexandra Hasluck and others wrote of the early women, mainly of the upper class, recording the history of the colony and acting as educators of the children. Rica Erickson revealed the different life of labourers and their womenfolk.

Mary Durack's sympathetic portrayal of Aboriginal men and women brought more understanding of their culture and problems. Nene Gare, writer and artist, looked into the lives of Aboriginal fringe dwellers and showed their warmth and humour, but disclosed their tragic plight. Lyndall Hadow told me she was named after Olive Schreiner's heroine in *Story of an African Farm*. Lyndall's short stories took up women's social problems, and in *Don't Cry for Me* she showed poignantly how an Aboriginal girl's thirst for education was frustrated. Hearts and minds were won by Mary Gilmore's compassionate poems and articles, by Miles Franklin's defiance of convention, Christina Stead's understanding of women's oppression, and the social causes behind the tragedy of *Coonardoo* depicted by Katharine Susannah Prichard.

Reaching towards Working Women
It is 1959, and Australian leftists are still under threat from McCarthyism, as in the United States. But Irene Greenwood is widely respected as one of Perth's leading feminists, while her mother, Mrs Mary Driver, is the redoubtable campaigner of the WCTU. Irene and I consult each other frequently on problems: political, literary and feminist. (Sometimes she is in tears over her son's male chauvinist put-downs.) We discuss overall aims and tactics on immediate issues in the organizations to which we belong, plan to introduce new ideas that are within their constitution. We often seek Katharine's opinion. Our discussions range the world — defending a writer against censorship, a delegation to the Soviet Women's Committee, a possible visit from her friend Jessie Street (who is now Australian delegate to the United Nations), an invitation from Dymphna Cusack to meet the ship that is taking her on a visit to the USSR.

When Jessie Street arrives, she pelts us with questions and reminisces with Irene on their work for the 'Sheepskins for Russia' campaign during the war. 'We've come a long way', she says, her clipped diction redolent of an expensive education, as she puffs at the cigarette that eternally dangles from her mouth. But she is one of our sisters, not a snob. She is much sought after as a speaker for International Women's Day, which leftists are battling to make popular, but which is regarded with suspicion by leading women's organizations and the media. International Women's Day originated with German writer and socialist politician Clara Zetkin. At the Second Conference of Socialist Women in Copenhagen in 1910, Clara called for an international day of action by women to be held on 8 March every year. All over the world women have been celebrating the day ever since.

In the 1950s the worldwide petition to ban the A-bomb draws housewives and working women into action for peace. We support a new progressive national organization, the Union of Australian Women (UAW). Its policy includes price control, equal pay and opportunity, friendship with the women of socialist countries and world peace.

Although immediately branded a communist-front organization, the UAW is an independent body, but includes party members in the rank and file like Katharine Susannah Prichard and myself, and the Secretary, Mary Lester. Work on practical issues — child care, better living standards, equal pay — wins support; housewives, though new to politics, are quick to understand their oppression.

Women in the UAW leadership like Mary know they must listen carefully to those making their first step outside the home. The organization has strong links with trade unionists and their wives; in the long metal trades strike of 1953, UAW members help distribute meat, fruit and vegetables. It is the beginning of a new kind of women's committee that we want to develop in the unions, a body not restricted to cups of tea and socials. This structure is already federal policy in the militant Waterside Workers Federation (WWF). The UAW members help me set up a women's committee in the Fremantle branch of the WWF during the national strike of 1954 over union rights. Our core of staunch wives struggle on two fronts. They battle both the communist bogey and the male chauvinists who view us with suspicion. At the same time they understand the need for strike action for better pay in 1956, and are eager to counter vicious press attacks on our menfolk.

We draft a leaflet explaining why we support our men and hand them out in Fremantle streets. Our solid work on strike relief begins to break through prejudice. We march with the men to the Town Hall, united and determined. Our members are invited to speak to the orderly meeting of 2000 strikers. We forge links from Cairns to Albany at national conferences of WWF women's committees. In later years, when wages and conditions have improved, our committee winds up. But I know that, despite some of my high-handed mistakes as President, it filled some of the needs of the time, broadened the vision of our members and many other women and helped overcome some of the entrenched male chauvinism among workers.

In the recent national dispute between the Maritime Union of Australia and Patricks Stevedoring, I joined the picket line with many wives and supportive women from the community. On one stormy evening I was invited into the windswept tent where today's women were setting up the West Australian branch of Women of the Waterfront. How wonderful to see it take off like a rocket in the hands of a new generation of determined women. How I admired the wife with a baby at her breast discussing not only practical matters like catering and childminding at the picket centre, but also stress counselling for partners whose menfolk had been locked out without pay. How wonderful to see this new generation of women so confidently taking on leadership and responsibilities in what they saw as a struggle not only for their livelihood but for the basic democratic right to organize!

Back in the 1950s, left-wing activists in the UAW consciously try not to dominate but encourage a wider range of political activity, including peace and friendship, involving exchange delegations with socialist countries that are eye-openers to both sides. We find that timid women are enthusiastic about making paper flowers and painting banners, and will march with them on May Day, although they have never marched before. And on practical issues like a bridge for children over a busy highway or air-conditioning for the King Edward Memorial Hospital for Women (KEMH), they will demonstrate and not be driven away until they get satisfaction. They go shyly from door to door selling the UAW national magazine. Lyndall Hadow holds the Western Australian portfolio. Other West Australian contributors include Katharine Susannah Prichard, Madge Cope, Dorothy Hewett (who later becomes editor) and myself.

The Second Wave
By the late 1960s the second wave of feminism has reached Australia. Germaine Greer's book, *The Female Eunuch*, explains the role of the patriarchy and the psychological sell that cripples women. A younger, highly educated generation recognizes the origin of their exploitation and oppression. I talk about the book's revolutionary impact with Irene Greenwood, sitting in her pleasant home, under one of Elizabeth Durack's early paintings of Aboriginal women. Others drop in — aspirants for parliament; Rosalind Denny, progressive matron of KEMH; writers and poets also. Irene chuckles wickedly as she pours her favourite vermouth bianco saying, 'Mother wouldn't approve!'

I have just come back from Sydney, fired by the new Women's Liberation movement, in which a comrade, Joyce Stevens, has a leading role. I tell Irene how politicians in the New South Wales Parliament were shocked as women waved banners demanding the right to abortion. We rejoice that a new force of women, determined to take fate into their own hands, has arisen.

I find that in Perth there are already two groups, who don't know each other, discussing the new wave of radical feminism. After talking it over with the Communist Party Secretary, Madge Cope and I bring them together — academics, students, housewives and radical and closet feminists. We organize furiously, if not very efficiently. Our public meeting draws an enthusiastic audience. Women's Liberation WA is on its way in May 1971.

Discussion rages on discrimination, the right to work, equal pay and opportunity, child care, abortion on demand, free or cheaper contraceptives, repeal of legislation which discriminates on gender. Groups are set up on political action, commercial exploitation of women, child care, 'demos', and of course, consciousness-raising. 'Womanpower' is our slogan on banners and T-shirts; we excitedly discuss each new feminist book, and study Engels' *Origin of the Family*. We boldly nominate a Women's Liberation team for election into local government: Leila M.

Soerink, Patricia Giles, Penny Marsh, Eleanor Humphreys and me. Our policy includes safeguarding the environment (before many knew the meaning of the word) and adult franchise on a residential basis – the property vote disenfranchised the bulk of women. We aren't successful, but a year later I am voted into Melville City Council on a women's program.

We assemble outside State Parliament with placards demanding, 'PASS THE BILL — ADVERTISE THE PILL', to monitor voting on a Bill to legalize the advertising and public sale of contraceptives. We conceal a banner, hang it over the balcony at the appropriate time. We are ordered out.

Supportive students arrange for a Women's Liberation issue of The University of Western Australia's Student Guild newspaper, *Pelican*. Called *Ptarmigan,* it is edited by Cheryl Meinck. The front page aims to reverse the stereotype of women with a full frontal photo of a man in a short fur coat pushing a shopping trolley. Outrage! But it is a medical article on self-examination by women that lands the Student Guild in the police court, with a fine to match. The press whips up a 'bra burner' furore when we give out a leaflet on female health to girls outside a suburban high school. It seems that education about their own bodies is taboo. We launch a campaign to remedy sexism in the language. Spokeswoman, chairperson, Ms, and so on; small points, but how the patriarchy resists! An influx of young radical women breathes new life into International Women's Day. Overjoyed, we march and demonstrate in a sea of banners. The radical feminists and lesbians initiate the Reclaim the Night march, more colourful and inventive, especially in the use of a high-pitched ululation that scares the police horses.

Our members are determined to get rid of masculine-structured forms of organization: no movers of motions, no seconders, just free-for-all discussion out of which agreement on action will emerge. But eventually it is the 'tyranny of structurelessness' that emerges and a few dominant women are making all the decisions and disheartening others.

The setting up in 1973 of the Women's Electoral Lobby (WEL), a more structured organization, is something of a relief.

Those of us who don't want a split join up; we see that WEL will be able to reach out wider, and find our militancy is quite welcome. WEL draws in many highly qualified, often ambitious young women. The initial lobbying of election candidates on women's issues brings much publicity about politicians' backward attitudes. In the next election, many candidates put our questionnaires in the bin, rather than be exposed as neanderthals, but political parties begin to court the women's vote. In the same year, Elizabeth Reid is made Adviser on Women's Affairs to Prime Minister Whitlam — a lead for the world. Irene Greenwood becomes a heavyweight in the National Women's Advisory Board, where she is a mine of information, an initiator and an astute tactician.

International Women's Year 1975 brings marches and banners galore, leading up to the first truly national conference of women in Australia. Delegates from the whole spectrum of women's organizations flock to Canberra on government subsidies, or under their own steam. A huge reception by the Prime Minister in the Houses of Parliament! The media pounces on an opportunity to savage Whitlam. Horrendous headlines exaggerate divisions between conservative and radical women. Jenny Beahan leads a march of about a hundred delegates waving feminist banners and placards. They surge into the offices of the *Canberra Times*, demanding unbiased coverage. The editor quails. Though progress is often difficult in the conference because of the wide range of opinion, the new points of view, and the vitality in discussion, the agreements reached are exciting and newsworthy but mostly ignored by the rest of the media.

In a climate of Federal Government attention to women's demands for child care, health needs, environmental protection, and affirmative action to get more women into parliament, the blow falls. The Whitlam Government is dismissed by the Governor-General. Many of us feel it is a coup and that swift action will be taken by democratic forces. We can give leadership, some of us think, to those who want the Whitlam Government's progressive programs for women to continue. Out come the feminist banners, and a male partner does an overnight run of slogans on newsprint in huge type. A hundred or so women march around the city. But where are the other protesters? Where are the militant unions and their leaders? Bob Hawke, leader of the Australian Council of Trade Unions, has said 'Do nothing'.

It is a hard lesson in leadership, of going too far ahead without gauging support. Despite this setback, we are confident the second wave of feminism will continue the practical and theoretical struggle against oppressive patriarchal attitudes.

Women in the Peace Movement

We have opposed the Vietnam War since it began in 1964, and now members of the Union of Australian Women are marching in our capital cities against it, following the example of the 'Save Our Sons' movement in Melbourne. In Perth they don't carry banners because they will be arrested if they do. Instead they wear aprons painted with anti-war slogans, and are charged. A progressive lawyer, Lloyd Davies, takes their case to the High Court and gets a decision in their favour, a decision that also opens the way for the gutsy T-shirt slogans of later days. Through all the years of war in Vietnam, we continue to march. Our sons' marbles were drawn out of the conscription barrel, and hundreds of thousands marched with peace banners, a flow that did not stop until, after the election of Prime Minister Gough Whitlam in 1972, Australian troops are withdrawn.

Attempts to show how war preparations cut down the money available for women's refuges and other needs came up against the cry, 'Peace isn't a women's issue'. But in the early 1980s, with the Indian and Pacific oceans bristling with guns and huge nuclear warships and aircraft carriers entering or standing off Fremantle, women began to take the lead in the peace movement. Nancy Wilkinson, Olive Lachberg, Jo Vallentine and I worked on the Peace and Disarmament Committee of the United Nations Association of Australia which, because of some dependence on government grants, was hesitant about demonstrations.

The threats of the cold war turning into a hot war led a small group of us to form a branch of the Australian Peace Committee. I was Secretary. We began handing out leaflets against visits by nuclear warships, which broke new ground. However, we soon saw the need for a broader organization and helped form

People for Nuclear Disarmament (PND), a one-issue body in which women like Jo Vallentine and later Dee Margetts played an important role.

In support of PND, thousands marched with colourful banners against nuclear warships and faced arrest if they raised them on the wharf. The Australian Peace Committee, though small in number, was a force in organizing the annual Palm Sunday Peace March and Rally, and also in encouraging friendship with socialist and Indian Ocean countries. However, it was the Greenham Common Women's Peace Camp and the National Women for Survival Camp at Pine Gap that turned peace into a feminist issue.

The Sound Women's Peace Camp, a national feminist action against Cockburn Sound (seen as a de facto war base), unleashed astounding fury from media, male chauvinists, local government and federal forces, while demands to close it grew and the State Labor Government wavered. The camp was made 'women's space' and the banning of men aroused particular animosity, threats and attempted break-ins. WEL participated in a birthday party given for Irene Greenwood and there was considerable unity among diverse participants from all over Australia.

The test of leadership came after many days of hardship, excitement and resistance to provocation, as our opponents raised public pressure to close the camp. Enlisting support from other women in the community unfortunately had a low priority, but explanatory leaflets distributed through the Australian Peace Committee were snatched up inside and outside the camp.

The considerable unity of the women in a tense situation was put at risk by a premature decision to march on the base. It was steamrollered through by an extremely radical group from Sydney. The majority considered it was wrong to act before the deadline given for a reply from the federal minister. But we all marched in solidarity. As the leaders began to climb the gates, there was an eruption of police followed by arrests, injuries and screams. Further alienation of the public followed through selected television footage and headlines about violent lesbians and women in war paint. Today, looking at the banner I carried, I see more of the strength and bravery of the women than the mistakes, and again hear our wonderful chant:

> We are the flow,
> we are the ebb,
> we are the weavers,
> we are the web.

We have inched forward for two decades. There is a pause. It will be harder now. Are we looking at the third wave, the struggle to keep the gains we have won? Who will give leadership? Will it be women who are tempered in action, and are learning to apply tactics within the long-range goals of the movement? Women who share the activity, ensure that it's not the prerogative of an elite few? Women who aren't concerned with power, but who have the courage to take a leading role? Women who listen to others and look for consensus, who know how to delegate, but will not hesitate to take on difficult or boring work themselves? Women who are optimistic but know when to retreat and when to move forward again? Women who learn from their own experience and past history? Women who share the vision and commitment to the end of oppression by the remnants of patriarchy, dying but dangerous? Can we pass on our experience? Learn from our mistakes?

From my study window I see a big ute turn into our drive, long white plastic pipes jutting behind. Our grand-daughter jumps down with a thump of heavy workboots, streaks of grease on the T-shirt that flaps around her slender waist, tattered shorts exposing tanned legs. She is apprenticed to a plumber and laughs about the surprise on men's faces as she lifts heavy equipment.

She is not yet a leader, but is quick to rebel in her own way. She accepts as her right the gains we fought for. And I'm confident that any attempt to take away these gains will make young women of her generation sooner or later take up the banners we carried. They will do things differently, but perhaps my grand-daughter will hear an echo of a poem I wrote for her and others:

> We are making ribbons to encircle cities,
> ribbons rich with birds and flowers, dreams
> of mothers, grandmothers, innumerable children,
> women painting their symbols of love and caring ...[7]

1   Justina Williams, *People & Peace: Selected Poems*, Lone Hand Press, Willagee, 1986.
2   Justina Williams, *The First Furrow: A Radical History of Western Australia*, Lone Hand Press, Willagee, 1976.
3   Bertha Walker, *Solidarity Forever!* National Press, Melbourne, 1972.
4   Verna Coleman, *Adele Pankhurst: The Wayward Suffragette*, Melbourne University Press, Melbourne, 1996, p. 31.
5   Lesbia Harford, 'Machinist's Song' in Marjorie Pizer (ed.), *Freedom on the Wallaby*, Pinchgut Press, Melbourne, 1953.
6   R. Throssell, *Katharine Susannah Prichard: Straight Left*, Wild and Woolly Pty Ltd, Glebe, 1982, p. 106.
7   Williams, *People & Peace*.

ONE GENERATION AFTER ANOTHER

PATRICIA GILES

Born in 1928 in South Australia, Pat moved to Western Australia in the early 1950s. Her early education was intended to groom her for domesticity. In addition to rearing five children, however, Pat became a Labor Senator for Western Australia and served from 1981 to 1993. A trained nurse and midwife prior to entering parliament she completed an Arts degree, worked as a trade union official, and chaired national committees concerned with discrimination and the status of women. While in the Senate, Pat led the Australian delegation to the United Nations End of the Decade for Women Conference in Nairobi in 1985 and was Australian parliamentary representative at the United Nations General Assembly in 1992. Besides chairing many other notable government committees Pat was the inaugural Chair of the Women's Electoral Lobby in Western Australia in 1972 and an inaugural member and President (1988–90) of World Women Parliamentarians for Peace. Since leaving the Senate Pat has held numerous national and international positions, predominantly in the area of women's health. She is currently President of the International Alliance of Women. In 1996, Murdoch University awarded her an honorary doctorate.

A daughter, I forget which one of the four, pinned me with a steely eye. 'Mother!' she accused me, 'fear of success?' At this point in my career I faced the real possibility of being elected to parliament, after several gestures which never had any hope of success but were not without purpose. I loved my job as a union organizer, but was very conscious of the need for the women's movement to increase its parliamentary voice, and for women's policy to become more firmly established within the Australian Labor Party (ALP). My daughters had no doubts about my capacity, nor where my duty lay.

Having by then served an intensive apprenticeship in the party, the trade union movement and within the community, my credentials were not bad. Except, that is, for my blatant feminism, which was used to justify some virulent opposition. This came to a head as the preselection ballot loomed and encouraged a host of contenders at the last moment.

That year, 1979, was to be a turning point for me. I succumbed gracefully to going grey, had a hysterectomy which greatly improved my health, and yes, I was preselected, and subsequently elected to the Senate, where I served from 1981 to 1993.

My career as a public person started in committee work associated with a local kindergarten, then primary and secondary schools as my five children progressed through the State school system. Consequently, I progressed to positions on the WA Council of State School Parents and the Australian Council of State Schools Organisations. Appointed to the WA Health Education Council as the parent representative, and working regularly as a volunteer with the Spastic Centre and Meals on Wheels, I edged towards party politics via the campaign for federal funding for State schools, and joined the ALP in 1971.

Active in Women's Liberation, the Women's Electoral Lobby, of which I was the inaugural convenor in Perth, and the Abortion Law Reform Association, I was among those women who were thoroughly reviled by the right-wing Democratic Labor Party, at that time running candidates in every seat in every election and demonizing everything and everyone associated with feminism.

Servicing my large and busy family of adolescents still required a considerable amount of time and energy, as did continuing voluntary activity while completing a full-time Bachelor of Arts degree in 1974 at The University of Western Australia (UWA). Moving on, I gained a very satisfying job with the Hospital Employees Union of WA (now the Miscellaneous Workers' Union) which I held until entering the Senate.

Having trained as a nurse and midwife, I was employed to organize so-called unskilled nursing home and private hospital workers. The first woman to be employed by the union in this role, I was less likely than the traditional male organizers to be intimidated by ferocious nursing administrators who in this industry were frequently also proprietors. I was ready, willing and able to stand eyeball to eyeball, or bosom to bosom, with these ogres as necessary.

In the course of constant monitoring and enforcing award wages and conditions I was instrumental in the demise of the worst nursing homes. At that time there was no other way of enforcing good standards in an industry where some proprietors were notorious for exploitation of their workers, and inevitably, their patients.

Later, as a senator, opportunity to influence national nursing home policy arose when I was appointed as Chair of a Senate Select Committee of Inquiry into the industry. The resulting report recommended wide-ranging reforms which were implemented during the next few years. The last and most contentious of these was for a Charter of Residents' Rights, which raised the possibility of aged consenting adults sharing rooms in nursing homes to the shock and horror of a few operators.

Another high point of my union career was the titanic clash in 1976 when the Western Australian Government announced its intention of moving profoundly disabled young people from the Tresillian Nursing Home in the salubrious Perth suburb of Nedlands to a location remote from transport in the foothills. The domestic and nursing staff, suddenly embroiled in a political fight and with their jobs threatened if they took action, needed moral support. In a wonderful show of solidarity, this support was readily provided not just by the hospital unions, but by the whole trade union movement. As their organizer I was at Tresillian every day for about three weeks, including weekends. As the drama unfolded, I helped with the usual routines, and at one stage retrieved desperately needed clean linen which had been diverted by the government. The courage of the families in taking on the government attracted wide community support, forcing it to yield to public opinion, and the move was cancelled.

During these years I was frequently the only woman on committees, including the Executive of the Trades and Labour Council of Western Australia (TLC), the Administrative Committee of the ALP in Western Australia, and later the National Executive of the ALP. Invariably, for the first few meetings I would be totally ignored, invisible and inaudible. Persevering, I would be heard, contradicted and dismissed out of hand. Finally, I would be more or less included to enjoy hearing my views recycled as the perceived wisdom of my comrades. This, of course, is not an unusual experience in many partnerships, except that I had to simultaneously tolerate the insecurities of up to fourteen male colleagues.

Despite strong support from a few union and party leaders, women were only gradually accepted in such positions. Almost always, however, constructive and enduring working relationships developed. Being well into middle age and not so subject to testosterone-based reaction as were younger women, I had an advantage over most of my women colleagues at that time. Later, the grey hair proved to be an asset, especially when dealing with expensively educated young conservatives. My divorce in 1976 left me free to do the normal (male) thing of hanging around in the pub after evening meetings. Making one beer last for hours, I would patiently explain the issues that women activists then were busily promoting, such as equal pay, maternity leave and part-time work. In short, I pressed for a union movement sensitive to working women's needs.

In 1974 the Whitlam Government appointed me to chair the WA Committee on Discrimination in Employment and Occupation. The committee's select membership consisted of four: two departmental heads and the presidents respectively of the Employers' Federation and the TLC. Chairing this small high-powered group often meant sensitizing them to sex discrimination in its many forms. Our task of dealing with complaints was complicated by the lack of any powers except those of persuasion. As my first prominent public appointment, it apparently merited an interview by the Australian Women's Weekly, to the thinly disguised disgust of my offspring, not all of whom were prepared to cooperate. As I recall it, the one who objected most had just been elected to the new position of Women's Officer at UWA.

I spoke at the Australian Council of Trade Unions (ACTU) Conference in 1977 when women were rarely seen and hardly ever heard, and in 1978 was selected to chair the ACTU's first ever women's committee which focused initially on maternity leave, child care and part-time work. The following year, I became an ACTU nominee to serve on the National Labor Consultative Council which produced a policy on the elimination of sexual harassment in the Australian Public Service. Early discussions on affirmative action were led by Gail Radford, who was rapidly becoming a world authority on equity in public services, and one of the many talented 'sisters' of that era.[1]

The ACTU, represented by Jan Marsh, now a Vice-President of the Australian Industrial Commission, conducted a successful National Maternity Leave Case in 1979, and in a welcome gesture of confidence the TLC of Western Australia nominated me to lead the State's Maternity Leave Case. Headed by a notoriously reactionary chief commissioner, the Full Bench of the West Australian Industrial Commission produced a predictably grudging and mean-spirited determination. However, at least West Australian women workers in private employment were now entitled to job security when they became pregnant.

Encouraged nationally and internationally by preparation for, and participation in, the first United Nations World Conference in 1975 and the United Nations Decade for Women 1975–85, activist feminists were developing policy in the women's movement, paralleled by remarkable progress within both the ALP and the trade union movement.

My introduction to the art of drafting policy came while sitting next to the President of the Victoria Mothers' Clubs Association, Joan Kirner. I learnt that making progress usually entails reducing differences to a minimum in order to maximize the strength of the document as well as making the occasional sacrifice for the overall good! Success can hang on a few words, or punctuation, or the order of paragraphs; it requires competence in the subject under debate, patience, and unfailing good humour when dealing with uncongenial adversaries. One of my union colleagues described these skills as 'the art of being nice to nasty people'.

Later, during my parliamentary career, I would have the privilege of participating in international policy making through United Nations conferences and preparatory meetings, and also in executive positions in national and international non-government organizations.

When working in a global context, one learns to treasure apparently tiny increments in the hope they will eventually affect much wider and diverse constituencies. One can expend a great deal of effort in simply maintaining a principle, let alone progressing. During a particularly tense preparatory meeting in 1985 prior to the United Nations End of the Decade for Women Conference in Nairobi, a Japanese diplomat walked past as I sat furiously knitting for an expected grandchild, wishing that certain delegations would disaffiliate from the United Nations forthwith and let us get on with the job. 'At least there's something productive going on here', she muttered.

Nationalism is unavoidably part of the exercise, but personal territorialism can also intervene, especially when enthusiastic amateurs get involved. At that same meeting Maureen Reagan, a committed advocate for women's rights and leader of the sixty-strong Republican delegation from the United States, announced that when we arrived in Nairobi she would organize 'chat sessions' on selected issues, horrifying one of the Australians who was justifiably sensitive to the trivializing of women's conferences at which the world's media (still) excels. She suggested mildly to Maureen that perhaps 'chat' was not the best word to use, but was squelched by a snarl from the impeccable Reagan: 'Sister! You're treading on mah toes'.

Elections and appointments by governments and international bodies have given me the honour of serving on a multitude of committees, chairing many, pioneering in such cases as the early days of the Women's Electoral Lobby in Western Australia; the WA Committee on Discrimination, and the inaugural ACTU Women's Committee. Relevant skills had been sharpened during the years while I kept the peace at the dinner table among my five vociferous and strongwilled children, and between them and their similarly endowed father.

In 1981 when I took my seat in the Senate, it was during the decade of a dramatic increase in the percentage of women in Federal Parliament, from 2.5 per cent in 1975 to 12.5 per cent in 1985, and the institution was becoming more woman friendly. Indeed, once elected, one acquires a very privileged status regardless of sex or any other distinction, and the only personal hostility of which I was aware was from senior male ministerial (conservative) staffers. Everyone else was helpful and courteous, regardless of political differences, at least in the corridors. Although the working conditions were atrocious for everyone in the old Parliament House, there was and is considerable goodwill and friendship between parliamentarians and the many people who provide the wide range of supporting services. There is also an abundance of sisterhood between the gifted women who have increasingly featured more strongly in parliamentary departments.

On one occasion I was especially grateful for this warm relationship. While parliament was sitting in the winter of 1987 large numbers of 'Women for Survival' had camped on the lawn opposite the old Parliament House, reasonably comfortable there despite hostility from some press, some parliamentarians and a few hooligans from Duntroon. Late one night, however, driving rain and gale force winds having demolished most of the tents, I offered the shelter of my home to whoever needed it. Catering for breakfast for the nineteen people and a dog who accepted my offer did not really pose a problem because as soon as they knew what I was doing, attendants quietly began scrounging around Parliament House to excellent effect, no questions asked! Next morning, breakfast in my small house was crowded and basic, but plentiful.

Parliament and its services, to my amazement, was geared to providing a complete support system for presumably helpless males marooned in Canberra far from their domestic routines. I had never in all my life been waited upon, and never took the attentiveness for granted. It was always amazing and delightful to have something returned to me before I was aware of having lost it! Apart from attending divisions, one need never have ventured out of one's room, and could have continued to function in lonely state.

In the Australian Parliament in 1983 we Labor Party women parliamentarians and senators established the inaugural caucus committee on the status of women. Our first challenge was to reconstruct our male colleagues, starting with the ministers in the new Labor Government. I chaired this group — 'the powerful status of women committee' as the press occasionally would report — until I retired from the Senate in 1993. We had some remarkable successes.

For a start there were memorable occasions upon which the committee was able to move a minister. During the massive 1987 federal reconstruction of the Education and Training Portfolio, we were disturbed to find there were very few women among those appointed to the board which replaced other consultative bodies. Additionally, the composition of the board did not inspire much confidence among feminist educators. Our appeals to the relevant minister appeared not to impress him greatly; but lo and behold, we were soon into the 1987 election campaign with the government promising to establish another board, and the all-women Women's Education Employment and Training Group was duly delivered.

In 1984 Australia ratified the United Nations Convention on the Elimination of All Forms of Discrimination Against Women but reserved its position on two articles. One of these dealt with paid maternity leave, the other required women to have equal access to combat and non-combat duties. The former would need quite drastic social and industrial reform, not yet completed in 1998, but the defence force issue we attacked immediately.

Minister Kim Beazley and subsequent ministers arranged for the caucus committee to meet with senior defence personnel, and supported the reduction of classifications which were 'combat or combat related' so that women were excluded from fewer and fewer positions. This strategy has continued, and it should be possible now for Australia to withdraw this reservation with little uproar from the traditionalists.

I will never forget our first meeting with an air vice-marshall. He was obviously uneasy, and sweated profusely as twelve Labor women parliamentarians challenged his deeply felt convictions about the place of women generally, and in the defence of their country in particular. He seemed genuinely puzzled when we failed to be moved by his emotional declaration that he would strenuously oppose the notion of his wife or daughters piloting an F111.

As in the previous decade, there was continuous development and refining of the status of women policy. Post-1983, with the ALP in government, we began implementing our feminist policies. There was significant progress, some of it incremental, such as changes to the *Family Law Act 1975*. However, many measures were revolutionary, like anti-discrimination legislation, community child care, the Family Support Allowance and the Child Support Levy, as were consultative committees of indigenous women and women of non-English-speaking background. In 1987 a National Women's Health Strategy was the result of nationwide consultations, and from 1988 to 1993 national consultative councils on violence against women were developing ground-breaking policy.

A major problem in ALP policy is the continuing existence of the 'conscience vote'. However, this particular aggravation was largely overcome in 1991 at the ALP's national conference when the notion of 'the rights of women to determine their own reproductive lives, particularly their right to choose appropriate fertility control and abortion' was endorsed. Despite inconsistencies between the various State legislatures, access to both family planning and abortion are now accepted as services to which women are entitled. Women's struggles have thus ensured that governments now recognize liberal opinion on this issue.

Australian official delegations were therefore authorized to attend the Cairo Conference on Population and Development and the Fourth United Nations Women's Conference in Beijing as firm supporters of the principles of sexual and reproductive health, and worked hard to ensure that strong language to this effect was widely supported by not-so-convinced delegations.

It has been very gratifying to see international recognition of Australian initiatives regarding the status of women, and of well-qualified Australian women. For example, in Beijing during the 1995 conference, panel discussions on a wide range of issues affecting women were organized by intergovernment organizations, and speakers were chosen from among the world's most prominent authorities. These sessions included three which occurred simultaneously, and which were moderated in each case by an Australian: Justice Elizabeth Evatt for the United Nations Commission on Human Rights; Anne Deveson for the United Nations Educational Social and Scientific Commission; and me as chair of the World Health Organisation's (WHO) Global Commission on Women's Health. For a relatively small country, Australia makes a disproportionately large contribution to such activities — another story waiting to be told.

Although never a minister or likely to be one, from 1984 onwards I was chosen by the Australian Government to lead a number of international delegations. The first were preparatory meetings in Tokyo and New York, followed by the United Nations End of the Decade for Women Conference in Nairobi in 1985, and also at that time the first Commonwealth Meeting of Ministers for Women's Affairs. These ministers subsequently met in Harare in 1987 and Toronto in 1990, and again I represented Australia. In 1992, I was government representative to the General Assembly of the United Nations (UNGA 47), which entailed three months of demanding and exciting work with our Permanent Mission to the United Nations. While I was in New York the Minister for Health, Brian Howe, deputed me to represent him at a meeting of Commonwealth Ministers for Health in Cyprus, which decided that its next meeting would be on women and health. In my role as a WHO adviser I attended that meeting which was held in Cape Town in 1995.

UNGA 47 included Special Sessions on issues which had been very high on the ALP's agenda (and mine) for many years, so it was an extraordinary privilege to give the Australian address at the three Plenary Special Sessions on People with a Disability, Aging and Indigenous People. Over the past decade the Australian Government, in consultation with non-government organizations, had introduced measures of social reform which received wide commendation from the global community. It was particularly gratifying to be able to report to the United Nations that our *Disability Discrimination Act 1992* had become law on the day on which I spoke.

There are many other unforgettable experiences to add to these. The stimulus of joining many new groupings such as

Women for a Meaningful Summit 1984 and World Women Parliamentarians for Peace (WWPP) 1985 for example, as well as making many new friends and colleagues.

Valentina Tereschkova, the first woman in space and also President of the Soviet Women's Union, was at the first WWPP meeting in Stockholm. I met her again in Nairobi with other Soviet women, some of whom had paid us a visit in Canberra. As the old Soviet Union began to disintegrate, and the collegiate system of elections was dismantled, the Soviet Women's Union called upon women parliamentarians in Australia, and elsewhere, to advise them on strategies to elect women in the new Russia. In response to this, in 1990 I led a politically disparate delegation of five Australian women parliamentarians to St Petersburg (then Leningrad) and Moscow for a series of formal and informal meetings. The Russian women whom we met were mostly without party backing, and needed to learn from scratch how to raise funds, develop support systems, approach an electorate, deal with the media, and rally the support which we take for granted as party members. At that time their own new electoral system was unresolved.

On this occasion, the Russian women raised another serious concern. Although a high percentage of them had degrees in the arts and humanities there were none with accounting and other business skills which would help them to survive in the new entrepreneurial Russia.

We proposed a modest scheme. We Australians would set up a bilateral 'train the trainer' scheme which depended upon an Australian teacher and a small amount of Australian funding, while the Russian Women's League would choose and provide accommodation in Moscow for students from Russia and all the newly independent states. After some hard work at our end a teacher was found, and Cavan Hogue, Australian Ambassador in Moscow provided the money. He and I had worked together when he was the senior diplomat on the Australian delegation to Nairobi. 'How could I possibly refuse?' was his very welcome response.

As a result, the first class of fifteen women graduated in small business skills in June 1992 at a grand occasion in the

Australian Embassy in Moscow which I attended like a proud grandmother. Within a year the original group had between them trained another 300, and the project has continued to blossom throughout the region, even to the extent of private enterprises themselves linking to the scheme. Ambassador Hogue who watched (beamed actually!) as this project blossomed, deserves a lot of the credit for its success.

In my electorate office the staff consisted of mature women, all of whom were in constant touch with the community through their own and their children's activities. A good working relationship between local, State and Federal Government authorities enabled effective networking between services, and via such networks my staff could readily identify gaps in community services and often initiate action to remedy such gaps.

Gratifying recognition of such cooperative achievements include my name being attached to a women's refuge, to an annual award by and for ALP women in Western Australia, and the recent award of an honorary doctorate from Murdoch University.

My forte, I think, has been as a facilitator rather than a leader. Leadership has been far from my mind, and even now seems alien, a masculine construct which bears little resemblance to what I have been doing for the last twenty-five years. Elections and appointments have led me into privileged and enjoyable positions, in all of which I represented one or another constituency.

Such challenges often carried awesome responsibility for I was under considerable scrutiny. But I was always conscious of the support or sponsorship behind and around me, and increasingly I was aware of the fact that no-one ever reached prominence on personal merit alone.

The philosophy of the modern women's movement, that we work cooperatively, sharing skills and rotating executive positions, is one with which I am perfectly comfortable. Obviously this does not translate easily into bureaucratic systems, but I am frequently reminded that women together often work in generous and constructive ways, circumventing hierarchical barriers and log jams. Many, if not most of us, who have been richly rewarded within the women's movement, have not sought prominence for its own sake. Pausing to recollect, satisfaction comes from having spread a little empowerment, as this is the means by which all women's lives can be enhanced. This is a vastly different concept from that of self-promotion.

My mother, a schoolteacher and a 'blue stocking' as a young woman, was a very conservative person and quite bewildered by my political activism. She would make disparaging remarks like, 'Well, you certainly have the gift of the gab', implying a regrettable trait which I must have inherited from my paternal grandfather, a prominent Methodist clergyman. Her empowerment was zilch when she was deserted by her husband in 1931 and left with two small daughters. She had no recourse but to return to her parents' home, humiliated and penniless. That leading clergyman, her father-in-law, made no move to help her, then or later.

If I am a leader, and if my genes owe him anything, I think perhaps I've used my version of his skills to redefine the conventional meaning of leadership in a way that can make more effective women of us all as we cope with disasters and enjoy everyday living, and plan a better society for coming generations.

1   Marian Sawer, *Sisters in Suits: Women and Public Policy in Australia*, Allen & Unwin, Sydney, 1990.

ACROSS THE DECADES

DAME RACHEL CLELAND

Born in Perth in 1906, Rachel was educated at Cottesloe Primary School and Methodist Ladies' College. She studied at Meerilinga Kindergarten Training College, then taught six-year-old boys at Guildford Grammar School. As the niece of Bessie Rischbieth and the wife of the Director of the Liberal Party, Rachel has lived a life inspired by liberal politics and is a prominent Liberal Party supporter. She was made a Dame of the British Empire in 1980 for her services to the people of Papua New Guinea. Currently, Rachel is active in the environmental movement, where she has become a prominent leader in the struggle to preserve Western Australia's old growth native forests.

I was born only seven years after the colony of Western Australia reluctantly gave women the right to vote. I say reluctantly, because continual pressure from the Women's Christian Temperance Union for most of the 1890s had failed to produce female suffrage by 1898, as had lobbying by the Karrakatta Club and two motions by Walter James. By 1899, however, West Australians (who did not want to federate with the rest of Australia) were becoming worried that the new population of Kalgoorlie might outvote them in the upcoming referendum. It then occurred to Premier Sir John Forrest that if women were enfranchised it would increase the anti-Federation vote. When Walter James again introduced the amendment to the *Constitution Act 1889* in July 1899, the Bill was passed. The decision made Western Australia a pioneer, after New Zealand and South Australia, in votes for women.

My mother Olive and her sister Bessie were reared by an aunt and uncle, Louise and Ben Rounsevell. Uncle Ben was Treasurer when Alexander Downer's grandfather was Premier of South Australia. A passionate federalist, and living in a large household, there was frequent entertainment of political figures from South Australia and other States. His forward-looking ideas were unusual for his time and were no doubt influenced by the work of early feminist, Catherine Spence. He made sure my mother and aunt had a good education and took an intelligent interest in the politics of the day. Even as children, they had a stool each side of the fireplace where they were encouraged to sit and listen to history in the making.

By 1894, when South Australian women won the vote, the two girls were young women. Aunt Bessie was among the first Australian women allowed to vote. Quite a milestone. After marrying Henry Rischbieth, Bessie came with him to the West. Early in the century my mother came to stay with her, met my father, William Herbert Evans, and married him in 1905. They promptly had six children in seven years, making me the eldest of four at two-and-a-half and giving my mother rather a handful. So my aunt and uncle, who grieved being childless, borrowed me from time to time to help relieve my mother. All through my childhood I periodically stayed with the Rischbieths, whose beautiful house and garden was near ours in Peppermint Grove.

The two sisters were very close. Both were foundation members of the Women's Service Guild (WSG). Founded in 1909 at a meeting called by Edith Cowan and chaired by Lady James, the WSG constitution was adopted at its second meeting. It included the pledge that: 'Every member of the Guild must undertake to exercise her vote, whatever her views, at parliamentary or other elections, and to aid in every way the objects of the Guild' (Article 3).

For many years Bessie Rischbieth was President of the WSG. She was creative in her vision of what could be done and had the ability and tenacity to achieve it. Mother was the intellectual who thought things through. They respected one another and made a wonderful team, constantly discussing the problems they were tackling. The resultant information and attitudes were absorbed by all of us children and became part of our background knowledge.

When living with my aunt as a small child, she took me with her to the Friday meetings of the WSG in their headquarters in a large pleasant room, upstairs in Barrack Street. I would be given a picture book and seated on a chair at the side of the room. I would watch the women, fascinated by their personalities. Some were real characters and became very familiar.

They were a remarkable group of women from all walks of life. With differing political affiliations — or even none at all — they worked together with drive and enthusiasm to found many of the institutions we now all take for granted. They had an enormous influence on the development of social welfare and became brilliant parliamentary lobbyists. Their work completely altered the political attitudes towards the needs and rights of women and children. The WSG was instrumental in getting discriminatory laws changed and in educating the public.

After studying at Meerilinga Kindergarten Training College, I taught six-year-olds at Guildford Grammar Preparatory School. In 1925 this was quite an experiment, engaging a woman to teach in a boys' school. In 1927 I met Donald Cleland. Don was a young lawyer with considerable drive and leadership, and prominent in community affairs and politics. I think I was the first girl he met who knew what he was talking about, and we married in 1928.

The National Party and the Country Party were in opposition and Donald was a close friend of the National Party leader, Ross McDonald. With other young men, Don worked hard to build up the National Party and get them back into government. In 1931 he stood for the Labor-held seat of Victoria Park, with many of his colleagues helping. I had my first experience of door knocking. Most enlightening. By then we had been plunged into that awful Depression.

I remember the despair and political muddle and the efforts to cope and bring about change, so difficult when each State had different parties with different names and policies; most were pre-Federation. This disparate group joined together in Canberra as the United Australia Party (UAP). It was always tough for federal members with no party organization in Canberra to support them as a group. Difficult in government, this situation was worse in opposition.

When war broke out in 1939, Don joined up as soon as the Australian Imperial Force was formed. He served in the Middle East, then back in Australia and Papua New Guinea (as a chief of staff) until his compassionate leave in early 1945.

Prime Minister Menzies had lost the wartime election of 1940, but Labor did well and the country was proud of Prime Minister Curtin. From the beginning, Australian unions had formed Labor's parliamentary wing. Among non-Labor voters, however, there was a lot of concern and discussion about the future. Everyone wanted a better world and a better party. As war drew to its end, Menzies launched the new Liberal Party. The name was right, denoting progress and openness to change and reform. To be Liberal meant social and global generosity. A wave of hope swept round Australia for it expressed the spirit of the times. And for the first time there was one conservative party for all Australia, instead of six.

Both Don and I were enthusiastic about the new Liberal Party. Late in April he returned from the war in Papua New Guinea to find he had been elected Vice-President of the party. He subsequently became involved with drafting a new Liberal Party constitution. Shortly afterwards the news that Curtin had died shattered Australia. In the by-election for Curtin's seat, Menzies persuaded Don to lead the Liberal ticket. Labor selected Kim Beazley, a lecturer in politics at The University of Western Australia, as their candidate. His extension lectures made him very popular with the public and our friends commented: 'How awful to have to choose between Don and Kim'. The odd thing was that Don did very well in Fremantle and Kim polled well in Dalkeith! Not so surprising if you were to read the policy and pamphlets of that first election for Fremantle, which today make Menzies and his new Liberal Party look left of Hawke and Keating. During that short four-week campaign in July, Churchill lost the British election, the bomb was dropped on Hiroshima and the war was over. Don managed to reduce Labor's majority from 30,000 to 7000. No mean feat.

In August 1945, Don was offered the position of Director of the Liberal Party, with the task of creating the new secretariat. He accepted the offer and left for Sydney in September. The two boys and I followed in January 1946. It was a bewildering move for us as a family, but we eventually settled down and ended up loving Sydney. Apart from building up a staff of talented people and creating an effectively functioning secretariat, Don spent a lot of time either in Canberra or visiting State branches to develop an all-Australian outlook. By the end of 1948 the federal secretariat was a smooth-running organization. When Menzies romped home in December 1949, starting his seventeen-year reign as Prime Minister, there was great jubilation. They were indeed exciting days.

I was often in Canberra during those first years, when there was quite a different atmosphere and relationship between the parties than there is today. There was more dignity in parliament and more honesty. Debating was tough but it kept more to the point and didn't try to win by crude denigration of the opponent. Voters on both sides had more trust in their politicians and respect for the other side.

With Menzies in power and relations between the secretariat and the government working effectively, Don felt that his work in this area was done. Feeling a strong pull to work again in Papua New Guinea (PNG) he applied for, and won, the job of Assistant Administrator. We left for PNG in 1951. Two years later Don was sworn in as Administrator and we moved to Government House. Then came fifteen full, challenging and fascinating years. Don's work — governing a war-ravaged country with most of its towns and many villages destroyed, its people badly affected by war and poverty and one-third of the country, in the wild highlands, not even explored — was indeed a challenge. He was responsible for the work of the PNG Public Service and its House of Assembly, of which he was Speaker. Therefore, apart from all the other duties, we lived within a political world. Australian ministers and opposition politicians visited PNG frequently. Since they stayed with us we got to know many of them well and saw them again when we visited Canberra.

Don retired in 1967. We built a house in Port Moresby and our son and grandchildren lived nearby. Don was taken ill quite suddenly and died a fortnight before the Independence Celebrations in 1975. The grief shown by the people was profoundly moving and a solace to his family.

I remained in PNG another four years and returned rather reluctantly to Perth to live close to my brother and sisters in Peppermint Grove. Being away from 1945 until 1979 meant that I came back to a different world. It wasn't easy to settle down and become a West Australian again. About a year after I returned, I was horrified that Fred Chaney was not selected as a Liberal candidate for Curtin. Disturbed at the circumstances surrounding that decision, I wrote to the *West Australian*. The letter caused quite a stir, with people saying that I had expressed what they felt, and I was persuaded to become active in the party. I therefore became very involved with the Women's Section, locally and right up to the State Women's Council.

As time went on, I found puzzling aspects which I didn't like. I found other like-minded people also. It was then that the influence of Noel Crichton-Browne became apparent and for some years we worked hard to counter it. But it was never referred to publicly. I resigned over a matter in the Women's State Council with which I couldn't come to terms. I kept on working with the Cottesloe branch, however. Through this experience I was saddened to find how far the party had drifted from the forward-looking vision and practical good sense once so much part of the Liberal Party Menzies had created.

At the same time I became involved with my old Kindergarten Training College, Meerilinga. Founded in 1914, Meerilinga was the flagship of the community-based kindergarten movement, with 390 groups all over Western Australia. As it grew the government employed a senior advisory teacher for kindergartens and my sister, Margaret Evans, was appointed. She remained until she retired in 1970. In 1976, the Minister for Education, in an authoritarian and arbitrary decision, turned the kindergarten movement over to the Education Department, along with its assets, its teachers and the highly trained and experienced director and headquarters' staff. The bureaucrats assumed it included the college buildings, a lovely old house in large grounds in Perth's Hay Street West, with a postwar two-storey college built from funds raised by great public effort plus a federal grant.

Late in 1980, I was concerned by a well-publicized kindergarten to-do. Teachers and mothers with their children, led by

Betty Lefroy, kindergarten-trained and a noted volunteer, were marching on Parliament House and achieving some success. Some time later, at a gathering of supporters called by Betty, we learnt that some public servants were in the process of trying to claim the buildings for the government. However, Betty and others believed that the original purchase had been made possible by a 1925 legacy from my uncle, Henry Rischbieth. They found the relevant parts of his will in the Battye Library and showed them to Premier Sir Charles Court. Fortunately, he saw the point. The upshot was that the child-care course could remain in the college for which the public had raised the money, while the heritage building could be used as the headquarters for various voluntary organizations for young children. From that gathering I became chair of the Friends of Kindergartens.

Thus began a long, tough and fascinating ten years working with a wonderful group of people. Shortly after the building was vacated, four organizations moved in. When the child-care students moved out we could expand, and over the years we began to fill all sorts of gaps in the community needs for young children. Now there are fifty organizations there. The time came to recruit a responsible management committee.

Watching this develop, we began to dream dreams. Pat O'Sullivan's vision saw a Meerilinga Early Childhood Foundation, with a staff of highly trained professionals to carry out research and run seminars, workshops, discussion groups and find other ways of educating the public and people responsible for children, including parents. The foundation was formed in 1987 with a director and staff and a very good board of which Pat was the chair and Margaret and I were members. Back in the mid-1980s the Education Department swapped the deeds of the five blocks of land from the Kindergarten Board to the Crown and we faced an ongoing struggle to have our titles to the property restored to us. Excuses, excuses, until finally, in 1989, it was done. Then I felt I could retire. The foundation is now almost ten years old and has grown enormously in scope, responsibility and public recognition. It works closely on projects with each of the universities, at two of which students of early childhood study for their degrees.

About 1988 I began writing a book and resigned from most outside activity until it was finished in 1994. When I began, in the same year, to work again in the party I was horrified to find that our branch was dominated by Crichton-Browne adherents. Several of us attended a branch meeting to assess things. We decided that we must alert our 300 members to the situation, and ask them to attend the 1994 annual meeting. We also approached a member who was highly respected by the public and he agreed to stand for President. Members rallied with over a hundred attending and voting in our new President, office bearers and committee, which included some of us who had worked to bring this about.

In the new group considerable responsibility rested on our shoulders, not only in developing a strong branch, but also to raise money for the imminent State and federal elections ahead. The fundraising was successful, but we began to worry over aspects of the way the party was run. We found that many of the flaws came about by some curious defects in the constitution which had been amended many times through Crichton-Browne's influence. We then found that people in other branches were also concerned. The need for change swept through the party and led to State Council setting up a group early in 1996 led by a notable outsider, Harold Clough, to examine the constitution and report their recommendations for change.

Many consultations and submissions led to a comprehensive report which went to branches for comment. When the final report was tabled, State Council organized a two-day constitutional conference to discuss and pass or reject each clause. The difference in thinking between the followers of Crichton-Browne and the rest became very obvious. He didn't appear, but from a room upstairs he organized his followers through his mobile. It was a tough battle. They had the numbers to water down quite a lot of the recom-mendations, but we managed to pass enough to weaken the hold of the Crichton-Browne members. And matters have certainly been better ever since.

A few years ago I was caught up in a series of happenings with quite spectacular results. Early in 1995 while visiting Canberra, a friend in the Press Gallery invited me to spend the day in Parliament House. Oddly, it was the day of speculation about whether Alexander Downer would stand down as Prime Minister in favour of John Howard. A dramatic day indeed. Having lunch, Julie Flynn asked me if I thought John Howard would be able to win back government. My reply was that I didn't think the Liberals would win as long as Crichton-Browne operated in parliament. Julie exclaimed in surprise. I filled her in with some background on the way he controlled the Western Australian Liberal Party, and suggested that she did some investigation.

Some months later, a State Liberal member tabled in Western Australian Parliament a leaked court document showing that Crichton-Browne's wife had once taken out a restraining order for violence. At last his doings were open to public discussion, but it seemed to me for the wrong reasons. There was much public fuss and discussion and Julie's friend, Pru Goward, rang me from Canberra quite late one night asking about him. I would not comment on the violence aspect, but spoke of the way he operated politically. She then asked if she could interview me for Radio National's morning program, 'AM'. Thinking, 'Oh Gosh! But I suppose it's time somebody spoke out', I agreed.

She asked many questions and I felt the interview went all right the next morning. By mid-morning, Alan Carpenter of ABC television had rung to ask if he could interview me for the '7.30 Report'. After some thought, I agreed. The phone kept ringing that night with support from viewers. Two supporting letters appeared in next morning's *West Australian* and the support continued all week, with more in suburban papers. After Channel Nine interviewed me for '60 Minutes' I received letters of congratulations from other States. Instead of public silence and constant private discussion about the way Crichton-Browne operated with such detriment to the party, there was now public knowledge and open discussion. It was quite extraordinary. People known to be under his influence suffered politically with this exposure. But a few weeks later, he was expelled from the party. There was great public relief, but even without party membership he nonetheless still operates behind the scenes.

Trees and the forests have been a lifelong love for me. Over the last six or seven years, my concern has been the recent rapid loss of the remaining old growth South-West forests. My activist line has been to concentrate on forest economics and employment. Standing forests are necessary to many other industries, I argue. Cutting down the forests will give huge profits once, then after replanting ninety years will go by before they earn again. It seems to be unsound, even stupid economics to me. Why not leave the remaining karri, and replant round Northcliffe and other areas of empty karri ground left by the failed group settlement scheme of sixty years ago?

My work mostly has been getting people interested by talking, lobbying, writing information handouts, using the media, and supporting other groups. I joined a committee of seven members from the city and forest areas, proposing changes to the Department of Conservation and Land Management (CALM) which administers the forests. The new policy would be profitable to the timber companies without logging any more of the remaining old growth unlogged forest. It indicates advantages to other industries, and was designed to have a marked influence on the salt problem of farming land and river systems. This policy would also increase the workforce in the forests. After nearly a year's work, a very attractive document was launched to an interested crowd in the Alexander Library in 1995. It received a good review in the *West Australian*, each member of parliament received a copy, and it was widely distributed. So far nothing has happened. But the document is there for people to see the possibilities.

In January 1998, as patron of the Walpole Wilderness Protection group, I launched the proposal for conservation of old growth forests in the Walpole area. We drew a very supportive crowd at Fremantle's Esplanade Hotel. Earlier I had inspected the Rocky Block forest, a unique ecosystem of old growth jarrah. Rocky Block is heritage listed by a federal conservation body, but it is still being clear-felled. A lot of wonderful people, many of them well known and all of them determined, are protesting loudly. The original Walpole proposal group met in my home late in 1997. It included dress designer Liz Davenport, environmentalist Shirley de la Hunty, Fremantle mayor Richard Utting, artist Robert Juniper, Subiaco mayor Tony Costa and environmentalists Patrick and Maggie Weir. In 1999 many others have supported and joined in our protests, including Eagles' coach Mick Malthouse, Sister Veronica Brady, John Quigley QC and Janet Holmes à Court.

Some of these people gathered at my house for a re-run of that first meeting, when ABC television filmed our battle for the old growth forests for an 'Australian Story' segment. By bringing together all these well-known Australians, we hope to persuade the government to protect our West Australian heritage.

I often feel lucky to have lived into my nineties while keeping both physical energy and quite a lively mind. It is fascinating to look back over the decades since early in the century. I remember when the Rischbieths sold their carriage and horses and bought two cars. We children loved the coachman and horses and missed them. But we had our ponies and mother drove her sulky to Perth every Friday until after the First World War. It's something to have lived from the horse and buggy age to the age of space travel and instant world communication. The change has been so rapid. But reviewing the political scene, it hasn't changed much at all. One political party in power follows the other into power in a sort of rhythm. Labor looks after the people, staggers into debt and loses. Liberals tighten our belts and get money in the kitty, and they lose. Labor goes its usual way again and the Liberals come back and get the economy right once more. We never learn. There have been four federal cycles in my lifetime and no doubt it will go on into the future. Alongside, you have the 'money-economy cycle'. My father spoke of the crash in the 1880s and 1890s, and fifty years later I lived through the 1930s Depression. And now, after another sixty years, we are entering another crash.

The great change in this century, which marks the subject of this book, is that women for the first time in world history are gradually taking their place beside men in society as persons of equal value, equal ability and equal responsibility. It is important that this equality comes about with women being accepted with all their femininity and men with all their masculinity. The qualities of both are needed for a balanced and happy world.

IN LABOR

CARMEN LAWRENCE[1]

One of seven children, Carmen was born in 1948 in the small wheatbelt town of Morowa, north of Perth. She gained a PhD from The University of Western Australia in 1983. Carmen's parliamentary career began in 1986 when she won the seat of Subiaco. She became Minister of Education in 1988 and Minister of Aboriginal Affairs in 1989. In a leadership change on 12 February 1990, Carmen made history by becoming Australia's first woman Premier. She moved into federal politics in 1994, becoming Minister for Human Services and Health, and Minister Assisting the Prime Minister for the Status of Women. In opposition from 1996 Carmen was appointed Shadow Minister for the the Environment; the Arts; and Assistant to the Leader of the Opposition on the Status of Women. She held these positions until she stepped aside from the shadow ministry in April 1997.

Discussing Carmen Lawrence has often been a national pastime. Observers watched her meteoric rise to political prominence in Western Australia and then speculated about how far she would go on the federal parliamentary bench. The media saw her as star quality from early in her career. They appraised and scrutinized her, praised, patronized and condemned her. Headlines such as '"Tootsie" is tipped to be our Premier',[2] and 'Why Carmen is teflon tough'[3] help fashion her public image. She has been called everything from 'Pearl Pureheart'[4] to 'Typhoid Mary'.[5] Until early 1995, journalists described her political path as a series of 'miracle milestones'. One writer lists her achievements as follows:

1986, wins the seat of Subiaco, wrested from the Liberal Party after 27 years; 1988, becomes a state minister in her first term; 1990, becomes Australia's first woman premier; 1993, becomes state's first woman opposition leader after narrow election defeat; 1994, replaces John Dawkins in federal seat of Fremantle, making Australian political history by increasing Labor's winning margin in a by-election. Soon after: cabinet minister 'most likely to' candidate for deputy prime minister and, even, first woman prime minister.[6]

Then came Easter 1995. The Minister for Health in Lawrence's cabinet, Keith Wilson, challenged her account of Cabinet meetings preceding the 1992 suicide of Perth lawyer, Penny Easton. At the centre of the tragedy was a petition to parliament by Easton's ex-husband, complaining of unfair treatment by the Family Court in the matter of his wife's divorce action. Lawrence had repeatedly insisted that she only knew of the contents of the petition just before it was tabled in parliament, and then only in the briefest of terms. The controversy gave Liberal leader Richard Court, Lawrence's successor to the West Australian premiership, the opportunity for political gain of the highest order.

Premier Court called a royal commission into the 'improper or inappropriate use of executive power', or 'improper or inappropriate motivations'[7] in parliamentary events surrounding the Easton petition. In November 1995, Commissioner Marks decided, on the basis of the allowable evidence, that Dr Lawrence had been untruthful about having prior knowledge of the petition before it was tabled. He did not go so far as to claim that Lawrence's untruths were wilful.

Lawrence's electorate office claims that: 'For cynical political reasons, the Liberal Party has always encouraged the idea that Dr Lawrence was personally responsible for Mrs Easton's tragic death'.[8] A marker of the political capital the Court Government stood to gain from Lawrence's fall from grace was their willingness to spend $6 million of taxpayers' money on the royal commission. These highly charged events gained enormous public attention across Australia. Only French nuclear testing and Bosnia rated more commentary from print and television during 1995, and Lawrence was talkback radio's most popular topic for the year.[9]

With what seemed to many like another miracle, Carmen Lawrence's political career survived the 1995 onslaught by media, lawyers and political adversaries. Until Labor lost the federal election in 1996, she kept her ministerial portfolio. Moreover, polls showed she had wide public support for retaining that status.[10] Lawrence remained a shadow minister until she was charged by the West Australian police on 21 April 1997 with the misdemeanour of giving false testimony to the Marks Royal Commission. Charged on three counts, she faces a maximum penalty of five years' imprisonment. The case is scheduled to come to court in July 1999.

Throughout her trials and inquisitions, Lawrence has had both strong and mild support from the Australian Labor Party (ALP) leadership. Paul Keating was publicly loyal in 1995, stating emphatically that the charges against her were politically motivated and promising that the government would foot the bill for what turned out to be $4 million of legal fees. The succeeding Coalition Government has not been as generous. As this book goes to press in May 1999, litigation over whether the Federal Government is responsible for the costs drags on. Kim Beazley, Leader of the Opposition since 1996, has been more cautious than Keating. When Lawrence was charged with giving false testimony in 1997, Beazley said he was worried about her political future and 'hoped she could survive the charges'. The ALP, he said, would not be sponsoring a fund to help Lawrence cope with the potentially massive legal charges.[11] Having just scraped over the line in the 1996 election (in his marginal seat of Brand), Beazley faced pressure from the ALP right wing to dispatch Carmen Lawrence and gain for himself preselection for her safe Labor seat of Fremantle.[12] The 1998 election vindicated the opposition leader's decision to ignore that pressure when he turned his marginal seat into a triumph for the ALP vote. Carmen's strongest support is from the left of the party. Right-wingers have never forgiven her for instigating the WA Inc Royal Commission, and 'dropping her mates in the drink'. Two of the 'mates' in question are ex-Premier Brian Burke and ex-Deputy Premier David Parker, both of whom were subsequently gaoled on charges arising from the commission's findings.

By contrast, Carmen has had vocal and unwavering support from a number of Labor women. Pat Giles, for example, believes that the attacks on Lawrence carry 'an element of an attack on women'.[13] More importantly, however, Pat believes they arise because, 'Carmen's position is unique. She's such a target. The biggest you can imagine'.[14] Joan Kirner agrees: 'There's a great feeling of anger about what many regard as a witch-hunt, a lack of justice ... When you have a Royal Commission into recollections and a misdemeanour charge laid over recollections, it would be farcical if it wasn't so serious'.[15]

According to *HQ*'s journalist (who interviewed Joan Kirner and Pat Giles), all the Labor women she spoke to 'insist that the disputed facts of the Easton affair have never been the issue for them'. Instead, it is 'the tragic pointlessness of Lawrence's undoing ... and the sense that somehow Lawrence must be made to pay for the — in their eyes — unrelated suicide of Penny Easton, that has them seething with rage'.[16]

Carmen herself protests her innocence on all counts. She had committed 'no offence' in the events leading up to the tabling of the Easton petition, she told the press in April 1997, 'or in any subsequent action.' She would defend the charges against herself while continuing to 'vigorously represent the people of Fremantle in the Federal Parliament. Since I'm innocent, I intend to get on with my job, and with my life'.[17]

In a written statement, Lawrence's electorate office claims that: 'Disbelief of her evidence, honestly given, by the politically motivated Commission has since been used as the basis for laying charges. *An offence has been created where none previously existed.*' The statement also claims that 'saturation publicity and media comment in 1995 and since about the veracity of Dr Lawrence's evidence ... casts doubt on any prospect of a fair trial'.[18]

The document goes on to reveal some little-known history of the Easton affair. Rather than the Family Court dispute between the Eastons being introduced with the petition, it claims, a Liberal parliamentarian first raised the matter in State Parliament in 1987. Moreover, Penny Easton's mother, Mrs Barbara Campbell, who held Lawrence culpable for her daughter's suicide and stood against Lawrence in elections, is claimed to have introduced the Easton divorce into the public arena almost a year before Brian Easton's petition was presented. In January 1992, Mrs Campbell gave evidence on her daughter's divorce proceedings to the Parliamentary Select Committee of Inquiry into the Official Corruption Commission.[19]

The legal and political mudslinging has so far cost Carmen Lawrence her shadow ministries. When she comes to trial she stands to lose large sums of money in legal costs, her life as a politician and at worst her freedom. Despite the political and media pressure Lawrence continues to convey an air of calm authority. Mixed with an ability to represent her constituents with intelligence and hard work whatever the odds, her demeanour wins loyalty from her Fremantle electorate and admiring observers, and grudging respect from her detractors.

In March 1997 we conducted an interview with Carmen Lawrence. Apart from some updating of that information in early 1999, much of the material outlined below comes from that interview. Given the highly personalized nature of the criticism that has been directed towards her, we were intrigued by Lawrence's reputation for public composure, hence our opening question:

EDITORS: How do you keep emotional control in the face of such a political battering?

LAWRENCE: I don't always keep that control. When I gave a press conference after I was charged in 1997, I worried that I might dissolve in a flood of tears. Perhaps my usual serenity is because as a child, particularly a 'middle' child, I learned how to maintain a level of poise under pressure. At boarding school and subsequently I learnt to be self-reliant. I think I've travelled a spiritual journey, for want of a better description, which insists on aloneness. Not loneliness, but aloneness.

It's not so much that I'm not subject to the same emotions as anyone else. But I have always maintained the distinction between who I am and who others think I am: both the exaggerated praise and the unjustified criticism. Neither of those is central to the 'you' that you are when you're staring into space.

EDITORS: Where do you go to stare into space?

LAWRENCE: I don't actually mean stare into space, I mean not being physically linked with anything. It might be through music, it might be through walking or through reading. I also engage in a loose form of meditation. Basically it's the ability to relax into oneself. You have to understand that there will be times of depression and sorrow and hurt. But you don't have to be fragmented and anxious and fall apart. I mean I've been all of those things. I'm not trying to suggest that I don't have those feelings, or that they don't disturb me.

EDITORS: How has the Marks Royal Commission affected your life as a politician?

LAWRENCE: The Easton business was designed to discredit me. And in some people's eyes I was discredited. So what I have to do is to rebuild my reputation. Not because I was ever interested in the political glory that the media love, but because in order to be effective you have to be seen as consistent, reliable, etc. I don't know whether this ground was necessarily lost to the extent that the media think. Nonetheless it's important that I do this rebuilding work to convince those who are still wavering on that question. I can't be an effective advocate on anything – the environment, in the arts or on behalf of women – unless there's a recognition that I'm a serious player, that I'm a long-term player.

Certainly I think some people who decided I was loathsome voted accordingly. But all the information we have within the party suggests that there were as many people who moved to support me as moved to oppose me. That's what our polling said. It says something about people's understanding of what was actually going on as opposed to what was said to be going on.

EDITORS: When your political career was in jeopardy in 1995 you reportedly said: 'People forget that I've always been a fighter'.

LAWRENCE: I think there was a view around that if it got too hard, and if I got pushed around enough I'd say it's all too nasty and go home. I didn't play politics in a way that was necessarily easily recognized and understood, particularly by some of the boys in the media. But whatever else they might have thought about me, I'm not someone who gives up.

In 1995 there was a time when I was the target of question time every day for weeks. I'd be called first and then the pressure would be on for the rest of the session. One day I wasn't sure I could do it again. Yet I made it, somehow. Can you imagine the scene if I'd fainted or burst into tears? What would have been made of that?

EDITORS: In December 1997, John Halden was acquitted on the charge of knowingly misleading a Royal Commission. What do you think that means for you, with your trial on the count of giving false testimony coming up in July 1999?

LAWRENCE: I don't really want to think, or talk, about it. I'm pleased with the results for Halden. And it is a bit reassuring, since politicians haven't been treated all that well by judges and courts over the past few years. But at present the less we all say about it the better.

EDITORS: Some political commentators say you came closer than any other woman to actually becoming Prime Minister.

LAWRENCE: I don't know about that. In some people's eyes perhaps. I think there were some in the party who saw me as a potential deputy. I don't think they had gone beyond that.

Being identified as a future leader is an incredible burden to bear, whether you're male or female. If you look over the years at the people who have been nominated as potential future leaders they often don't get there. There are too many uncertainties in politics to predict where you are going to end up. I never anticipated being the Premier of Western Australia. That was the result of a series of events which were beyond anyone's anticipation. In the federal arena I saw myself simply as someone who was seen as having potential.

EDITORS: Was it a hard decision to move from State to federal politics?'

LAWRENCE: It was hard in the sense that I thought the move was somewhat premature. I didn't want to be seen as deserting WA Labor in their hour of need, so to speak. But realistically, I could see that it was unlikely they would want me to continue to be leader and that maybe it wasn't a bad time to step aside and let someone else have a go. I probably would have stayed on another year before offering the party an alternative in the lead up to the next election.

Federal politics was an opportunity for me to be involved in the big policy issues. State politics tends to be a bit narrower, more constrained by what's going on from day to day. I saw this as an opportunity that wouldn't come along again.

EDITORS: What would you now do differently as a political leader?

LAWRENCE: As Premier I was criticized from time to time for not involving all of my colleagues in major decisions about policy. That was sometimes a reasonable criticism, and sometimes just based on a failure to understand that you need to keep things fairly close if you're going to have maximum impact on the community's response. But I think people would say that I always consider the issues carefully. In terms of leadership, I've always regarded my peers as just that. I assume that people will get out of their job what they put into it and that means that I am sometimes not as ready as others to congratulate or praise. It's not that I don't respond to what people do, but not as immediately or effusively as some would like and I think that was a difficulty that characterized my time as Premier. Nonetheless, I give people their own heads. I don't stand on their toes, I assume that they're competent, unless demonstrated to the contrary. Most of the time people respond well to that in preference to having someone who interferes all the time or tries to second guess them.

EDITORS: Have you always found yourself in tune with the Labor Party's policies on women in government?

LAWRENCE: Along with other women in the party, I've given a lot of support to women aspiring to political life. Emily's List is one of those projects.[20] It's a very deliberate strategy for providing money and other assistance for women trying to enter politics. The idea is to solicit financial and practical support from the wider community so that more progressive women are elected to parliament, not so that women are given special assistance which advantages them over their male colleagues (that's something which concerns our male colleagues).

EDITORS: Given that the Labor Party lost seats for women in the 1996 federal election, can you say that the policies to encourage women are working?

LAWRENCE: We lost a lot of people in that election. Basically it was a tide in tide out phenomenon. That's why people such as Joan Kirner and myself pushed very hard to get a rule change to ensure that at least 35 per cent of Labor members of parliament are women. We knew women would continue to be selected for marginal seats and only occasionally for safe ones. As long as they were sitting on the edge whenever the tide went out, they would go too — and they did. Conservative women also came in with the change of government in 1996, but they were just as vulnerable, as the 1998 election showed.

And we've had the same problem. I think we had twelve women in the House of Representatives before the 1996 election when we went down to four. Because most of them were sitting in fairly marginal seats. And that's why Emily's List exists. We wanted a network of people who would make sure women candidates got in and stayed in.

In the latest round of preselection for us federally there was a significant increase in the number of women in total, but more importantly in the safest of safe seats. Some of the jewels in the crown of the Labor Party seats — places like Sydney, Gellibrand, etc. — have gone to women which has helped increase our numbers since the 1998 election. With margins in the order of some 20 per cent those women can now participate fully in the political process without the incredible difficulties associated with sitting on the knife edge of a few hundred votes. So we have more women in those positions where they won't go out with the tide. We also have sixteen women in the Lower House — the largest number we've ever had.

EDITORS: How do you think your past has shaped where you are today?

LAWRENCE: The kind of upbringing I had was in many senses one of a pioneering family. I think it would have been economically very tough for my parents. They talk about the fact that when they first went to Gutha, where my father was a soldier settler, they had a suitcase full of clothes, two children, one on the way, and £50.

That was their total wealth. They tell stories of boiling wheat as a source of carbohydrate and shooting cockatoos. I don't think it was as terrible as it sounds now, but there's no doubt it was rural poverty. Everyone's ingenuity was tested in that environment. My parents could make a fist of just about anything. That was my model.

Growing up was a mixture of early separation, then a return home. I was sent away to boarding school at Dongara when I was six then came home when a Catholic primary school was built in Morawa. I returned to Dongara to complete my final two years of primary school, then went off again for high school in Perth.

Perhaps because of this I was more reserved as a child, more shy, than I am now. I think that made me more defensive when I was younger. I'm no longer defensive about that because now I feel more connected with people. Although in fact I'm actually more apart from them.

EDITORS: Where is home for you now?

LAWRENCE: Well, I guess I've got two. One is my own home, which is down here in North Fremantle with David. But in the sense of the wider family my parents, who are both still alive, live in Shenton Park. We get together with various combinations of family members once a week with my parents. In a way the closeness that was difficult when we were young because we were all over the place, due to both boarding school and the wide spread of our ages, has now been replaced by a level of closeness and contact that I guess I don't see in many families. My parents have been tremendously supportive of all of us in different ways and for different reasons, just as they were when we were young.

EDITORS: Did you ever think you would follow in your mother's footsteps and have a large family?

LAWRENCE: No, and I'm not alone in that among my siblings. We're all a disappointment to my mother: there are seven of us and only fifteen grandchildren in total. My marriage didn't work, so it wasn't possible to have another child. I loved having David and spending time with him. It was a fantastic experience, but I couldn't possibly have had seven children because I wanted to do other things. The women of my mother's generation were loving and giving, but I think with other options open to them they would have had fewer children too.

EDITORS: Do you miss the country you grew up in?

LAWRENCE: I have a very strong attachment to the Australian environment, which was one of the reasons why I wanted to take on that portfolio. My childhood was an experience of heat and dust, open spaces and blue skies, red dirt and brilliant wildflowers in spring. I'm really a bit of a nature freak, I think. I like nothing better than to spend time in the forest in the South-West. But the Kimberley is my favourite place in the world with its clarity and definiteness of colour and light.

I'm very much an Australian when it comes to the need for that space. I don't like being hemmed in. This office, for instance, drives me nuts because there is no window to the outside world. I actually feel physically tense, I don't like it at all. I spent twelve months in Italy, which I loved. But I found Europe too claustrophobic. There were too many people. You couldn't see the horizon.

EDITORS: How do you envisage your political future?

LAWRENCE: Within the parliamentary party I have positioned myself as someone who is prepared to do the hard work, both on policy development and in achieving specific policy objectives. In the first twelve months in opposition, I consolidated a new policy in relation to the Environment and the Arts. Although I was always very interested in these areas, I wasn't particularly familiar with them until I became shadow minister. Without a portfolio I've researched and developed policy concerns on a number of local and national issues. I also continue to work in the area of Status of Women.

In the latter case I consider that activists, feminists and others who argue for improving the status of women and oppose discriminatory actions are being demonized by the government and some parts of the wider community and the media. However, I feel part of the circular backlash against feminists and feminism stems from a failure to communicate. It's not the fault of individuals, it's just something that hasn't been achieved successfully and it's all the more pressing now. I think we need to ask the questions: 'How do we communicate our aspirations to the wider community? How do we strike a note that resonates beyond the converted?'

The very dangerous notion being spread by the current government is that women make up a noisy minority. My interest in women's welfare is making sure that we have good policy, but more important than that, communicating the need for a whole range of issues to be given adequate attention. Otherwise these needs are seen as special pleading and objections to so called 'special treatment' become the overt reason for pushing women back into a more subservient role.

EDITORS: Journalists have described the ALP today as the party taking its medicine, doing the 'hard labour' of winning back the Labor heartland — those battlers who defected to Honest John Howard. How much of the last few years has been 'hard labour' for you?

LAWRENCE: I have a vivid memory of myself as a young woman, abdomen extended two feet in front with a couple of pillows, on top of the St Catherine's float at the annual University of Western Australia Prosh procession. We were protesting about the paucity of women in our governments. My hair was tied up in a bandanna with a knot on top, and blazoned across my chest were the words 'In Labor', deliberately misspelt. You could say that the slogan proved prophetic. On a more sober note, it would be incorrect to label my political life as hard work. Pursuing the interests of my constituents and researching and developing policy that will improve Australian lives is too enriching and rewarding to be labelled 'hard labour'.

Carmen Lawrence's wide band of well-wishers will be hoping that the enriching and rewarding aspects of her political career continue to outweigh the costs of being a woman leader.

1	The material for this chapter was written by Joan Eveline and Lorraine Hayden from an interview in March 1997 and subsequent updates.
2	*Daily News*, 7 Oct. 1988, p. 11.
3	*Weekend Australian*, 2-3 Sept. 1995, p. 25.
4	*Australian*, 18-19 Aug. 1995, p. 27.
5	*Australian*, 26-27 Aug. 1995, p. 24.
6	'Carmen and Her Sisters', *HQ*, Jul/Aug. 1997, p. 57.
7	Terms of Reference, Premier's media statement, 9 May 1995.
8	Electorate Office of Carmen Lawrence, 'Marks Royal Commission/Easton Affair', Fremantle, June 1997, p. 2.
9	Susan Mitchell, *The Scent of Power: On the Trail of Women and Power in Australian Politics*, Angus & Robertson, Sydney and Melbourne, 1996, p. 235.
10	ibid.

11	Randal Markey, 'Labor "won't foot bill"', *West Australian*, 23 April 1997, p. 5.
12	Karen Middleton, 'The Big Bloke', Big Weekend, *West Australian*, 15 August 1998, p. 5.
13	'Carmen and Her Sisters', p. 57.
14	ibid.
15	ibid.
16	ibid.
17	Damon Kitney and Louise Dodson, 'Labor battens down for trial', *Australian Financial Review*, 23 April 1997.
18	Electorate Office of Carmen Lawrence, 'Marks Royal Commission/Easton Affair', p. 2, emphasis in original.
19	ibid, p. 3.
20	Like its counterpart in the United States, the Australian organization Emily's List, founded in 1994, is a fundraising body aimed at increasing the number of women in parliament. The group selects women for financial and practical support on the basis of their progressive politics and individual merit.

A TAPESTRY OF PASSION AND PEACE

JO VALLENTINE

Jo was born in Beverley, east of Perth, in 1946. A boarder at Loreto Catholic Convent in Perth she spent one year at a United States high school as a foreign exchange student. After training as a teacher at Graylands Teachers' College and The University of Western Australia, she taught in Australia, Canada and Britain. Jo's activism encompasses numerous community groups, including the Council for Civil Liberties, Aboriginal Treaty Support Group, Community Aid Abroad, People for Nuclear Disarmament, Quaker Peace Committee, Women's International League for Peace and Freedom, and the Peace Education Foundation. In 1984 Jo was elected to the Australian Senate on the single issue of nuclear disarmament. In 1987 and 1990 she increased her portfolio area to cover social justice and environmental issues to represent The Greens (WA). Jo now combines family life with a busy schedule as a volunteer. On 'those wretched forms where "occupation" is called for', Jo calls herself an activist.

Not surprisingly, some of my most exciting moments as an activist involve my two daughters. They are, after all, or should I say before all, my chief motivators. In fact, they are the reason I dared stick my neck out to work for peace and social justice in whatever way seemed right, appropriate, useful for the planet.

One such moment was at the Palm Sunday Peace Rally in Perth in 1985. The federal election of the previous December had seen a rank outsider, a peace activist, a woman, elected to the Senate on the single issue of nuclear disarmament. I was that woman.

It was an exhilarating time as about 20,000 of us gathered to let the government know we wanted some action to take the world away from the brink of the awesome possibility that we might blow ourselves to pieces. It was a beautiful day. I'd been asked to speak, and my supportive partner Peter Fry was there looking after our little girls, only five and three years old, who were eating juicy pears just in front of the sound shell in the Supreme Court Gardens. As I began to speak I felt a tug on my skirt, and there was Samantha, blond curls waggling at me. She wanted her mum. So I scooped her up, introduced her to the crowd, which roared approval, and continued to speak with her cradled on my hip. When I finished, there was a standing ovation. Now that is heady stuff. I've always given Samantha's presence credit for that. It still makes me sad and glad all at once to think of it — being a senator for seven years was very costly in emotional terms. I missed my girls so much in all the times I had to be away.

Another exciting moment was after I'd been arrested for civil disobedience at Pine Gap, and I got a card from Katy, then eight years old, which read: 'Dear Mum, I'm so proud (underlined) of you for going to gaol, love Katy'. It was mind-blowing. That still makes me weep too, because in those few words I knew that Katy understood why I'd broken the law, and been determined to go to gaol for it. Not bad for a little girl, who was teased about it at school.

My decision to be an activist for social change predated parenting, in fact it was a prerequisite. I couldn't consider bringing more children into an already crowded world without making a commitment to the future, that I would work for peace and justice till I dropped.

That was in 1978 when I heard the then Premier, Charles Court, announce that Western Australia would be the first State to have a nuclear power station. I didn't know a whole lot about it, but I started finding out and thinking, 'No way, Charlie, over my dead body will there be a nuclear power station in WA'. I think that's one issue which is safely behind us, although there are now moves afoot to use WA as a dumping ground for nuclear waste.

Many campaigns, and many groups later, there I was in the Senate, representing people around the nation on the disarmament issue. It was only after my seven-year stint, when I was doing what I labelled cupboard therapy (cleaning out my cupboards), that I began to sort out how it had all happened.

What I found were many boxes from various groups which had given me the chance to practise my lobbying skills, unwittingly leading me to be the one chosen to be the candidate for the Nuclear Disarmament Party in 1984. There were copies of letters, submissions, notes from meetings with ministers, sets of newsletters and other documents relating to People for Nuclear Disarmament, the Council for Civil Liberties, the Campaign to Save Native Forests, Community Aid Abroad, Women's International League for Peace and Freedom, various Quaker groups, and the Aboriginal Treaty Support Group. I realized how busy I'd been as a mother of babies, remembering that I'd thought it was better for the children to be at home in the evenings to settle them to sleep, so we often had meetings at our house — and I liked to have some home-baked goodies for each group!

Working in community groups was invaluable experience. It seems like I've come full circle because that is exactly what I'm doing again now, and enjoying it thoroughly. It's an often quoted cliche, but Margaret Mead's words ring true: 'Never doubt the power of a small group of committed individuals to change the world — indeed it's the only thing that ever has'.[1] What is it about working in small community groups which is so empowering, so effective and so much fun? Frustration should also be added as another essential ingredient.

There are many factors. One is the satisfaction gained from trying to do something worthwhile for the planet. Success is elusive, but at least there is a sense of integrity about having a go to change an unjust situation, a feeling that my children will understand that at least I tried to do something useful. We are called to be faithful, to witness truth and justice as we see it, whether or not we succeed. Often the process is more important than the destination, and great learnings occur along the way.

Another factor is the satisfaction from working cooperatively with others. The groups I have worked with have aspired to be non-hierarchical in structure, where jobs and information and skills are freely shared. It is amazing to see how often the emerging talents balance to produce the desired result, as if there had been some planning involved in the formation of the group, but mostly it's a serendipitous gathering of like-minded people who choose to work together for a common cause.

It was a real buzz in the 1984 election campaign, for example, to see women especially, who'd never been part of a political party or a peace group, come in and offer to help. They came in with their babies and were welcomed enthusiastically as co-workers. People found skills they'd never dreamed they had. Encouragement of newcomers was high on the agenda. Everyone could do something. They felt passionate about the nuclear issue, and suddenly found there were many others with the same concerns. It felt good not to be alone with fears about a nuclear holocaust, but to share the hope that we could turn a dangerous situation around. So, belonging to a group is an important element.

Vision for the future is vital to social change agents. We often workshop our ideal world, so that we don't lose sight of the big picture — what we're actually aiming for. Again, sharing hopes and dreams which sometimes become reality is a bonding experience, without which small community groups often perish.

Planning strategies and education campaigns, drafting leaflets and press releases, training public speakers, organizing events, and doing the hard work of collecting signatures, lobbying decision-makers — this is the stuff of campaigns.

An occasional victory does wonders for the sustainability of a group. However, we're often so busy moving on to the next issue that we forget to celebrate our wins. Constant deadlines can be draining, as can the fact that it sometimes seems an issue we thought we'd finished with keeps turning up for us to campaign about all over again. Quite exhausting!

How we deal with each other and with society in general is also important. A commitment to truth is basic, and the other fundamental element is a commitment to non-violence. This commitment is a way of life, as well as a strategy for operation. It is based on respect for oneself, for others, for all life forms; it is based on an integrated understanding of the connection between all living things.

Coupling commitment and respect leads to spirituality, which I consider a vital aspect of leadership. There is the spark of the divine in each of us, whether we label it or not. I find a recurring need to dip into the well of spiritual renewal and feel gladdened by Quakers' (mostly) silent meetings for worship, during which insights often occur. Increasingly, people around the planet are realizing that the materialistic, mechanistic systems by which society has measured success and lifestyle since the beginning of the industrial age leave a great deal to be desired. As people give more attention to values like fresh air, uncontaminated soils and food, water quality and quantity, care of forests and endangered species, there is an increasing understanding of the need for nurturing, rather than exploiting ourselves, each other, and all species.

This is where the leadership of women is particularly relevant. There is no doubt that women generally reach conclusions about the nurture of our shared nest sooner than men. There are obvious reasons for this, including the conditioning to which men have been subjected for centuries. The revolution — still underway — which attempts to gain equal opportunities for women, has made it possible for women to articulate values which are different from those expressed by the patriarchy. Not that there's been immediate or overwhelming response, sadly.

However, it is not helpful to get into blame mode because we can stay immobilized there. Women have shown that they want to change things, and have often encouraged the men in their lives to see things differently from the way their forefathers did. It is more useful for everyone if we attempt to work in partnership with men towards a more equitable situation for everyone, rather than be separating, criticizing, and getting stuck in negativity.

Riane Eisler showed that a partnership society existed in Minoan culture about 5000 years ago.[2] No evidence of weapons has been found from that society. There is a great deal of evidence to suggest there was respect from each gender towards the other, and from all people towards the earth and its resources. That is my aspiration for the future: to move beyond the dominant model of society, where one group lords it over the rest, whether that be men over women, the wealthy over the poor, whites over blacks, or any other group of oppressors over the oppressed. I believe it to be possible, indeed imperative, that we learn to live in partnership.

How we get from where we are to where we want to be is a big question. It requires support for everyone, whatever their starting point, as they embark on the journey towards sustainability and an integrated wholeness of individuals which would allow for everyone's needs, but not everyone's greed. It is necessary for women, who I believe have innate wisdom on the subject, to be gentle and encouraging of men who are just beginning the kind of revolution women bravely engaged in a generation ago. It requires all of us to make a conscious effort to consume less, for all our sakes.

So what influences shaped my thinking towards these understandings? One of the most important would be an inquiring mind. All the time my mind buzzes with questions, ideas about how things could be better, fairer. I remember as a child, always working things out as I was driving sheep along the dirt road from one part of our farm at Beverley to another. Figuring out how it might be possible for everyone to have enough to eat. Thinking about helping women get the education to which we are all entitled. The nuns at Loreto — where I was a boarder attending daily Mass for six years — certainly gave us a strong indication that women could do anything. But there was a very mixed message: motherhood was a high ideal, and so was embarking on a profession. True, but never was there any indication about how one person could do both simultaneously.

I knew from an early age I would be a teacher. I could get people to do things, by having ideas, and telling people about them. I read whenever I could extricate myself from the work of the farm and the busy household. Gutsy girls were my heroines, like George in the *Famous Five* books, and Anne of Green Gables. I identified strongly with the Billabong books of Mary Grant Bruce, imagining myself riding out in the Australian landscape (which I learned to love deeply, and to which I shall always return), doing 'men's work' with the boldest, bravest and best of them.

The example of a strong work ethic from both my parents encouraged me to be persistent. I cannot recall either parent complaining about tiredness and they both worked extremely hard over many years, on the farm and in community service.

Then there was the independent streak. I was nine years old when I started at boarding school. Although I had older sisters there, it was an early start to learning to fend for oneself. Also, I had two grandfathers who were the types to make things happen. In very different ways, they'd spoken out, and done things which they strongly believed in – one as an Anglican missionary in Africa, the other as an Independent member of parliament in the north-west of this State for thirty-three years. During my first year at Loreto I engaged in my first social action campaign, which was cleaning other kids' shoes for threepence a pair to raise money for missions in Africa.

An important event in my teenage years was an exchange scholarship to the United States. This was with the American Field Service (AFS) which had begun between the two world wars as a way of bridging the gap between German and American young people. The original 'AFSers' had been ambulance drivers during the First World War. They had wanted to do something towards reconciliation and their motto was, 'Walk together, talk together, all ye peoples of the world, then and only then, shall ye have peace'. I was privileged to be a representative for Australia, and was delighted to meet so many foreign students from other countries, as well as learning to appreciate a great deal about the American people; this has been important for me to keep in mind when I have been so critical of the United States Government's foreign policy. It was an internationalizing experience, and I shall never forget Robert Kennedy speaking to us in July 1964 in place of his assassinated brother, who was to have addressed us. He suggested that some of us would be leaders in our own countries in the future and asked whether any of us could imagine pitting our people against one another in war. 'No!' was the resounding response, 'Never!' That has stayed with me in all the years I've worked for peace. All people are valuable. All people have rights. But not all people have opportunities.

Most of us in Australia have many opportunities and enormous privileges, which bring with them enormous responsibilities. Being aware of the gross injustices towards the indigenous inhabitants of this country, I believe we will not have true peace in this land until we are reconciled with Aboriginal people. And that means accepting the basic concept of belonging to land instead of owning it.

Opportunities coupled with ideas, having something to say, and some notion of how to go about working for change, plus boldness, seems to me to be the combination for leadership. Where the boldness comes from is something of a mystery, but it's something I've got, and I feel at times obliged to use it. Perhaps it could be described as having the courage of conviction. Others would describe it less kindly. For example, at times I feel led by a force outside myself to take a certain course of action. So I meditate on it, mentally prepare myself for it, figure out the likely consequences, although I can rarely predict them all. Then, if it feels right, I go ahead. A lot of the decision-making is therefore intuitive. Getting into the Senate was like that. I felt led to take the chance. Once my hat was thrown into the ring, I knew I was going to end up a senator, against all odds. I knew it was right. I was even clearer about getting out seven years later, having done my best to be a community educator in difficult circumstances, such as being on my own in a hostile environment.

As for what was achieved? Well, not much in tangible terms. But surely something in creating a greater awareness about nuclear, environmental and social justice issues, although such changes are difficult to measure in the short term. All the time I was aware I was but one among many working for that awareness which might lead to a change in behaviours. And all the time I was working closely with not only my team, but a whole host of community groups who were feeding me ideas and information and suggestions, and which were also informally monitoring my activities. For most of the seven years, I was an Independent. But I knew the time was coming when I would need to vacate the position, for the sake of my family, my health, my soul.

The obvious move was to form a Green Party which would be able to continue the work both inside and outside the parliament. This was no easy task. People who worked with me did an enormous amount to assist the process, which involved getting four separate groups to cooperate to form The Greens (WA). Not surprisingly there was some resistance to the merger, as well as great enthusiasm, as each group wanted to retain its independence to some degree.

Once the party was formed and launched with great gusto on 1 January 1990, we faced an election almost immediately. It soon became obvious it was to be the most difficult of the three elections we had faced. My office team, with one notable exception, consisted of a bunch of women. We had shared jobs, equal salaries, and we supported each other. We had also been successful in two elections. We had regular evaluation and planning sessions and focused on community campaigns rather than point scoring in parliament. I had always considered the community work more important than Senate chamber work, realizing the limits on one person working independently of the party structure. It was very disappointing that the team was not respected for its expertise in running elections, and that there were arguments at almost every turn. These were generated almost exclusively by men, who were either jockeying for position in the newly formed party, or jealous of women being seen as successful.

Success sometimes seems as much of a dirty word amongst Greens as leadership. Put the two together, in the shape of a woman, and it's potentially an explosive situation. Thankfully the fireworks were short lived. Before the year was out, almost all the men who'd behaved churlishly actually apologized and said they'd grown to understand how our team operated and to appreciate what we were trying to do, and in fact they began to work with us. The Greens (WA) make a very good effort at a flat structure, with attention to gender equity, and respect for everyone's input. Participatory democracy is one of the four foundation pillars of Green Parties everywhere.

An inspiring member of the British Greens (formerly the Ecology Party), Sara Parkin, spoke about the issue of leadership within Green movements when she visited Australia in 1990. She pointed out that it was unrealistic to talk of leaderless groups, to promote the notion that everyone is in the same boat as everyone else. Of course there will be leaders, she said, and there need to be leaders to inspire and to organize. They should be chosen by the group, with their roles clearly defined. And they should be accountable to the group. This process should also be set out, so that the office bearers or leaders know what is expected and how they are to report to the wider group. If they don't measure up, then they should be replaced, but with some sensitivity and dignity.

It's a good idea to share roles and tasks and to rotate people through them, in order to train more people for leadership roles. But everyone is not suited to upfront speaking-out roles, so it is not advantageous to insist on everyone taking their turn. Each person in a group has talents and skills to offer, and if these are valued, there is less likelihood for people to jockey for position, or to undermine those who do have positions, whether official or unofficial.

In 1995 I attended a workshop led by Glen Alderton, a wonderful facilitator from Commonground, home of the Australian Non-violence Network. She talked about the circles of concern and circles of influence which we create around ourselves. The circles of concern can be immense and overwhelming, including everything in the world which worries us. The circles of influence, on the other hand, are closer to us, and limited to issues where we can actually do something to make a difference. Depending on circumstances, we can move issues from one circle to another, and awareness of the big picture is helpful to figure out the best use of personal energy at the local level.

I believe this theory is aptly demonstrated by a recent anti-uranium campaign, which began in 1997. I was asked to assist the Gaia Foundation in organizing a fifty-five-day pilgrimage round Australia under the banner, 'Stop Uranium: Reclaim the Future'. We travelled to Aboriginal communities at risk from uranium mining, taking with us two people from the regions of Russia affected by Chernobyl. They exchanged their stories with the Aboriginal people we met.

We were in turn moved and inspired by the Mirrar people's struggle to protect their country against the government and Energy Resources of Australia. That led to the formation of the Jabiluka Action Group WA which aims to build community support to stop a uranium mine from desecrating Kakadu. One of my daughters is a start-up blockader, and she is prepared to stay for the duration. Kakadu is one of only seventeen World Heritage areas listed for both cultural and ecological values.

For me this describes the dynamic way in which local issues, such as nuclear mining, connect with global experiences and vice versa, shifting issues like conservation and land rights from worldwide circles of concern to local circles of influence. My five-week journey to the blockade with my other daughter was well beyond my physical comfort zone. It was worthwhile, however, in terms of a useful arrest, and for the strong support shown for the Mirrar people. The struggle continues in the cities during the wet season when the blockaded area is flooded. Despite the Coalition Government giving the go-ahead to uranium mining, CRA — the mining company — may in the end find it is not economically viable since the Mirrar people are standing firm on their legal right to disallow milling at the Ranger mine.

Above all, I think it's important to listen to the still, small voice from within, which is a gentle and discerning guide to what is right. I often suggest to young people, find your passion, whatever it is that really excites you, as long as it's something good for the planet as well as for yourself, and go for it with all your heart and mind, body and soul.

1   Margaret Mead as quoted in Paul Loeb, *Hope and Hard Times*, Lexington Books, Lexington, Mass., 1987, p. 232.
2   Riane Eisler, *The Chalice and the Blade*, Harper & Row, New York, 1987.

My Place, My Work

THE COLOUR OF STORIES

JOSIE BOYLE

Josie was born in the Western Desert outside Kalgoorlie in 1941. She belongs to the skin group Booroongoo whose roots stem from Maralinga. Josie grew up on a desert mission where her 'mission mother' arranged for her to be with her Aboriginal mother as often as possible. She first learnt to sing on the mission, but it was her mother who passed on to Josie the rich heritage of her Aboriginal storytelling. When she and her family moved to Perth in the 1970s Josie's initial impulse was to communicate via songs, which she translated into Wongi. Josie lives with her family in Perth, where she is enriching her singing and storytelling with a new-found love of artwork.

When I tell stories I use a red background, mainly because I come from a red place. My country, on the edge of the Western Desert, is coloured with shades of red ochre. Mothers would roll their babies in the red bulldust as soon as they were born, to let them feel the colour of their land, our original mother. The midwives would rub the new baby with emu oil and red clay, to keep their skin soft and safe from insects and weather. The dominant flower and colour of my childhood, at Mount Margaret, was the Sturt desert pea, a brilliant red with a shiny black centre. We call it 'Goo-roo-Daan'.

There is always a beautiful black background to my thoughts. A persisting pattern of blackness. It is the colour of my race and my racial memories. I see smooth dark skin that does not fear the blazing sun. Black is the colour of life to me, a mix of different hues that I recognize and love.

In our culture, yellow is the colour of the beginning of time. Our people worshipped the sun; they saw the sun as a powerful light and the creator of life itself. The beautiful yellow ochre is therefore special to us, and we use it to decorate our bodies for important dances and ceremonies. Yellow is the colour of the desert buttercups, which match the polished gold of sunlight glinting on the stones and leaves. When I was growing up, some of us went hunting for the mineral glitter of gold. It's hard to find in the desert around Kalgoorlie these days, which is why it is worth money.

When the Sturt desert pea was flowering, out in the red desert country, we gathered great armfuls of it. What a happy sight — that vast expanse of desert covered with red pea flowers. When we saw the desert in full bloom, adults and children would run and sing and shout; the quiet plain would ring with sound as we laughed and rolled in that wide red sea of flowers.

There was a beautiful pearly white desert pea, also, that grew on the nearby claypans. These claypans were areas of land slightly below the level of the rest. They were dotted with marda marda (kurrajong) trees. We used to dig up the roots of these trees and drink their ice-cold moisture. Our mothers used the fibrous bark of the marda marda roots for bandages, to cure our wounds, bites, burns and infections. Those roots were always filled with juice, but women had to dig down a long way for them.

As children, we copied the grown-ups and drew our stories in the rich red dirt: we drew with sticks. The elders also painted on bark, on stone and on people's skin. They did the traditional dot paintings and they used the traditional colours of red, black, yellow and white. Many years later, I was amazed to find out that these same colours are always used in traditional paintings of colours on skins of people around the world.

When the Mount Margaret missionaries sent us to school they gave us paper and crayons, and some of these materials also went to the elders. The elders were often expert artists in the white tradition, with a natural ability to portray beautiful scenes of their country on paper. Their minds were full of their country, like a camera inside them; they did not need to have the land in front of them to copy it down on paper. We can see this when we look at what Albert Namatjira did.

Most desert people still draw the Seven Sisters Dreaming Story and the Waddee Gooth-thadda (Two Wise Men) who gave them their law. At the beginning of time the Waddee Gooth-thadda and the Seven Sisters were sent to create and generate the earth. It is the belief of the Western Desert culture that Bunaga, the seventh sister of the group in the Milky Way, produced children by the Two Wise Men. The Two Wise Men did their bit and formulated the system of skin groupings to stop too much intermarriage between families. They set up six kinship groups (skin groupings) and strict laws about heredity following the line of the mother and the skin group of the grandmother. I am the same grouping — Booroongoo — as my grandmother, who lived in the desert around Maralinga.

Our people were lucky when white people came to this land. The desert was not a place the whites grabbed. Instead, they settled in the greener, more fertile parts. The drier regions were rejected, or at least not coveted by the invaders. This is why the culture and language of the desert people are intact today. My mother, who is more than eighty years old, still lives in the desert country behind Kalgoorlie. She lives the traditional life, on red land under blue sky. She eats bush tucker, and talks to her beloved trees and wind, as well as to others of her tribe, the Wongi, and her skin group. She is healthy, strong and happy.

When my mother visits me in the city, she becomes miserable and a bit afraid. But in her own country, she is a strong and respected leader. Her leadership is linked to her storytelling. She is a very good storyteller. Her stories are about our people's origins, laws and traditions, but also about the patterns you find in the bush: the cracks in the dried-up mud flats, circles in the grass made by the wind, ridges in the red sand of the desert. After I came to Perth in the late 1970s, I too began telling stories. I love it when everyone says to me, 'You're just like your mother', because I love telling stories.

Unlike my mother, who was born at Maralinga in South Australia, I was born out of Kalgoorlie, in Wongi country. My father was the leader of his tribe. My mother, along with other young women of her skin group, came across the desert to marry among the Wongi, when there were no suitable men outside her skin grouping at Maralinga.

In many ways my life was quite different to my mother's, because I floated back and forth between two mums. I had a white woman who treated me as her own. Yet she allowed me the freedom to live with my first mother, and family, whenever I could. I was one of the lucky ones. My mother took me into the Mount Margaret Mission when I was young, because I was very ill. I'd caught one of the white man's diseases and needed the white man's medicine to fix me. Instead of being put in a dormitory, and experiencing the agony of being cut off from my loved ones (like my best friend was) I was brought up in the household of a missionary. But I spent most of my time with the Aboriginal people who lived on the mission reserve.

At and around the mission, I saw those strong women leaders with bones in their noses, the ones who had passed all the endurance tests and were the best fighters, the best midwives, the best storytellers and the best healers. They walked with authority, those women, with long and powerful strides. When you saw one of them in full deck with markings, you really knew you were seeing the most powerful. They all had the breast tucking, to raise their breasts from hanging down too long in old age. They did that thousands of years before the plastic surgeons started doing it in white culture. Those women could stand up and stop a willy-willy, turn it to the side; they took their clothes off and sang the rain or sang it away. That is the way they believed and healed each other.

On the mission I also saw how the women taught the children to be leaders, almost from the day they were born. They showed us how to survive in, and respect, the desert. They taught us how to know our feet, for bonding and tracking. They would sit for hours bonding little ones to others of their skin group by matching their little feet and hands in the sand to those of the grown-ups, and then telling their babies who they would grow up to be like.

Women taught us how to find and recognize insects in the trees, on logs, under leaves; how to find and catch goannas and honey ants, where to find the wild silky pears, budga budga berries, mugoo (witchetty grubs), quandongs, and thulloo (bush potatoes); how to collect eggs, from emus, mallee hens and goannas; how to look for signs of life — kangaroo dung, eggshells, footprints; how to recognize the footprint of every member of the tribe; how to distinguish sounds, small sounds, background sounds, to know the importance of listening; how to read the stars and sky for weather signs and for navigation; and how to use all the signals of our senses to read and know our natural surroundings until it became as natural as breathing. And they did it by talking to us all the time, telling us what we would do and who we would be when we grew up. So I was not deprived of my culture. Rather, I lived and breathed it alongside the things I learnt from and about white people.

Today, some of my happiest times are when I pass the richness of my culture on to white people. I do this in my songs, my storytelling and in my workshops on music and Aboriginal women's folklore. I did it some years ago when I published a Wongutha (the Wongi language)–English dictionary with my white husband, John. More recently, I am learning to do it with my art and painting. Schoolchildren tell me in their many letters that they love my stories and songs. So do the people I give talks to in clubs, shopping centres and workshops.

In the 1950s, moving from the mission to the towns was not easy, but like many young women of my time, I earned a living doing housework and child care. The owners of the kindergarten where I worked treated me well, but most white people gave us no real respect. Many of us took on that disrespect as a people. In fact, we were often taught to deny our Aboriginal heritage. Aborigines who wanted to get a house or a flat usually pretended they were Indians. To be an Aboriginal was a guarantee of exclusion from privilege.

Marrying a white man, who I met while I worked at the kindergarten, took me further away from my culture, at least in the beginning. In the end, though, it was John's support and interest that made me see that white people would also appreciate my people's art and knowledge. That culture was in many ways like breathing to me, and I thought most white people would treat it with the same lack of respect they often showed me and my skinfolk. Instead, I found in time I was able to treasure my world openly. I could now pass on what I knew of survival, and of leadership, in my own country and culture.

In my early married life I worked hard so people would treat me like a white woman. I built my life on white people's terms, bowing to white people's ideas of rightness and leadership. When my husband and I lived in Hall's Creek, I learnt all about taking the lead in business. We owned a motel, and I had to prove I was the best cook, the cleanest housekeeper, the perfect mother and the best tennis player, before people would come to eat. We did it. It was hard work. We made money, though, and owned a flash car. During those years I put my own culture on a shelf; instead, I got on with the business of proving myself in a white man's world. That all changed when we shifted to Perth. We left the North so we could be with our girls while they went through secondary school and university.

John's influence on my life was tremendously important. With his encouragement I learned to think — to some extent — as a white person does. But I also learnt, once we came to Perth, that I could be proud of my cultural heritage. We Western Desert people, if we went to school, learned the English language and English ways. But there were very few white people who knew anything at all about our language or culture. John helped me see that the knowledge I took for granted would be of interest to white people in the city, who had never been in contact with people of the desert. John would say, 'Tell them about the skin groupings, tell them the goanna story'. So I would tell the laws and stories to friends and all-comers, who would sit there goggle-eyed.

My ability to sing was another asset. On the mission, we sang in choirs and I loved it. But I put that on hold when I left Mount Margaret. When we got to Perth in the early 1980s, I went back to the pleasure of singing. Nobody was doing Aboriginal things in those days and I translated country and western songs into Wongutha and sang them. We put our money into recording those songs and then I hawked them round the radio stations. I was so proud when 6PR played them for the first time, and soon the radio stations were all having a go. People around Kalgoorlie especially loved them and the money started coming in.

Before long I had $2000, earned by my own efforts. This was a very new experience for me. In the business we had in Hall's Creek John looked after the money side of things, and the mission had held my little bit of wages in the days before I was married. So I never really learnt to handle money. But this lot was mine and I was going to spend it as I wished. I gambled it all away. That was a big lesson, and I'm not sure if I've learnt it properly yet.

These days I don't go for flash things — the material world is too damaging to our culture. I used to work at making a white image of myself in the motel business. Now I work a lot harder at ambassador work. Why do I do it? I like people to know how I've survived. But it's not my way to focus on the victim. Instead I focus on art. Art is a beautiful way to show how we've survived, and the art I know best is songs and storytelling. Of late there is also my drawing and painting.

I laugh when I see how I create work for myself out of being an ambassador. You might say I am a bridge between my culture and whites. I have my tapes to sell, and I put them out when I do talks and workshops, depending on whether I think people can afford them. When I want a bit extra, I ring up a few women and say, 'Come around and help me make some canvas bags'. They all turn up and we make them and paint them. I put the bags out when I give my talks, and people often buy them. I also ring up a shopping centre and offer to do a demonstration on how to make screen-prints of Aboriginal stories, for example. They pay me for the display and then I charge customers for the screen-prints. And if I need more money in a hurry I ring around to people who know me and say, 'I'm running a one-day workshop. It's on Aboriginal storytelling, or on Wongi women's culture'. They chase up the numbers and before you know it I've earned $1000. And at those workshops I can also put out my tapes and bags.

Every now and again I have to go walkabout. My body and spirit call to me and I have to get away from the material things of city life, even though I don't have many of them. I get out where the wind and the trees can talk to me and I can talk to them. We all get that call, and if we don't answer it we lose something: our health, our identity, our spirit.

There has been no clear knowledge of what Aboriginal people are doing when they go walkabout. It's quite simple. The people are going walkabout to experience the silence. To ask and find: who am I? To sit still in a particular place and meditate. Spirituality is like a plant. It needs nourishment. It is a beauty that enriches our lives. Every feature of the land is important in understanding its spirit. When I was a child in the bush, you wouldn't kick a stone. It was there before you came, and you would honour its age. The beauty is in the age. When you take something out of the ground, cut down a tree, the conscious spirit of it will still be there. If we do not have that experience, it is because we do not want it.

Theatre starts in the bush, in the landscape, in the ocean. The theatre of the bush and the ocean goes on all day. You watch it, it is never the same again. Every time you look at its shape, colour, contours, shadows, objects — it has changed. This theatre is full of symbolism, mythology and wisdom. Dance relates to everything in the landscape. All the movement in dance — the stances, the poses and so on — are there in the landscape, and we just act them out. We act out the animals, the rocks, the trees, the birds, while the wind blows around us and passes on our thoughts. The wind is always there, from the time we are born. It is responsible for our lives. We must respect it. And fear it too at times.

Whether on walkabout or not, the goanna is my inspiration. It is an ancient reptile, still surviving from the Dreamtime. The goanna is my identity, the key to who I am. It is also the key to every woman's identity. Every day, I look at this ancient reptile. My mission is to survive like this goanna. I can enter my path by going through the circle the goanna is guarding near her head. In there I can learn my lessons about who I am. Then I come out from where its tail is and go and find my many paths in life. But I will always take the path back to my Aboriginal culture.

We Aboriginals know a great deal about sharing. You could say that is the part of our culture that has helped us to survive.

This explains why there is no Wongi phrase for 'thank you'. We do not need one.

It would be nice to meet at the season when the seeds of the wild rye grass turn brown and are ready for harvesting. We women could gather a quantity of seeds and, in the old way, we would pound them between stones and so make a sort of flour or wholemeal and bake it into a loaf or a cake-type of food. These are my wandering thoughts started off by the word 'sharing', and by thinking about the work of women in the future.

There are more Aboriginal women exercising influence nowadays than there were in the past. Depriving us of our land was almost a deathblow to us as a race because the land was our life, you could say. History cannot be undone and I want to see our women develop strong racial pride. If they could be inspired by the old spirit of our Dreamtime and walkabout maybe we could set an example to the world in ways that would save our sacred but damaged planet.

MAKING STRIDES

SHIRLEY DE LA HUNTY

Born in Perth in 1925 Shirley grew up on her parents' farm in East Pithara. Educated at Northam Senior High School, Shirley followed her early interest in science and gained an honours degree in Nuclear Physics from The University of Western Australia. Better known throughout Australia and the world as Shirley Strickland, an exceptional athlete, her record-breaking list of achievements in track and field events includes London in 1948 where she became the first Australian woman to win an Olympic medal. In national sport Shirley is known as an athlete, a State and national coach, and for her administrative contributions. Shirley was awarded the Member of the Order of the British Empire in 1957, and the Advance Australia Foundation Award in Sport and the Community in 1987. In between she won several 'Sportsman' of the Year awards. The environment is now Shirley's greatest love. She was a founding member of the Tree Society and the National Trust of Australia (WA) and is currently President of the Foreshores and Waterways Protection Council.

Women's struggle to be admitted to the domain of athletics has been long and tenacious. Until 1938, no women's athletic organization existed in Western Australia. As a woman, outstanding local athlete Decima Norman was ineligible to be a member of the men's WA Athletic Association; this meant she could not be considered for the Australian team. Incensed at this inequitable state of affairs, some amazing young women set up the Australian Women's Amateur Athletic Association that enabled Decima to compete. She won five gold medals and broke three world records.

Despite the energy and dedication women brought this new association, the International Athletic Federation denied them any powers (other than domestic ones, which could relate only to women). All overseas teams were chosen by men, all programs were designed by men, all control was given to men. This status quo reigned for over four decades. The origins of the term 'amateur', a lover of sport, rooted in the tradition of a nineteenth-century upper-class male elite, mark sport as the recreation of the rich; those who had to earn a living were all but excluded.

One Step Backward, Two Steps Forward

Athletics became my world in 1947. Through sport, I learnt to be grateful for the patronage of male administrators. They controlled my athletics events, my selection in overseas teams and my employment opportunities. They even decided whether I had professional access to my own name. Athletic success came early, and in this climate of male advantage I learnt to be obedient, grateful, acquiescent, decorative and winning. As such I progressed, but I was unaware of the history and existence of the male hierarchy that dominated the Olympic movement, the Commonwealth Games, and the then Australian Athletic Union.

Following my medal-winning performances in the Olympic Games of 1948, 1952 and 1956, I addressed hundreds of groups, extolling the spirit and vision of the Olympics. In particular, I applauded the far-sightedness of Baron Pierre de Coubertin, the man who initiated the revival of the Olympic Games in 1896. But I would not have extolled the Baron's virtues if I had known more of his history. For a while the good man promoted the Olympic ideal; he also, with great success, fought to keep women out of the Olympics. De Coubertin described women as a 'regrettable impurity', yet he accepted their attendance in the valuable role of 'applauding and rewarding the victors'. Even after his death, his followers ensured that women's participation was marginal and tenuous. Throughout the 1950s, the decade in which I competed in the Olympic Games for Australia, there were only four track events for women. Times have changed slowly even though there are now many more events.

When, in April 1996, I helped celebrate the re-enactment of the 1896 Olympic Games in Athens, it was my task to represent track medal winners in the Australian Games of 1956. I was grateful for the invitation. Later, however, I discovered that I was selected because Greece had requested a gold medallist from the 1956 Olympics who could carry a torch 200 metres. Had there been a male track medallist with those credentials I am sure I would not have been the one chosen. It is a bittersweet feeling to know I represented my country at a re-enactment of the 1896 games in which no women competed. A gap of one hundred years seems to have made little dent in the forces that keep women out of the upper tiers of sport.

By the 1970s, my understanding of the deterioration of the world environment was a far more compelling concern than sport. The environment, and what we do to it, impacts on all species, and all humans across this unique and fragile planet. I became an environmentalist, and my new public face gained credence from the fact that people knew me as a sportsperson. At that time I was also sought by the three main political parties as a candidate. While I recognized that temporary politicians have inordinate influence on our lives and direction, I could only agree to that role if I was allowed a 'conscience' vote. I declined the invitation of politics until the Australian Democrats, incorporating such a vote, was formed.

Before then, however, women's athletics did see some changes, particularly in Perth. In a sense, we women spat the dummy. Tired of the dominance, the broken commitment, we took our program into our own hands. For a start, we acquired the lesser venue at Perry Lakes Stadium – the warm-up track. In place of the grace and favour minimalist programs offered to us by the men, we set up a program that provided all events to women every week. We took our officials, spectators and workers with us, and to our great joy we thrived. The statistics showed that more females were competing than males, and that officials, spectators and other supporters ran at 60 per cent female. While all entry fees and other funds had previously gone into the men's finances, we could now retain our income and build our own funds. Our performances and records rose dramatically. The men, by contrast, were in deep trouble. Their life energies, previously supplied by women, had been removed.

In the 1970s, Prime Minister Malcolm Fraser threw a spanner in the works. He directed that only one State organization would be eligible for any federal recognition. Members of the women's association knew what this meant; we would have to regroup. We would not survive in this new climate if we tried to stay separate. The men were already threatening to register women in their membership and only allow such members into international competition.

With a large amount of effort, we reached a workable compromise. A group of three women (of which I was one) and three of the younger men spent many hours together, designing a combined organization that would serve both sexes equally. It was to have equal sex representation on the board, and equality throughout the organization for three years. The Perry Lakes athletic track is a stark reminder of the success of this agreement as it has twelve lanes in both straights, to enable all events of *both* sexes adequate event opportunities. I doubt that any future stadium will provide such a grand scenario for athletics competition and display.

Six years later, however, the three women who had taken the initiative on gaining a gender-equal association were exhausted. Because we failed to replace them with other similarly motivated and dedicated women, men won back their power, and the association reverted to male control. The source of stress for these pioneering women was the climate of relentless antagonism and lack of male cooperation, generated by the orthodox males who remained after the younger trailblazers retired to further their non-sporting careers.

I was appointed one of the first national coaches in athletics in Australia. I owed this honour to my 'dedication and excellence in coaching', to quote the first Australian Institute of Sport Director. At times my athletes formed over half of the State team, and I was made National Event Coach in sprints and hurdles, then National Coach of the 400-metre hurdles. Time and again, my coaching performance was proven by the successes of my athletes, yet not once was I selected (despite the mandatory applications) as accompanying coach to an overseas team.

After years of superior coaching services, and patiently waiting while coaches with little or no status or record flew off with a series of Australian teams, I finally popped the question at one of the many conferences I attended to present lectures and make assessments at the three levels of coach development. I was told 'there is an embargo on you'. Short of undertaking legal action I have been unable to resolve the truth of this hurtful and damaging statement. I may never know the reason why I was refused this recognition, despite a record of athlete and coach development second to none; the administration remains tight-lipped. But it could well be that I was assessed as outspoken, scientific, knowledgeable, a successful athlete *and* a woman.

Soon after this event, I retreated from the status and gender politics of athletics coaching, but I still maintain personal involvement with athletes in the top echelon. Australia's sex-divided sports scene has still not shifted from its male-dominated scenario. One finds the occasional woman decision-maker, but she usually garners the votes through acquiescence, by projecting herself as no threat to the incumbent males. Women can be strong on the sports field, but in this male-dominated activity they must not show their strength other than as competitors, if they are seeking recognition and position.

First Steps

My childhood farm life — warm memories of a wide expanse, of unfettered space and a sense of solitude — developed in me a need to understand my existence, my space, my world, my role. Perhaps from this I developed a great thirst for knowledge, for understanding, and to justify my space and use of the planet's resources. So while I acknowledge the gains hard-won by our sisters, and I thank them, I now march to a different and more insistent drum.

My mother grew up with an aloof English father who reflected the standards of his time. Although expected to financially support them, he showed little warmth to his family until it was too late. When money was short wives were to bring up the children with whatever money was made available. My tall, blonde Norwegian grandmother is my idea of a leader. Married at eighteen and transplanted to the summer of west Queensland from winter in Norway, I remember her as a wizened old lady of immense dignity. During the Depression she lived in desperate poverty with her husband and only son in the north-eastern wheatbelt of Western Australia. I now realize that she must have gone without food to support her men's appetites and chronic smoking habits. She died at about my age, but half the height she was earlier.

My grandmother was a source of wisdom and love for her two daughters, who also shared the disaster of trying to make ends meet as pioneers in the north-eastern agricultural area. My mother endowed my middle-aged 'newland' pioneer father with enormous love and respect. Their pre-wedding letters, which I found recently, are outpourings of love, life and vision. Not until her family commitments were complete did mother explore her wealth of interests and talents in art, pottery, travel, spinning, bookbinding, upholstery and leatherwork.

When I was a child, poverty was a way of life, and sadness a daily trial. My father was much older than my mother when they married, and he suffered serious collapse and depression when the realities of drought, flood, market variation, the vagaries of climate, and a wife and five children to support took hold. My eldest brother ceased his education at sixteen to run the farm and support the family. My first twelve years were spent on the East Pithara farm that my father tried to carve from the bush with mere physical strength only. Neither he nor my mother realized the immensity of the task they faced: an uncertain rainfall, a property that had never been cleared, no machines, no animals, a stone and tin room for the family, and no doctor or hospital within cooee. They had a horse and cart to take them the 16 miles they had to go for other food, to collect the post, or to see other faces.

I grew up in a boys' world, knowing no other children than my four brothers. My eldest brother helped to bring me up. I was his playmate and he helped to stamp-wash my nappies in my mother's washing trough. I did all the things the boys did, but they did not do all that I did — I do not remember them learning to cook, for example. Like the boys, I could drive farm vehicles before I was nine, and I never sat a driving test for my licence. I knew I was different, but special, in my family.

Mum struggled desperately to raise the funds to send me away to school. The bank, which had complete control over our finances, refused to help fund the 'unnecessary expense' of educating 'the girl' in the family. 'Keep the girl on the farm', they said. I had to leave home as a shy child of twelve-and-a-half years to attend Northam Senior High School, financed by farm produce and my mother's other fund-raisers of pigs, butter and artworks. My only respite were holidays home. Even those holidays demanded a good measure of self-reliance, for they involved an all-night journey home alone by train.

I hated nearly every minute of wartime Northam and its boarding, but its high school was excellent. I am flooded with memories of homesickness, of loss of freedoms at the country boarding establishment, and of the uncertainty about my own and my country's future. I had to face the trauma of those early teenage years virtually alone, and this was not really helped by knowing there were others like me. It wasn't until my own daughter travelled back through those years with me that I was able to look at and understand my pain. Despite the trauma, however, I have been eternally grateful to my strong, wise and selfless mother who insisted 'the girl' would not be denied her education.

What I find most admirable about my mother and grandmother was that neither was tempted to reduce or blame their husbands for their lot in life. By the same token, however, they helped teach their sons a different male model. This may have been because the growing up was happening in a later era, when change was underway. But I also like to think that the strength and wisdom of these formidable women played a major role in shaping a new generation of men as well as women.

Although Northam was not among the high-cost private schools of Perth, I received nonetheless a first-class education, under the tutelage of superlative teachers. Nearly all my education took place under the shadows of the European and Pacific conflicts. Away from home, I was thrust into independence, but I held my strong maternal models before me like my own secret beacons. Then, too, there were my teachers who inspired me to test, train and use my brain and body at every opportunity. It was my English teacher (a Miss Jackson) who taught me the Greek ideal of fitness of mind and body (although nothing of the excesses of the early Greeks).

But how were those opportunities to be realized? My first attempt to capitalize on my education was when I tried to enrol as an engineer at The University of Western Australia. This was firmly rejected. 'There is not a toilet for women', I was told. Fortunately, the Science Faculty did have a toilet and I took an honours degree in Nuclear Physics.

I resisted marriage for several years. Laurie and I both came from families of five children, so we had much in common. As a returned serviceman Laurie was anxious to catch up on both his lost tertiary education and his perceived ideal of family life. Although I craved the closeness of family life and hoped to have many children, I was worried by the commitment of married life. When I finally took the plunge, our relationship was warm, supportive, and produced our very much desired children. We had little money but there was enough. As parents, we immersed ourselves in the richness of a shared creation: a home and family. There was no way either of us, although distracted at times, would have put our personal aspirations above our commitment to our children.

Finding My Stride

A seminar, given at the Australian National University by Dr Stephen Boyden in 1970 on behalf of a group called Australian Frontier, greatly influenced my course of action on the environment. This group has disbanded, as groups tend to do, but their message that worldwide environmental degradation was serious hit the spot with me. The cause and effect of such environmental damage was evident in all communities to some degree. The rapid rate at which environmental problems multiplied was exponential. Only drastic changes to the way humans impacted on world environmental cycles could stabilize the very environment upon which we humans depend.

In the years since, science has done little to vary that gloomy prognosis. So I remain committed to exerting whatever influence I can towards elevating people's conviction that humans have a limited existence on this planet if we go on multiplying at the current rate and fail to preserve our base environment. How will future generations find the necessary food and sanctuary?

Trees and conservation became my passion. I was a foundation member of the emerging Tree Society, and as President I conceived and initiated the Conservation Council of Western Australia (Inc.) as a forum for nature conservation groups. I was also a foundation member of the National Trust of Australia (WA) and the Australian Conservation Foundation. As the first Secretary of the new Wildflower Society, I campaigned with others against freeways on foreshores and power plants in the Swan Valley (to name just two of our many causes).

I found my profile of sporting excellence no drawback in these public campaigns, and I was prepared to use it in what I saw as the common good. I lectured, I addressed groups, I refused no opportunity to discuss the issue. What sort of a parent would I be not to attempt to reduce and reverse the destructive effects of the industrial and modern global age?

Our family is now into its fourth generation of strong women who follow the changing times and do their bit to change gender role expectations. Living with me are my daughter, and her husband and family. She plays a full part in their business decision-making, they jointly provide family income, they have three small children, and they share family decisions according to their personalities and relationship. They need and appreciate the mutual backup and support they give each other in all situations, and central to their lives is the sharing of time with the children and in their work.

I am not a feminist of my time, although I accept the female imperative to refocus on oneself and pursue one's own future. I am not a feminist because I am aware that in certain aspects of society the feminist pendulum has swung too far. A proper statistical and sensitive survey, I believe, would reveal that many men, if they were allowed by today's society, would opt for the trendy 'sensitive New-Age guy' concept of ironing their own shirts and doing the cooking. Not only that, but I think that men would also swap with relief the role of provider, director and enforcer. Many men not only want more time to be a child carer, they also want to take on that powerful caring role of developing their progeny without the threat of being seen as uninterested in a career.

Even though feminism is not my thing, I am grateful to those women who have committed themselves to the further recognition, the equality, welfare and prospects of women. Theirs was and is a continuing challenge. In the past I too have been active in the cause of women in sport and education, but my conviction and moral commitment to local, national and global environmental concerns elicits my available energies today.

So back to the future of women's leadership — is there anything like a change at hand? Do we see the power passing from male to female, or is it best to look for it emerging among joint parents? Do we need to establish firm legal and social mores with respect to children?

KEEPING THE FLAME BURNING

HELEN CREED

The Secretary of the Australian Liquor, Hospitality and Miscellaneous Workers' Union in Western Australia, Helen was born in Melbourne in 1953. She gained a degree in Social Studies from the University of Melbourne and worked as a social worker in Melbourne, before moving to Western Australia in 1977. She has a high profile in the union movement, serving as Senior Vice-President to the Trades and Labor Council of WA, holding the position as Director of the TLC Building Society Group and chairing the Community Services Health and Education Industry Training Council. In 1990 she was the recipient of the WA Women's Fellowship. Central support in Helen's life has come from the women in her extended family and from her mentor, Pat Giles.

The Miscellaneous Workers' Union (Missos) is one of Western Australia's largest trade unions. It covers a broad diversity of workers, many of whom are women. After a varied community work career, I started at the Missos in 1985 in the position of Children's Services Organiser. In 1988, I was elected Assistant Secretary and two years later, the Secretary. Since then I have been elected Vice-President of the Trades and Labor Council and, more recently, the Vice-President of the Australian Council of Trade Unions (ACTU).

At the time I was elected Secretary, replacing Jim McGinty, a number of people commented that it was a very rapid rise. In the male-dominated world of trade unions, perhaps it was. This chapter explores some of the influences on how I got there and some of the strategies I use to help me remain.

The Community Sector

Like many women of my age, my feminist consciousness was raised during the 1970s when I was at the University of Melbourne and involved in the women's movement. That was an exciting, challenging time. The lateral thinking of the women's movement in developing innovative strategies to deal with issues like equal pay and child care have stood me in good stead. But also there were more symbolic issues on the agenda such as women not being permitted to drink in a public bar. And while many trade union leaders learnt their skills 'on the job' — coming up through the ranks as job delegate, through honorary positions in the union and so on — it was the years of activism in the women's movement and community sector that provided my grounding.

However, the relevance of that experience is rarely recognized in the union movement where 'commitment to the cause' is so often measured in terms of length of time working as a full-time union official rather than recognizing the breadth of contribution. This often disadvantages women.

One of the most useful theoretical conceptions of this issue comes out of the work of an English feminist, Elizabeth Wilson. In 1977 she argued:

> It has been considered one of the positive aspects of women's involvement in union struggles that they do in fact raise issues of the social conditions of work, instead of sticking to generalised economic issues, so that far from being negative, involvement in personal problems may represent a higher level of political consciousness.[1]

Wilson's argument has only been appreciated within the Australian trade union movement in recent years. Child care was one of the earliest and most obvious examples of this link. Improvements in wages and conditions for child-care workers have sat side by side with the Missos' involvement in policy matters such as the quality of child care and lobbying for increased funding. Currently, the link between conventional industrial campaigns and more community oriented activities is being well demonstrated in my union's long-running campaign against the Western Australian Government's privatization of hospitals. We have used lightning stoppages complemented by petitions, surveys of public opinion, media exposure and so on.

At the Right Time

With Jennie George as the high-profile President of the ACTU, the role of women in the trade union movement has received greater attention over recent years.

Trade union women celebrated the election of Jennie George onto the ACTU Executive in 1983 and since that time there has been a remarkable transformation at the peak body, which will see women comprise 50 per cent of the ACTU Executive by the turn of this century.

Jennie's endorsement as president-elect at the 1995 ACTU Congress was itself a remarkable event. Ross Martin has described it in a way which captures the mood at the time well:

> When the time came for Bill Kelty to move his resolution, he made the bare statement that he was asking Congress to 'endorse' Ms George as a 'president-elect' — then the cheering overwhelmed him. The delegates stood and applauded as the hall was invaded by masses of balloons in the suffragette colours of purple and green (with an added touch of white). The cheering and applause went on and on. It was almost five minutes before the secretary could resume and talk of 'an historical day for us all', 'a new day'. His seconder, Sharan Burrow (Australian Education), upped the diurnal ante and spoke of 'a day that is hugely symbolic' — because 'if it's possible to shift the male culture of the trade union movement [in this way], then it's possible to shift anything!'. The applause following this remark swelled again to greet Ms George herself as she moved to the rostrum. In the tumult, Mr Ferguson, in the chair, understandably did not try to put the resolution before she replied to it. Twenty minutes later, after a speech marked by a skilful blending of the

personal and the political, there was more cheering, another standing ovation, and delegates sang along to a recording of Helen Reddy's 'I Am Woman'. The occasion, as a demonstration of enthusiasm, exceeded any other in the forty years that this observer has been attending ACTU Congresses.[2]

Jennie George talked about these changes at the ACTU in a paper she presented to the Women, Power and the 21st Century Conference, held at the Victorian Arts Centre in December 1993.[3] Jennie identified the four major steps taken to change such a predominantly male institution and movement as follows:

> (i) There was a need to align the cause and case of women with the overall objectives and vision of the organization. Thus, for the union movement to survive and grow it became obvious that change was needed. One of the newspaper headlines at the time of the 1989 ACTU Congress captured this theme with the words: 'ACTU sends SOS to women'.
> (ii) The change had to be supported and led by senior people with credibility. The Secretary of the ACTU, Bill Kelty, took a prominent role in the debate, arguing at the 1989 ACTU Congress:
>> It is simply not good enough for us, year after year, Congress after Congress, resolution after resolution, to talk about it. It is about time we started to do it. That is, we have to ensure that women are seen and involved in unions as equal partners. Anything less is a failure.[4]
>
> (iii) A strategy was formulated to achieve these goals. The key points included:
> - The creation of three specific and 'tagged' positions for women on the ACTU Executive.
> - Of the six vice-presidents, three were to be women.
> - All unions must include at least one female on their delegation to the ACTU Council.
> - Targets were set for the representation of women on the ACTU Executive to rise, in a staged increase, from 25 per cent to 50 per cent by 1999.

(iv) Credibility. Jennie George argued that this strategy had already worked because the women on the ACTU Executive had demonstrated their competence, ability and merit.

Changing the Culture

In institutions like the ACTU, the rules have changed to reflect women in leadership positions. The culture in most unions, however, is still overwhelmingly male.

The images that are conjured up when the term 'secretary' is applied to men in the union movement — people like Bill Kelty — are images of power. When the term 'secretary' is applied to women it is often a very different image of a clerical worker running around catering to the needs of a male boss. In one of a number of similar situations I experienced after I became Secretary, I had a heated discussion with a representative from a company from whom the union was leasing equipment. He insisted that if I was the Secretary, there must be someone else above me who could authorize the documents. Eventually in desperation I asked him: 'Have you ever heard of Bill Kelty?' He had, so I continued, 'Well he's called the Secretary, that's what the senior person in a union is called; and I'm in the same position as him'.

After my election as Secretary (which saw Sharryn Jackson elected to the vacancy of Assistant Secretary) the journal of another union headlined its article, 'Women take over at the Missos', and an employer organization referred to us as the 'Ms cellaneous Workers Union'.

On several occasions, male shop stewards in government hospitals expressed a similar view after meetings attended by the relevant officials, namely the Secretary, Assistant Secretary, Organiser and Industrial Officer for Health, all of whom were women.

In the debate about the representation of women in politics, the figure of 30 per cent is seen as a critical mass — the possibility of change from which there will be no return. Apart from changing the trade union culture through sheer numerical strength, women have also been instrumental in changing what is defined as the norm for union activity.

On 17 June 1993 there was a rally at Parliament House over the first round of industrial amendments. It saw barricades installed at Parliament House, a violent confrontation between police and union, and women unionists alienated by it. Such was the concern that one teacher, in a letter published in her union's magazine, called for a change to the 'male culture in unions' and concluded with the following:

> It has often been said 'if you can't stand the heat, get out of the kitchen'. A cliché obviously invented by a man. Women who are all too familiar with kitchens would say that there is a far more simple solution. Open the window, get rid of the hot air and let the fresh breeze in.[5]

Subsequent rallies at Parliament House against the proposed second and third wave legislation have been markedly different and characterized by singing, street theatre and a gender balance in the speakers. Many have been led by women. Most recently, activities around the maritime dispute have been conducted in a similar vein.

Survival

As a trade union leader, I am very much part of the struggle to change that culture. It is not something that can be done alone, and there are some important survival techniques.

In the corner of my office is a toy witch riding on a broomstick which moves in the slight current from the airconditioning. It was a present from a group of women officials, known affectionately as 'the health hussies' after a comment made to a newly appointed male official. Rather than asking him 'How is it going?' his former Secretary inquired, 'How's life at the witches coven?' While to some extent you get used to the labels of witch, bitch, lesbian and so on, every so often you need to laugh to diffuse the comments.

On another occasion, in the midst of an action involving hospital workers, one of the State Liberal politicians, Ross Lightfoot, said in parliament:

> That was a disgraceful episode, where there was tonnes of unwashed linen. In fact, the linen looked a bit cleaner than

did the union leader, Ms Creed, who was a disgrace. At least she should have had the decency to do her hair. She was a dishevelled looking person, and how anyone could follow someone like that, I do not know.[6]

Several of my colleagues reflected on the likelihood of a male union leader ever being told to do his hair before appearing on camera. This comment also drew a humorous response from one official who provided me with a fold-up brush, complete with a mirror in the handle and several hairclips, which she dubbed the 'Ross Lightfoot Survival Kit'.

Whether or not they plan to have children is also a question male trade union leaders are unlikely to be asked. The actual or potential family responsibilities of women is, however, an issue. At one workplace I visited shortly after being appointed Acting Secretary prior to the formal election process occurring, I sensed considerable anxiety among the shop stewards (all male) who were present at this meeting. Eventually the reason emerged, best captured in the words of one delegate: 'Well, what's going to happen if you go off and have a baby?' To this I replied that I had already made a decision in relation to having children and there was no need to worry. That workplace and those representatives have been a source of great support to me as Secretary ever since.

Although we have not been very good at documenting our women's history we should not underestimate the importance of role models or mentors from the past. When I first became elected to the position of Secretary we believed that it was a first. This was not the case and with the assistance of the Australian National University's Business and Labour Archives we discovered the first woman to lead a Missos Branch was Florence Anderson.

Florence was a schoolteacher. After a few years of marriage her husband died, leaving her with three young children. Now the breadwinner, she failed in several attempts to gain re-employment in her vocation. Instead she worked as an office cleaner.

In those days, although not an award condition, it was common practice for employers to expect women cleaners to take the office towels home to launder, 'or else'. She soon put a stop to that! Florence Anderson is on record as saying: 'Women cleaners are not fair to their families if they bring into their homes towels soiled by others, particularly in homes where there are young children'.[7]

It was Mrs Anderson's advocacy on behalf of women cleaners and her activity as a trade unionist which was responsible for her being elected as Secretary of the Victorian Branch of the Miscellaneous Workers' Union in the early 1930s — a position she held until she retired in March 1946.

The Labor Party has attempted to redress the invisibility of working women's history. In 1993 Victorian women members of parliament published *At Home in the House*, and in 1994 West Australian member of parliament Judyth Watson published *We Hold Up Half the Sky*. Both publications, through the medium of Hansard recorded speeches, provide an indication of the depth and breadth of these women politician's interests and work.

Until the publication of the latter I did not know, for example, the fascinating history of May Holman. May was the first Labor woman elected to a parliament in Australia, in 1925. She then became the first woman in the British Empire to hold her seat for a decade, an anniversary which was widely celebrated.

May was the oldest of eleven children. Her father was Secretary of the Timber Workers' Union and she started working for the union as a secretary at the age of seventeen. She became her father's Assistant Union Advocate and succeeded him as Secretary when he was elected to parliament. He died in 1925 and May won endorsement for his seat in a contest with eleven men. One of the things she is best remembered for is the introduction of the *Timber Industry Act 1926* and her two-and-a-half-hour speech, built on her experiences in the Timber Workers' Union and particularly her emphasis on occupational health and safety issues. May was fatally injured in a car accident the evening before the 1939 election — she died three hours after hearing that she had been re-elected.[8]

Inspiration

Every so often we need to recharge our batteries, relight the fire of enthusiasm. This is even more the case if part of the leadership role is to provide that inspiration to others (which I believe it is).

In 1995 I was privileged to be in South Africa at a very exciting time, which provided a source of that renewed inspiration for me. I had the opportunity to work closely with the African National Congress through a Work and Study Brigade arranged by WA South Africa Solidarity.

While the monumental victory of the democratic forces in South Africa had marked the end of a long and bitter struggle against apartheid and colonialism, it also saw the beginning of a new struggle: that of rebuilding the country. South Africans have such an enormous task to redress the legacies of apartheid. But the level of commitment from so many people to do just that was awesome. In the words of Cheryl Carolus:

> We are a very fortunate generation. We have experienced the full brutality of apartheid, we were there in the forefront to defeat the beast and we have the privilege to build an alternative.[9]

Like the women in South Africa, we undoubtedly have pretty high expectations of ourselves. I will conclude with a quote I keep on my wall which summarizes where I'm coming from. It is taken from an American book on women in unions and is one from which I draw inspiration:

> The best of today's emerging women leaders, concerned with family and community, with a social conscience and political awareness, supportive of education and training, skilled in coalition-building and collective styles of work, driven to work twice as hard and be twice as good, often underestimating their own ability and skills while encouraging and acknowledging others' accomplishments, depending on others and fostering involvement, represent an important force for rebuilding a broad-based, independent and powerful Labor movement in the decades ahead. They will add numbers to the ranks of labor, but it is not their numbers which matter most. What matters is their ideas, their energy and commitment, and their approach to challenges.[10]

1. E. Wilson, 'Women in the Community' in M. Mayo (ed.), *Women in the Community*, Routledge & Kegan Paul, London, 1977.
2. R. Martin, 'The ACTU Congress of 1995' in *Labour History*, No. 70, May, 1996.
3. J. George, 'Affirming the Future', presented to the Women, Power and the 21st Century Conference, Melbourne, December 1993.
4. Cited in Jennie George, 'Affirming the Future', p. 2.
5. J. Broz, 'Letter to the Editor' in *Western Teacher*, State Schools Teachers' Union, August 1993.
6. *Western Australian Parliamentary Debates*, 31 October 1995, p. 9998.
7. Federated Miscellaneous Workers' Union (WA Branch) 'Union History: Our First Woman Secretary', in *Union News*, 1990, pp. 16–17.
8. J. Watson, *We Hold Up Half the Sky*, Australian Labor Party (WA Branch), Perth, 1994, Introduction.
9. C. Carolus, in *Women and Reconstruction*, ANC Women's League, Johannesburg, 1994.
10. R. Needleham, 'Women Workers: A Force for Rebuilding Unionism' in *Labor Reseach Review: Feminizing Unions*, Midwest Center for Labor Research, Chicago, Illinois, Spring 1998.

AN OUTSIDER ON THE INSIDE

MARY PATETSOS

Born in Sydney in 1964, Mary is a product of the public school system. After attending various universities and living overseas for a couple of years, she moved to Perth in 1989. Mary's main motivation for this relocation was a desire to 'move out of home'. Since then she has worked, researched and lobbied in the areas of multicultural health, aged care and human rights. Mary thrives on pushing herself and the people around her to the outer limits of tolerance and doesn't mind some conflict if it gets things moving. Her passions include exploring places, people and interactions. The key influences in her life have been her mother's strength, her father's humanism, her friends' persistence, her aunties' tolerance, her partner's energy and her child's curiosity. Mary is currently working as a principal consultant with a group of four women. Their consultancy works on projects that have a social justice and human rights focus.

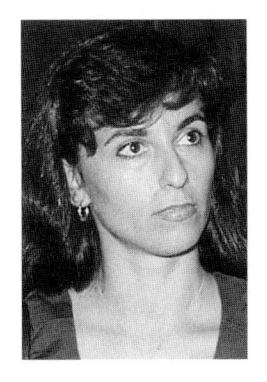

I've always found talking to be my favourite way of communicating. This may have something to do with early childhood experiences which encouraged verbal rather than written communication. This preference for speaking is one of many experiences that reflect my early years as the first child born to migrants.

My parents came to Australia from the Greek island of Lesbos in 1962. They shared two languages with their children: Greek, and to a lesser degree, English. Both were only shared as a verbal means of communication. So, having to write anything sends me into a bit of a spin. It's not that I can't do it, but that it isn't as much fun. And I don't believe that I'm as good at it.

My parents arrived with very little, leaving all their material possessions behind. At least they were in love. That fact is significant, because many postwar migrants were married via proxy. I was born in Sydney in 1964. My parents wanted to name me Ariadne. However, it was not to be. The midwife thought the name Mary was 'less woggy'. She chose the name because it was Christmas. I guess I am lucky; she could have preferred Santa.

We lived in the Sydney suburb of Hurstville, a suburb overrun by lots of other working-class migrant kids. No-one had high expectations of life, least of all upward and outward mobility. My experience as a child born to migrants, my cultural differences to others, and my position in society's pecking order (often referred to as my class), continue to impact on how I interact with people. These experiences have shaped my attitudes and responses to Anglo-Celtic men and women, and in turn, how they see me. The type of 'leader' that I may be seen to be today needs to be understood in this context. Essentially, while I have succeeded in doing a few good deeds, these deeds are also testimony to my feeling that I am still the 'outsider'.

I first realized that life was going to be a challenge when I was six. I remember how fascinated I was, for instance, that my best friend's parents spoke the same language as the teachers at school. I was astonished to find that my friend spent hours with her parents talking about school work and, moreover, that they understood and helped her to do her homework. My parents loved me. However, I was the one who helped them learn English.

In retrospect, I was lucky that I didn't 'dream the suburban dream' of secretarial work, marriage and children. This was not a conscious choice. It was just that it didn't turn me on. Not that I ever knew what would or could turn me on. Like most young people I sought out role models with whom I could identify. There were not many around. With hindsight this was a good thing; at least I was able to form my own images of leadership and success and not cling to starry-eyed perceptions of others. Once again, the sense of being an outsider was reinforced.

So, these early childhood experiences heralded for me what would be a lifelong feeling of being the 'outsider'. These images of myself *looking into* the Australian community still persist. It was difficult to accept that my hair and my skin would not get lighter and whiter; that I wouldn't get vegemite sandwiches for lunch; and that I couldn't go out till dawn and then bring the boyfriend home. I saw myself as an outcast, adrift between a community that did not mirror my life experiences and a cultural and family environment which was alien to the broader community. Rebelling against both, I was fortunate in that I saw myself as *different*, rather than *disadvantaged*. The truth of it was that in many ways I was both. I remember describing myself as being 100 metres behind before the race even started. These feelings of being on the 'outside' made me feel that I might not be able to achieve as much as I wished in life. So I worked harder, and persisted, probably knowing that I needed to. Twenty years later and things have not changed that much.

My personal baggage included a sense of being different, feelings of being on the margin and a sense of being proud of being an Australian from a non-English-speaking background. All of which made me rebellious, stubborn and arrogant. In short, I had some attitude and this helped me at school, at work and in my private life.

I have worked in the area of multicultural and ethnic affairs since I graduated. Both my chosen profession and my area of work, therefore, have been a direct consequence of my life experiences.

As a child my role was to assist all family members, including my extended family, with every aspect of their lives which involved interacting with Australian society. It's amazing how big the 'family' became at that time. I was involved in property exchanges, banking, medical visits, employment disputes, social security negotiations, workers' compensation cases and the list goes on ... and this was before I finished high school. I needed to either escape from the entrapment of being a migrant kid through the study of accounting or engineering, or I had to seek some framework in order to understand what my experiences were really all about. So I studied psychology, politics, philosophy, economics, history, government, sociology. I needed the 'big picture' then and I still need it now.

After university, where I completed a Bachelor of Arts in Social Work, I was sure of one thing. That there was no way that I would work as a caseworker or as a counsellor. With my background of supporting my family and community, I had already done enough social work to last me a lifetime. My motto was, 'your individual problem, however significant, ain't my problem'. Someone else could sort out all that individual casework. I knew that if I continued to do casework I would be drawn into it, consumed by the load. I would never have the time or the energy to impact on the Australian community in the way that I wanted to. Life was too short.

My main concern was that I would be sidetracked and would not be able to tackle the broader structural policy issues which needed radical surgery. I also didn't want to lose sight of the political and economic imperatives. I wanted to know about aggregates and trends, research and analysis, community and society, economics and politics. In time I learnt about political activism, structural change and lobbying. It has been moments in my life where these three combine that have defined the experience of leadership for me.

I decided early on to work as a community worker, rather than as a public servant. I didn't want to feel the pressures of accountability, loyalty and obligation that seem to crush bureaucrats. Many of my friends are public servants, and while I have a great deal of admiration and respect for them, they do spend a great deal of time compromising. Community workers can also feel the same pressures if they place undue importance on maintaining funding, and hence their 'job'. Most community workers have a transitory work history, and I am no exception. In my case, my disinclination to compromise has made my work history even more transitory.

Working in the multicultural and ethnic affairs area is complex, especially if you don't swim with the tide, and particularly if you challenge the boys. It is even more dangerous if you dare to make public the reasons why you differ from the rest. There are the usual power games and the factions with the accompanying confrontations and backstabbing. The field is just as diverse as any other with the usual gender, class, age, ethnic, race and ideological divides. It may come as a surprise to outsiders but not everyone in the field is a crusader for social justice, equality and rights. Many work to maintain the existing order and to facilitate assimilation into the mainstream. Some of the people who are part of the 'ethnic lobby' are rigidly and unthinkingly conservative. Despite these and other obstacles, I feel that a few of us have made a difference. Our work has had an impact on both the structures and the internal workings of the area, and also placed on the public agenda in Western Australia the broader issues of social justice and race.

Like many, I was busy with my work and my committees, negotiating my role in a field where entry to the few senior positions available was jealously guarded. These positions were off-limits, especially to those who dared to rock the boat. It is interesting that the main agents of change were women. Younger women, in particular, challenged the tradition. But so did the new arrivals and refugees who may have been expected to be 'silenced' as a result of their previous experiences, but were not.

It was, and continues to be, clear that the field of multicultural and ethnic affairs is not unique in terms of gender relations. However, I have found that it is more severe. This is because of its low status, low pay profile, and the fact that the women in the area also have to deal with sexism, ageism and discrimination directed at them from both the Anglo and non-Anglo men in the field who dominate most of the senior positions (even though men comprise a smaller percentage of the total workforce in the field). The battle was between ageing male status seekers, and a younger movement of predominantly women, who went in to bat with policy agendas and no time to waste.

I remember the day when the Aboriginal Affairs and Ethnic Affairs policies were launched by the Western Australian Municipal Association. I had spent twelve months drafting the association's policies with much of the time taken up negotiating with the key stakeholders. These were Aboriginal people, people of non-English-speaking backgrounds and representatives of local councils. The policies had to have meaning and substance, and they had to be practical. I thought the main opponents to the adoption of the policies would be the local council members.

However, this was not the case. The main critics were a few people in the multicultural and ethnic affairs area who were not involved but who felt threatened not only by a 'new kid on the block', but also by new ideas.

Some of the people working in this area really had great difficulty in understanding issues of difference. Instead of two policies they supported one multicultural policy encompassing both Aboriginal and ethnic issues. They did not understand the importance of land issues for the Aboriginal communities, nor did they comprehend the extent of underservicing of these communities by rural councils (for example: no rubbish collection on Aboriginal land). They believed that the cultural, linguistic and religious issues facing people of non-English-speaking backgrounds could incorporate 'black issues'. Aboriginal people, of course, would not stomach this and there was no way that I would compromise. I fought hard to maintain the two policies as they had been drafted. I lobbied councillors and staff and I wrote to the Minister for Local Government. We won. The two policies were launched without amendment.

As always when you defy the hierarchy, there is a price to pay, including personal attacks, vilification and attempts at employment destabilization. My opponents in the bureaucracy wanted me sacked. Their actions almost jeopardized the adoption of the policies by the association. There were also the moments when I doubted my own judgement; after all my detractors had all been working in the area for a long time. Stubbornly, I stuck to what I believed was the right thing to do, and the letters of support and thanks that followed proved that the outcome was the right one. I felt great and I felt like I had been a leader. I felt a sense of achievement. But I also felt that I should watch my back in future. You can't afford to celebrate your successes for long: governments, personnel, and political and economic imperatives change and what we fight for and gain can often easily be clawed back.

While my work has contributed to the Australian community I still feel like the 'outsider'. I remember the time I had an appointment to see the State Director of the Department of Immigration and Ethnic Affairs. I showed up at the office and walked up to the front desk to ask for directions to his office and was promptly told to take a number and sit down. The receptionist had assumed that because I looked 'ethnic' that I must have wanted to apply for citizenship or asylum status. In her mind, my request for directions to her boss's office did not match her image of me. I looked like a client. Despite my appointment, my clear request, my Australian accent, my briefcase, I was treated like the one who doesn't belong.

Then there was the time when I met the State Premier for the first time and he expressed surprise at my perfect English. In reply to his question, 'Where did you learn to speak English so well?' I answered, 'Hurstville Preschool in Sydney'. 'Well, you have done remarkably well to get such an authentic Australian accent,' he replied. What could I say! Then there was the time I was at a dinner function with a prominent federal politician. After discussing the levels of unemployment with other people on our table he turned to me and said, 'You know I can't work out how you Mediterraneans eat your spaghetti with a fork and spoon'. And they made him Prime Minister.

These experiences were as an *outsider*. In 1994, this changed dramatically, when it became known I was in a relationship with Nick Bolkus, then Minister for Immigration and Ethnic Affairs. Needless to say I didn't tell too many people about it until I was ready. Anyway I wanted to use my time well, and not disempower myself along the way. I knew that 'dating the Minister' would only complicate everything even more. Time would prove that I was right, because as soon as our relationship became public knowledge up went people's guards and on went the camouflage. Suddenly, everyone was my mate. My understanding of the type of 'leader' that I am, therefore, has evolved over time and includes the private and public domains. However, as we all know, any one action or thought in our lives can affect everything else and the distinction between the private and public can be blurred.

Although I still see myself in the same way, I am now perceived by others as an *insider*. Not much has changed really. There are many moments when I feel like I don't belong to the mainstream. There are also those rare moments when I have seen myself as part of the mainstream. These moments did not involve changing myself to fit, but changes in the broader community which accommodated me.

Reflecting on leadership has necessarily meant referring to the broader Australian community and to my own field of work. However, during these post-Keating years it is with caution that I discuss multicultural and ethnic affairs, fearing that its critics will use any inside information against the area. This concern is based on my belief that Australians will need to meet the challenge of race and social justice as we approach the year 2000 or risk being branded as an intolerant nation by some of its own citizens and by the international community. I hope that Australians do take a strong stance against the politics of exclusion and division which have resurfaced after the election of the Howard Government. Those of us who work towards harmonious community relations know that 'multiculturalism', 'self-determination', 'reconciliation', 'equity' and 'access to resources' are not terms of political correctness but concepts that captured the mood and direction of a nation.

In the broadest sense I've always believed that *for all of us* to feel as insiders we need to be able to relate to the symbols that represent us as a nation, including our flag, our constitution and our government. For all of us who migrated here we need to feel secure here, to feel comfortable and relaxed, and to reconcile ourselves with the Aboriginal people. To do this we all need to be leaders. That means we need to reject apathy and assert ourselves and our ideas.

This chapter was written during a series of thirty-minute time slots allocated to me by my daughter, Aria Christina, who was four weeks old when I commenced writing. She was three months old by the time I had finished. During this time she taught me about the leaders we all are as parents. She helps me dream, too, of the leaders that our children can be from the day they are born, if we encourage them.

INDUSTRIOUS WOMEN

LYN SHERWOOD

Now Chief Executive Officer of the Building and Construction Industry Training Council, Lyn was born in Perth in 1947. She attended Gosnells Primary School, then Perth College in Mt Lawley in order to pursue her aspirations of becoming a chemist. However, Lyn's interest turned to teaching and after completing studies at Claremont Teachers' College she started work at Armadale Primary School. Here she was encouraged to diversify and took secondments to teach in maximum security institutions. Later her administrative abilities led to her work in the Department of Education. Key influences in Lyn's life have been her mother and grandmother. Currently enrolled in a PhD at London University, Lyn has future dreams of training women in public speaking and mentoring skills.

Leadership is not so much about doing more, but about being more.
(Ancient Chinese Proverb)

Reading this chapter may be a bit like following the flight of a butterfly. It rests on defining moments and milestones which have shaped my ways of 'being more' while working within the building and construction industry. Thanks to Susan Mitchell's book, *The Scent of Power*, I feel quite free to fly as the breeze takes me rather than trying to make it appear that all my learnings have been linear and logical. As a listener it takes a while to realize that the teller imposes the order while she organizes a respectable retelling. No longer!

Friends will tell you what a bore I was over the Christmas break of 1995 as I savoured the insights Susan Mitchell was able to portray of well-known female politicians and political commentators. I have always been drawn to biography. Nowadays I connect with it, as though following biographical recipes can help me with whatever intricate management, board or industry issue I might be dealing with as Chief Executive Officer (CEO).

So what am I doing in the building and construction industry? My father was a carpenter and as a little kid I used to go onto the building sites with him. Dad would make a trowel out of tin for me, and I'd make a brick wall at the front of the house all day long. To this day, I cannot remember any of those front walls being knocked down. So, to be appointed CEO of a building industry peak body has completed a circle for me.

If I could have had one wish before gaining this job, however, it would have been to have read 'Beryl's Battle Rules' earlier in life. In *The Scent of Power* Beryl Beaurepaire provides twelve rules which all women should stick to their fridge door.[1] When you're working in the cut and thrust of industry negotiations, these tips are key pointers for a successful career. I'm going to add a few extras to Beryl's Battle Rules for 'How to get the best out of your situation'. These extras provide useful answers to that niggling problem, whether it be your secretariat, your board of directors and the constituency you're serving, or whether it be an industry, the government, the community, or your shareholders.

But first I will retrace some ingredient watchwords by which to lead, as I think they will empower women. I single out teachers in particular, who so often seem to undervalue the excellent training-ground teaching provides. As Janet Holmes à Court has said publicly: 'As head of a large international construction company I draw on my understandings gained as a teacher everyday'. The same, of course, can be said of all those women who raise families, and time manage their personal and professional lives.

'Learning How to Lead and Stay True to Yourself'
In the early 1980s I heard educationist John Nisbet analyse success in educational innovation. I was a deputy principal at the time and it was one of those Piagetian 'aha' learning experiences.[2]

Briefly, Nisbet found that successful innovations were typified by a working environment in which people were 'informed', 'involved' and 'supported'.[3] These three constellations became the identifying characteristics of successful innovation, with the degree of success being related to the quality of the information, the involvement and the support. Once you've heard these watchwords or ingredients you think of Peggy Lee's song, 'Is That All There Is?' I mean it stands so much to reason that you have to take time to inform and explain to others who will be working with you about the ideas and rationale for change. A leader portrays the vision. An excellent leader uses broad brush strokes and encourages others to add further details. If you want innovation to be taken up and to last, you have to involve your colleagues. Let them have a go, gain a bit of ownership. Then in order to reinforce the participation and growing ownership, you support those whom you're leading by providing the necessary personal back-up. In so doing you enable the innovation or change to be properly integrated in the workplace, rather than being treated as an add-on.

I was absolutely enchanted with these inherently sensible ingredients. I started including the relevance of informing, involving and supporting in seminars and talks which I was giving to various groups. I was still doing this in the late 1980s when I was the Superintendent of Teacher Development and speaking to many different types of groups. The same 'ahas' were evident in the audiences and I would encourage leaders to use these as a check list: 'Am I informing my staff? Am I involving my staff? Am I supporting them?' Quite tellingly the answers to these questions were more often than not, 'No'.

Not surprisingly, when I was in London a few years later, as a proud recipient of a Commonwealth Relations Trust Fellowship, I made sure that the final chapter of my master's thesis was riddled with references to Nisbet's ideas. By then, he had extended to the 'social infrastructure' of schools. You're right, further research had shown that those same characteristics of informing, involving and supporting impacted on the take-up of educational change. In Australia the same sentiments were coming from industry and the training reform agenda was pushing down the doors of traditional managerialism. Different ways of 'being more' were now required and a new era of chief executive officers was replacing older chieftains of the patriarchal style. In fact, the *Business Review Weekly* in 1994 carried an article on the change in competency profile for corporate leaders and chief executive officers. In the past, corporations wanted a person (usually male) who was good 'at the figures'. Now, in the run up to the twenty-first century, a chief executive officer is being sought for their interpersonal skills and their capacity to develop the organization.

My work in management led to a strong belief that the quality of workers' lives was important. So I added two other ingredients to Nisbet's recipe: 'resource' and 'publicly acknowledge'. My experience in management in the public sector, as a superintendent and director, was by then telling me that you need to really demonstrate you are serious about involving and supporting staff by allocating dollars, time and flexible work arrangements.

Publicly acknowledging staff members' ability to make something work really adds to the team and to your leadership. To this day I fail to see what people (mainly men) think they will be giving away if they publicly acknowledge staff members at every opportunity, whether it is in annual reports, launches, staff meetings and public addresses. Contrary to some male colleagues' fears, the staff do not immediately come into your office and demand a salary increase. What happens is that their notion of themselves, their capacity to achieve, is taken to new levels and the organization winds up with even greater output. Your staff may move on eventually, but it is always with a shared sense that you contributed to their next career step. These characteristics of successful leadership apply to all kinds of employment contexts, for organizational change as well as maintenance. The following example from the building and construction industry shows how these powerful effects work.

From Small Kitchen Company to Overseas Exporter

Early in 1996 I attended a seminar conducted by the Australian Centre for Industrial Relations, Research and Teaching at the University of New South Wales. They compared first and second generation workplace agreements. They wanted to see whether the parties were still heavily into trade-offs in workers' conditions. Someone presented a case study of a New South Wales kitchen joinery and cabinet making business. The principal of the company, a cabinet maker by trade, had stumbled across the idea of putting an additional line-item (of $16,000) into the company's administration budget, labelling it for 'staff innovations'. This line-item enabled the staff as a group to test, develop and apply their trade insights into the company's products and production methods. Apparently, the owner of this small family company constantly tops up this $16,000 throughout the year so that the flow in innovations from the staff can continue.

This single innovation has taken the company from a small business, with all the difficulties facing small business in Australia, to being a supplier and leading exporter of Australian-made kitchen products. The company's workplace agreements were generous in spirit, seeking 'not to muzzle the ox'. Consistent with that quote, the remuneration levels were designed to acknowledge the contribution of the staff to the increased productivity of the business. Even more importantly, the workplace agreements are structured to retain the company's best contributors.

The public acknowledgement and trust ingredient theme loomed large in this case study. The acknowledgement of the staff's potential by the drawing up of the budget to include the 'staff innovation' line-item recognized that the employees' ideas would be extremely worthwhile.

You can appreciate what the job satisfaction would be like for these tradesmen working in such a business. It would be a real buzz for them to see their ideas implemented, as it is for any of us. You could see how the Trojan horse of 'inventiveness' and 'continuous improvement' would have been parked right in the centre of the smoko, the tea-breaks and, probably, even the social gatherings. Recognition — there's nothing like it. If you're a leader or an aspiring leader, apply it in liberal quantities.

Thinking back on my own valuing of these leadership behaviours (or lack thereof), I suspect that one of the reasons I believe so strongly in them and stress that such behaviours should become part of managers and leaders 'being more', relates to an experience I had many years ago. I remember reassessing my sense of team loyalty in 1975, when I was working at a teachers' college in Perth. I wrote a paper for the head of department on the implementation of student identification badges. Basically, it was a well-researched paper saying, 'Hold off on investment, as machine readable badges are just around the corner'. I vividly recall my mixed feelings when I found my name had been removed from the cover of the report and replaced by the head of department's name. On the one hand, and I suspect this is part of our compliance with the pathology of gender construction, I was flattered that it was good enough to grab. On the other hand, as I had worked hard researching this issue from scratch, I was annoyed that I had not been acknowledged as author. For one thing, showing I had a head for technical and operational matters would have enhanced my career prospects.

As a sequel, I think that not long after the change of by-line the head of department actually believed he had written the paper! The incident provides a fascinating flashback. Clearly, it is also great fodder for how I would want to treat staff myself. As the CEO of an incorporated council (board of directors), I ensure that papers written by other staff members carry their own signatures. Acknowledging others' contributions creates a wonderful sense of partnership, and assists staff to manage their own careers.

A few years later I was delighted to find that Janet Holmes à Court, the owner of John Holland Construction & Engineering Pty Ltd, shared a similar staff-centred management philosophy. In an article in an issue of *Workplace*, Janet talks freely about what she sees as important attributes in leading a large construction company such as John Holland, as well as her other organizations, namely Heytesbury Enterprises, Drury Lane Theatre and the Swan Theatre Company.

> A well-trained, well-educated, highly motivated, happy workforce is one of the fundamental ingredients of being successful. I mean you can work people into the ground and ignore their wellbeing, but only for a very short amount of time.[4]

In the same article Janet talks about how she tries to value each of her workers. She states:

> I can't understand how people could believe that you could get people to work with you — under any conditions — without going around saying, 'G'Day, what are your problems, how are your kids, how can we work together to make this more exciting?'[5]

Janet is a boss who seeks to win her employees' loyalty by her leadership style, and by offering on-site training facilities. While building the Great Southern Stand at the Melbourne Cricket Ground, for example, her building company, John Holland Pty Ltd, had an on-site training room for workers to up-skill trade and personal skills. Janet Holmes à Court's view was that in this multi-million dollar project some of the profits should be invested in the upskilling of the workforce.

You can see why John Holland is the envy of many other major companies as it constantly wins contracts in Japan and Indonesia, as well as Australia.

Part of Janet Holmes à Court's strategy is to enhance the quality of experience for workers on John Holland jobs. This is the loyalty issue in practice. The John Holland contracts are undertaken promptly because subcontractors and tradespeople phone the company to get work there. This is extremely smart thinking. It means you have a labour line chasing you rather than you chasing them. The pay-off is that the large construction projects can be finished 'on time and on budget'.

Final Touches

I am in the Qantas Club business carrel on a Friday evening, surrounded by fax machines and suits attached to mobile phones. I have just added some editorial changes to this chapter, while waiting for my flight home from Melbourne. The day's business meetings have gone well. But I have barely had time to reflect before I fly off on the next round of meetings and decisions. The 'doing more' and rushing is a dominant and unavoidable part of this milieu.

Here in the hustle and bustle the emphasis in this chapter on 'being more' seems very abstract. But life in the executive suite is very much in the T.S. Eliot style: 'They had the experience, but missed the meaning'.

This chapter has been about the understandings essential in modern management. The checking, reflecting on how you and others experience your leadership role, the sense you are making of it, will add to the overall meaning of everyone's experience. The meaning you derive will affect the expanded sense of meaning you allow others through your leadership style. On the centenary of West Australian women's suffrage, the time is ripe for more women to join industry and boardrooms. My hope for you as we think back to the quality of life made possible by women's full participation in our society, is that your career in management will turn out even better than you could have ever imagined.

1 Susan Mitchell, *The Scent of Power*, Angus and Robertson, Sydney, 1996.
2 For an elaboration of Piaget's account of insightful learning see H.E. Gruber and J.J. Vonecke, *The Essential Piaget*, Basic Books, New York, 1977.
3 John Nisbet, 'Innovation — Bandwagon or Hearse?' reprinted in A. Harris, M. Lawn, W. Prescott (eds), *Curriculum Innovation*, Croom-Helm, London, 1994, pp. 230-241.
4 Quoted in A. Casey, 'One Great Mate', *Workplace*, Winter 1996, p. 15.
5 ibid., p. 12.

REINVENTING LEADERSHIP

DEBRA SHORTER

The daughter of a West Australian pioneering family, Debra grew up on a poultry farm in Canning Vale. With her husband Bruce, she has developed a successful and prominent marketing communications company, The Shorter Group. With more than twenty years' experience, Debra is well-known in many sectors of the business community and was the inaugural winner of the Australian Institute of Management's Excellence in Management Award for Women in 1988. Debra's long community involvement is associated with providing opportunities for women. She co-founded the Women's Economic Development Organisation and was a member of the Women's Advisory Council to the Premier 1988–89. President of the Australian Institute of Management Board 1995–96, she has been Chair of the Advertising Federation of Australia (WA Division) since 1997, and in 1999 is Advertising Person of the Year in Western Australia.

I grew up in Canning Vale which was, of course, vastly different then to the way it is now. It was a rural community. I lived on a poultry farm, a bit-of-everything farm really — mushrooms, dairy cows, watermelons, ducks, chickens. Like most people, I now only ever see my childhood in very romantic terms: long, lazy, idyllic summer days; chooks and magpies; Kielman's dairy; and the swimming hole at Sandy Banks on the Canning River. A favourite pastime was to pursue gilgies on a sunny afternoon with a lump of raw meat knotted onto a string bag and dream of the freshwater crustacean feast my mother would cook up when I returned home. I would lay on my belly at a Canning Vale culvert, legs straggled across a gravel road, with the absolute certainty that no car would come and if they did the slow pace would allow them to stop for me anyway. I could no more see the future of my own career or that of Canning Vale than I could stop thinking about the elusive gilgie.

One day Canning Vale would be just a suburb. One almost famous, or perhaps infamous, for a brewery, a prison and one of the largest supermarket operations in the southern hemisphere.

I thought then my life was mapped out for me. It would not have occurred to me then that girls could do anything or that I could do anything. In fact, quite the opposite was true. There were clearly things that girls did and women did. There were some small tolerances. The tolerances seemed to have something to do with money. A rich father might indulge his daughter's whim to go to university but by and large the rest of us, it seemed, had to choose careers that would suitably warehouse us while we awaited motherhood. As for women in leadership, that was clearly confined to areas of community benefit, like the Country Women's Association, the Red Cross, Parents and Citizens Associations, and so on. Career choices were offered accordingly. I've often wondered, if those choices had been different, how different would my life be today? Could I have achieved more or less? Did I succeed in spite of the limited choice or because of the limited choice?

There was another side to me that had nothing to do with career choices. As a little girl in primary school I knew exactly what I wanted to be. It was quite simple. I wanted to be a genius. I was so disappointed to find that I was not a genius. All those relentless school tests told me so every day. IQ tests and maths tests vigorously applied seemed to conspire to keep reminding me of this fact. I always had grave difficulty with Bob — 'If Bob had 2000 apples and gave away 25 per cent ...', and so on. Who was this Bob who kept cropping up in all my exams? I could never understand why Bob, having so many apples, would give them away. They'd be gone by winter. Such illogical thinking on Bob's behalf was intolerable. He should put some into the coolroom and sell the rest to buy apple seed. Alas, this was not the answer my superiors were seeking and my inability to conform was notable. So with continual reinforcement of my uninspiring place in life I cut my career cloth accordingly.

I was considered reasonably bright 'for a girl'. I could even be a schoolteacher if I worked hard and my parents had enough money to keep me at school, I was reliably if somewhat appallingly counselled. Well, my 'parent' didn't have the money and I was given three other very traditional choices: to be a hairdresser, a nurse or a secretary. No-one ever mentioned metallurgy or botany or economics or diamond cutting, and certainly not accountancy.

Despite this lack of choice, and this apparent predetermination of my place in life, I found a doorway. At fifteen or sixteen I bought a book called *Your Erroneous Zones*. Just a paperback. I thought it was a sex manual. I thought it said *Your Erogenous Zones*, a subject I was highly interested in at that stage of my life. Despite not getting what I thought I had paid for I did read it and in it was an important message for me.

It said, 'Intelligence is the sum total of your experiences'. I liked that. It said I could be a genius yet. It said that for every new experience, win or fail, I could add something to my intelligence. It is the credo by which I live my life.

It is satisfying now to see the paths which have opened up for women: better educational options, more diverse career options and less objection to stepping outside traditional roles, less pressure to conform. As far as we've come, however, women are still terribly under-represented in management and leadership positions.

Survey results for 1995 showed women represented 4 per cent of all board members and only 1 per cent of executive directors. In the private sector the figure for women's participation in management figures was only about 19 per cent in 1997. The figure is on the move but the movement seems very slow to those of us who have been around awhile.

In 1997 there were 36,519 female students in higher education, representing 56 per cent of the total student population. A vast improvement on my schooling of two decades ago. However, female enrolments are still dominated by the traditional female fields of arts and education. Only a small proportion of women are enrolled in science, engineering and business courses.

Despite a wider range of choices for girls, the environment in which those choices are offered is still often uncomfortable. During my time on the Women's Advisory Council to the Premier, I went out to speak to many people. At a school one day I was told the girls were needed to run the social club because the boys were too busy studying for their TEE. That seemed to sum it up. I hear the old catchcry so often, 'But we just couldn't find a woman interested in the top job', or 'We just can't get girls into computer or engineering classes'. 'They're not interested.' Not interested in positions of leadership in the community? Not interested in well-paid positions or rewarding and interesting careers? It is simply not true. But it's a myth propagated by both men and women. It's important to understand that a thirteen-year-old girl, finding that she might be the only girl in a class full of boys, still faces enormous social pressures, subtle pressures that give her clues very quickly that she'd rather not do it. It's the same in a boardroom or in a political party. The pressures to conform are still enormous.

The Brilliant Exceptions

It's lonely at the top for many women. During my time on the board of the Australian Institute of Management (AIM) I met many senior female managers. It wasn't hard to do. There weren't that many of them to meet. The tune was mostly the same. Often women in leadership positions are given credit as a 'brilliant exception'. Far from embracing the tall poppy syndrome, male colleagues and friends often speak proudly of their female colleagues' achievements but see them as being different to the vast majority of women. It's like being the bearded fat lady in the circus.

Some years ago a mild fracas hit the press when female Hansard reporters went on strike to earn the right to wear trousers. A male client of mine said that he would fire any woman who wore trousers to work. When I pointed out that he and I had professional meetings frequently when I was wearing trousers and it didn't seem to be a problem he said, 'Ah, but Debra you're different'.

At first I basked in the notoriety of being one of the few female executives in the advertising industry. Now when I look back and appreciate the pool of female talent I am simply saddened by the uniqueness of my position. There was no need for me to be the bearded fat lady in the circus; talent and ability abounded in young women.

Role Model, No Model
There comes a time when your career takes off, that people 'discover' you. The rush is on to turn you into that dreaded phrase 'a role model'. This happened to me. In 1988 I became the inaugural winner of the AIM Excellence in Management Award for Women. The invitations to speak and to sit on boards and committees came thick and fast. I loved the challenge and still do. I like to be a part of the fabric of the city and have the opportunity to change and develop new directions. Alas, it also delivered more opportunity to prove that I have feet of clay, that I am not a brilliant exception, just an exception. This is often where women are the least supportive of other women. The pressure is not just to be a leader in a public forum but to prove you are an excellent mother who always takes her own child to the dentist, can cook for six dinner guests on any night, hang out the laundry before work, bring it in at night, know what's in fashion, always look perfectly groomed, and drink with the boys. Woe betide any 'role model' who doesn't live up to these expectations. I wanted to be good at what I did, to make a contribution. Now people measure me, not what I did. They wanted me to be a role model, but in so many different roles.

My success in the advertising industry continued. My business grew and expanded into a total marketing and communications company — The Shorter Group — billing in excess of $17 million. My husband and I created an exciting entrepreneurial partnership which attracted business. We worked hard. It was a tough, competitive, male-dominated industry, but I thrived on it.

I worked at a furious pace. I realized often that I should cut down on my work load and give something up. People readily concurred with this. I always found quick and ready agreement to me doing less. 'You can't do everything,' they soothed. It was easy to establish that many people wanted you to slip back into their comforting conformity. These advisers were quick to suggest that I should give up my career or sitting on boards and committees, things that were immensely satisfying to me. No-one ever recommended that I give up the washing and ironing, the shopping or bussing my children around the suburbs. I never resolved this dilemma, although I was lucky enough to have some wonderful help in the home. By and large, like many career women of my generation, I continued to do everything, often at the expense of my health.

Reluctant Leaders
I'm astounded by the number of women who steadfastly deny they have ever encountered any sexism. I often wonder if the woman who loudly proclaims, 'Any women can make it if she tries', has the sensitivity of a rhinoceros or, more to the point, whether her denial is in some way useful in finding a pathway through her own male-dominated world. This denial lacks credibility. Heaven forbid that we should ask women to stand up and be counted as feminists, that politically unattractive word, but I think we are entitled to ask them for a little perspicacity and generosity. I can accept that a woman might consider she has never been discriminated against but it is hard to accept that she is not aware of the trials and tribulations of others. It's easy to see the discrimination from a female perspective. Women talk about it frequently when they gather together. They talk about it covertly, not wishing to make a meal of it or claim any specialness about their own personal situation.

   Women are all too often reluctant leaders. Those in senior positions are particularly sensitive to their position and have no wish to alienate men. Women don't want to take over the world but want a true, equal and happy partnership with men. We mostly tread carefully and quietly at the top because we are so acutely aware that many men feel uncomfortable when a woman leads or holds power.

   Many women simply zip up their lips and soldier on. I have some sympathy with this very war-like concept of 'soldiering on'. It's useful for flu, a death in the family and other tedious situations. I confess to taking this approach myself in the face of some very overt discrimination. It's not a cop-out. I like people. To give every individual a tongue-lashing over every sexist misdemeanour would reflect a bitterness that just doesn't reside in me. Having said this, I am no shrinking violet on this matter either and remain a constant champion of equality. More than once I have paid the price for it. A sense of humour goes a long way.

Businesses, organizations and political parties that are to succeed will need a genuine female representation, not just men representing women, although I would readily acknowledge many do well. Bias is a subtle and very human quality. It's too easy to unconsciously give low priority to issues which prevent women succeeding and see the status quo as evidence of, or justification for, the low number of women in leadership positions. Women are right to mistrust any political power which doesn't adequately present both men and women in positions of power and leadership. Choice isn't enough. Some genuine stepping stones need to be in place.

Reinventing Leadership
How far it's all come. From Bob and his apples to me and my Apple laptop. From gilgies in the creek to an office in the city. From ducks and chickens and watermelons to the World Wide Web. My life has changed dramatically from that of my mother's and that of our pioneer grandmothers before us. My grandmothers would have been thrilled to see the way in which women's roles have been reinvented. They were progressive, practical, get-it-done type of women who, one way or another, contributed to a better life for their daughters and their daughters' daughters. I think they would have been even more excited to see the influence a few women have been able to bring to change the leadership paradigm of the past.

Management studies have identified and acknowledged the contribution of a particular female style of leadership and its ability to benefit the 'new leaders' of the future. It's a style that's collaborative, tolerant, practical, inclusive – it's communicative. It's far from the testosterone-driven boardroom wars and the competitive, autocratic parliaments of the past. It's a style for both men and women. Unfortunately, still too few women get the opportunity to practice it.

My lovely daughter is sixteen. This story is for her. My wonderful son is also sixteen. Twins, of course, occupying the same space in time, the same family, the same world, the same scarce resources, the same trials and tribulations, the same love, the same admiration. This story is for him too.

Professing Difference

TAKING ON THE ACADEMY

FAY GALE

Fay Gale was Vice-Chancellor of The University of Western Australia from 1990 to 1997. Previously she held the positions of Pro Vice-Chancellor and Professor of Geography at the University of Adelaide. She was President of the Australian Vice-Chancellors' Committee from 1996 to 1997. Professor Gale chaired both the Festival of Perth Board and the Western Australian Symphony Orchestra Board, and was a member of the Prime Minister's Science Council. Fay has been President of the Institute of Australian Geographers, Chair of the Social Justice Advisory Committee and the Australian Research Council's Humanities and Social Science Panel, and a Commissioner of the Australian Heritage Commission. In 1989 she was awarded the Order of Australia for her services to Social Science, particularly in the fields of Geography and Aboriginal Studies. In 1994 Professor Gale was made an honorary Doctor of the University of Adelaide. She is President of the Academy of the Social Sciences in Australia and author of fourteen scholarly books, and numerous chapters and journal articles.

There have been many challenges for me during my career, but perhaps none as daunting as when I arrived in Perth as only the second woman to be an Australian vice-chancellor. Initially there was a strong reaction to the appointment of a woman as Vice-Chancellor of The University of Western Australia (UWA). I had stepped into what was perceived as a 'male role'. There was a lot of opposition from women as well as men, primarily from women who saw their own status and position as a reflection of their husband's. Clearly I was making a different statement. These women saw me as criticizing them because I was doing it without a husband.

There was also criticism from women who had expectations that changes would be made much faster: women who did not realize that change had to evolve through existing systems and structures. There is no point making instant changes which last just one year; it is crucial that changes are built in so they become part of normal procedures.

This was a very lonely time, a time with no close friends or relatives. Coming straight off a plane from Adelaide, I was wary of confiding in anybody, never sure who could be trusted. Throughout this difficult period I concentrated on setting goals and doing what I believed was right, shutting out criticism. This was actually very hard.

I introduced strategic planning and faculty restructuring, and through developing procedures for a range of staffing issues I set out quite consciously to raise the profile of the university. This was eventually rewarded in the success of the quality grading given to UWA by the quality audits. But there was a long road of criticism, self-satisfaction and complacency, not to mention chauvinistic conservatism, to overcome in the process. An interstate vice-chancellor said to me a couple of years along the track, 'You inherited a battleship with both its sea anchor down and facing 180 degrees off course'. It was somewhat of a comfort after the first quality audit to be told I had got both sea anchor up and turned the ship right around.

A vice-chancellor has to walk a constant tightrope, stepping the fine line between academic and administrator. It is a perilous task, with potential falls either way. But a successful leader picks herself up after a fall and gets back on top again. It is a lonely job in many ways because there are so many things that must be kept confidential. Most men in senior positions have wives they can talk to and they can go away on a family holiday and have a break. It is definitely more lonely for women at the top, particularly because most of us are single: senior women are generally either never married or divorced. Husbands do not tend to follow women at senior levels for many reasons. I remember going home very late one night to a dark, empty house and, as I drove in, the headlights revealed anti-Gale slogans painted on the front of the house and the front door. That highlighted for me the loneliness of being a female at the top and a target of abuse.

In my time as Vice-Chancellor, I had to keep quiet about many things, some of which were very difficult for me to suppress. For example, a case regarding an allegation of sexual harassment levied at a woman was highly publicized. But there have been other cases of sexual harassment, by men, both within the university and in other organizations in the community which have been suppressed by those involved. Many cases regarding sexual harassment by men never made it to the front page of a newspaper. Unlike the highly publicized case involving a woman, committees of inquiry are not set up in relation to harassment by men. This is because men protect each other. Men involved in sexual harassment at UWA have never been made publicly accountable. There have been some who have gone through disciplinary actions and have gone quietly, but they have never received intense public scrutiny through the media. Until 1995 the university had no sexual harassment policy. To rectify this, we introduced a policy on close personal relations and a policy on sexual harassment, so now there are clear procedures in place.

Throughout my career there have been individuals who really believed in what I was doing and came on side. They were different people for different situations. It is crucial that a leader has the support of her immediate team. The vice-chancellory had an excellent team whose members I could really trust and work well with. Together we were able to implement many reforms, particularly in the area of human resources. But this was not true in my early years where I felt conscious only of jealousy, criticism and downright antagonism. The undermining came from many quarters. How dare I, a woman, challenge their attitudes? They made it clear they thought they did not deserve a female vice-chancellor. On more than one occasion I was told to go back to the kitchen where I belonged.

In later years, my senior management team met every day. There are universities where deputies and vice-chancellors do not talk to each other for weeks on end, but as a leader it was my job to make the team work right, to make sure we all played as a team and not as individuals. This belief goes back to the days of being a varsity netball captain. You have to have a team with the proper square pegs for the square holes, which as a composite works really well. My leadership style is very team based, because no one person can do everything. No-one makes all the right decisions. You must have a balanced team. Women are better team players than men. Women have learnt how to be second fiddle to their brothers and fathers in the home. Women grow up with an unconscious feeling that maybe a man could do this by himself, but surely a woman could not. So women build teams around themselves, for support. This is not an easy notion for many men who have come up through academic streams with big egos and always expect to get individual recognition.

One of the most exciting tasks I have undertaken was that of President of the Australian Vice-Chancellors' Committee (AVCC). But dealing with so many vice-chancellors could be torturous and the AVCC meetings a delicate balancing act. Writing the West Submission, the Review of Higher Education Financing and Policy, was incredibly difficult because we were trying to contain within one submission the ideas of thirty-seven people with very different constituencies and a lot of self-interest. As President, I stressed that each of us had the opportunity to put in individual submissions and to be as self-interested as we liked. But the AVCC was responsible for the future of higher education in this country and we had to tackle the big issues: where we wanted people to be educated, what kind of education they should have, the role of liberal diversification in education, and the role of research in Australia. My task was to lift people from one plane to another, which was very challenging. Some men can rise to that and some cannot. Chairing these meetings was unbelievably exhausting. I learnt very early on that it was acceptable for men to lose their temper or swear or thump the table, but if a woman did that nobody listened. Women cannot weep or thump the table and get away with it. Men can put on a great turn and people respect them for their strength or emotion. An emotional woman is simply perceived as weak. Women have to be actors and we have to put on a theatrical show in order not to be hissed off the stage.

There were only two women on the AVCC when I joined: Professor Di Yerbury from Macquarie University and me. In 1997 we welcomed Professor Denise Bradley from the University of South Australia, Professor Mary O'Kane from the University of Adelaide, Professor Ingrid Moses from the University of New England and most recently, Professor Millicent Poole from Edith Cowan University. Four new women in one year was an enormous change and I am now a lot more optimistic about the future for women in higher education than I was years ago. During my first years as vice-chancellor I had serious reservations about what I had taken on. It seemed to be a lousy job that no-one in their right mind would ever do by choice. But now I believe we have broken another barrier. Not only are there more women vice-chancellors coming through, there is also a much better network.

Life at the top, however, lacked a women's network for me. In fact some women were openly hostile. I soon learnt that finding the right open-minded males was going to be the route to sanity. Such men did exist and to those, relatively few, I owe almost my survival. But for a long time I had been made to feel so unwelcome by the loud males that I was afraid to trust anyone. I recommend to all women leaders that they not only develop sound, non-competitive female networks but also actively seek out male supporters.

There have been periods, like in the late 1960s, when it seemed that things were going to be great for women. I had a fantastic job with a young family and a lot of encouragement. But then we went through a period where we plateaued. There was a bit of a jump in the 1980s, with affirmative action, but still it did not get the runs on the board that we expected. There were more women coming to university, there were more women getting their first degrees, but it was a pretty slow tackle to get them through their PhDs and into tenured positions. It was as though the barrier had moved to a higher age level, but we still had not broken through.

Affirmative action has a backlash. Consider what is happening to the Aboriginal people. In the early days we tried quite hard to implement affirmative action at the University of Adelaide but it did not take off and it got too much opposition. Originally, the thinking was that if we could get women applicants onto the short list, and on committees and so on, then of course it would be all right. But all that happened was we nearly killed all the women who got onto the committees and the short lists, without making real gains. These women were often already carrying families or caring for aged parents. Many single women take on family responsibilities, which limit their careers, because they are the ones to look after their sick parents or their older brothers. My commitment to having a woman on every committee wavered, in spite of the views of the equal opportunity people. I was heavily criticized for that. But I had been around long enough to see that it was not working: it was actually doing some women harm as they were being expected to do three jobs.

We had to change the definition of merit, rather than put women on all the committees. On selection committees I started asking myself questions like: 'Has this candidate had ten years' teaching experience, or one year ten times over?' We had to look at the unique skills women were bringing to these positions. Women looking after families learn a number of key skills important for a managerial position. Human relations, sorting out conflicts between children, or between sons and their fathers, personal skills, organizational skills, time management skills. When I arrived at UWA we had no selection criteria or interviewing formula, so it was inevitable that men would clone themselves. Now all appointments committees have selection criteria because they are written into the procedures. For the first two years it was extremely difficult trying to get some acceptance of that process. I kept on being told that it was not necessary, that the committees knew a good candidate when they saw one. There is a problem for women in defining merit primarily in relation to research. Women tend to be committed to teaching. Women are often given more teaching and they feel they should do it, because they see themselves as the carers. They also become the counsellors for women students. Certainly in my early teaching years I saw a lot of women students who never went to speak to their lecturers. They came to me, as a woman, with a whole range of personal problems.

There are now more women in the system. They are still at relatively junior levels, but there are more women. More women are breaking through. There is more notice being taken of teaching now. When I first went to UWA I was horrified to find that there were women who had been here for twenty-one or twenty-two years in a non-tenured position, teaching major first-year classes. Every time a position came up in one department, where they had only men on tenure, another man was brought in from outside. This has all changed now, it had to, it was so unjust. Now staff can no longer remain indefinitely non-tenured, departments cannot just roll contracts over year by year. And we managed to change the rules on promotion to take teaching into account. We introduced student evaluation of teaching and everyone applying for promotion or tenure had to put in a teaching portfolio as well as a research portfolio. Student assessment became part of the promotion process. Some men were horrified because they had not been promoted despite their strong publishing record, because their teaching portfolios were not good enough. These changes were essential, not just because it was disadvantaging women – it was also disadvantaging students.

    I believe we have to convert the men because there are too few women to make equality work on their own. You have to get men to have a burning desire for equal opportunity and for them to run with it. It is another important signpost, that men are being converted. As part of the Leadership Development Program at UWA we ran a mentoring program. Many of the mentors were men and a lot of them mentored women. That was a big breakthrough. I was pleasantly surprised by some of the men who nominated as mentors and subsequently told me how much they had enjoyed the experience, although I would not have identified them as being sympathetic to the cause. We must continue to recruit the positive men.

    I remember making a statement about equal opportunity, and women and different career paths, and I could see all the men's eyes just glaze over. They just totally switched off. But get a male colleague to say exactly the same thing and they will all listen. Part of the skill is in picking the messengers. Some men are already sympathetic because they have wives or daughters and they have witnessed at first-hand the obstacles they face. But many men simply have not thought about the issues. It never occurs to them that their wives would do anything else but give up their own careers to follow their husbands. The idea just hadn't been raised. These unaware men are the ones we need to target. Once these men's awareness has been raised they are like new converts and, funnily enough, these are the men that have gone out there and been fantastic.

I guess I first recognized the strength of women in my PhD days doing field work with Aboriginal women. Their stamina in the face of seemingly impossible barriers was inspiring. The discrimination they faced was brought home very clearly to me when I was in hospital having my first child. It was a country hospital where Aboriginal mothers were segregated. I learnt that a woman I had met in the field was giving birth in the same hospital. I asked to see her but was not allowed. Ironically, our babies were in the same nursery, so I saw the baby but not the mother. Just filling out the form, given out in the 'white' section, brought it home even more. The forms made it clear that I was eligible for maternity allowance and my baby for child endowment. Neither was available to women in the 'black' section. When I returned to academia after my family years I spent much more time on Aboriginal women's issues.[1] It was Aboriginal women who contributed so significantly to my book on urban people,[2] and it was because of these women, who were so concerned by the problems their teenagers were having, that I entered the juvenile justice arena.[3]

In all countries, indigenous women play a crucial role in the survival of their families, and the well-being of their communities. I recently toured South Africa, where I was privileged to visit a women's health program on the outskirts of Durban. There I met the most astonishing resilience, determination and humanity in the face of social disintegration, starvation, homelessness, and what I would see as desperation. This was a self-help project, set up by the women of the community, to improve the health of their children. There were several teams in the project, each using different strategies.

These women were running their health project in homeland areas, in places where they walk for miles to one tap to carry their water. On their backs they carry thatch for the roofs, and big bundles of sticks to make an open fire on which to cook. I never saw the men doing anything. But all the women were working incredibly hard, carrying big loads, carrying the water and essentially carrying the family. The whole place was made up of women full of optimism for the future. These women were really running with their ideas and activities.

This is common also in some Aboriginal communities, where there are women doing something about petrol sniffing and the alcoholism. I have seen amazing strength from groups of women when the situation looked so depressingly impossible and the men were drinking. But the women are getting together because they have the children and they have to build a future for those children. These women are wonderful. This is why I feel hopeful, because whenever the situation is really bad you meet women who are taking up the flame. These women will always be an inspiration to us all.

1   Some of the results are: F. Gale (ed.), *Woman's Role in Aboriginal Society*, Australian Institute of Aboriginal Studies, Canberra, 1970; F. Gale (ed.), *We are Bosses Ourselves: The Status and Role of Aboriginal Women*, Australian Institute of Aboriginal Studies, Canberra, 1983; F. Gale, 'Roles Revisited: The Women of Southern Australia', in Peggy Brock (ed.), *Women, Rites and Sites*, Allen and Unwin, Sydney, 1989.
2   F. Gale, *Urban Aborigines*, Australian National University Press, Canberra, 1972.
3   F. Gale, R. Bailey-Harris and J. Wondersitz, *Aboriginal Youth and the Criminal Justice System: The Injustice of Justice*, Cambridge University Press, Cambridge, 1990.

A VIRUS IN THE PRIESTHOOD

ANTOINETTE KENNEDY

Antoinette Kennedy was the first woman to become a judge in Western Australia, appointed to the District Court in 1985. Born in Perth in 1945 she attended St Kieran's Convent School until Year 10, completing her secondary schooling at Leederville Technical School. Antoinette graduated in Law from The University of Western Australia in 1966, and in her work as a solicitor and barrister she has been a long-time advocate of women's advancement in the legal profession. Key influences in her life have been her mother, who taught her to support herself financially, and her father, who believed that it didn't matter what people did as long as they did their best.

Poor Edith Haynes — she was a 'woman', not a 'person'. Having registered as an articled clerk in 1900, Edith worked for four years in a law firm, then in 1904 sought to be admitted to her intermediate examination to become a lawyer. The governing body, the Barristers' Board, refused to allow her this, being of the opinion that women were not eligible for admission as legal practitioners. The matter was taken to court but the Full Court of the Supreme Court of Western Australia agreed with the Barristers' Board. Their Honours pompously opined that, simply because the relevant statute said 'every person', that should not be read to include 'women'.

And so Edith Haynes disappeared.

One of the learned judges in her case, with suitably subdued horror, warned that if women were entitled to become members of the Bar, then they would be eligible to sit on 'this

Bench'. Subsequent events in Western Australia show that the good judge had nothing to worry about for a further eighty years.

Nineteen years later, the *Women's Legal Status Act 1923* (WA) was passed to prevent women's disqualification from legal practise and other areas of endeavour. This private member's Bill was sponsored by the first woman member of parliament in Australia, Edith Cowan.[1]

There is a note of familiarity in some of the comments made during the debate on the Bill:

> Mr Lathan: I support the second reading, and at the same time point out that I do not know whether it is a step in the right direction to try to bring about equality of the sexes. Women have more important functions to perform than to enter the professional world. They are the custodians of our race for a start. On woman depends the future of our race ... Our women, on entering professions, will be just about at marriageable age. I hope that before taking up professional careers they will seriously consider their responsibilities to the nation.[2]

To which Mr Underwood replied (presumably in jest), 'They ought to be compelled to marry'.[3] Later, The Hon. M.F. Troy remarked:

> I am sorry that women are entering into spheres to which they are aspiring. We find them now in Parliament. I do not personally resent the presence here of the member for West Perth (Mrs Cowan), but I think it is a pity that women should be brought into sordid competition with men. Men are the rougher creatures. We were made for the hurly-burly of life, whereas the rightful place for a woman is in her home, and with her children.[4]

Twenty-nine years after the Bill was passed the first woman appeared as counsel in the Supreme Court. Eighty-one years later the first woman judge was appointed. I was that virus in the priesthood.

When Lady Nancy Astor became the first woman member of the British House of Commons, Winston Churchill apparently greeted her after the first sitting with: 'Nancy, when you first entered the House, I felt you had come upon me in my bath and I had nothing to protect me but my sponge'.

My welcome was like that too. Male colleagues often resorted to sexual innuendo and lame jokes. When it was realized that really I was different, and worse, I really was staying, the joking stopped and the real trials began. Eleven years further on things have settled down but there were times when I wondered how Edith Haynes coped. What could other women have done to help her and others under siege? What of the future for women who follow?

A key factor in the advancement of women is the attitude of women to each other and to themselves. Women should like each other and make excuses for each other; that's what men do and women could learn from them. Of course, it is not enough that we should simply like each other and make excuses for each other; it is necessary that there be consciousness-raising. The need for this has been talked about since the 1960s but we have not progressed enough; women must see what is happening to themselves and to other women as it is happening. We need to be aware that different standards are being applied to women.

It is easy to demonstrate this by casting your mind to the appointment of a very ordinary male to some position in your own field. Ask yourself what would have been said by both men and women, had a woman of similar talent been appointed. If a woman is appointed then higher standards are demanded of her and no excuses are ever made for her. It is hardly surprising that most women cannot live up to the standards demanded.

I have on my wall the original of a cartoon by Nicholls from the *Australian*. In it two men are talking and one says to the other, 'You have to watch women politicians extra closely to make sure they don't get treated differently'. This scrutiny of women, looking for errors and applying a higher standard than would ever be applied to a man, happens in every field.

A recent example of this, albeit not on the highest end of the scale, has been the treatment of Judi Moylan, appointed Minister for Family Services in the Federal Government. This politician was given the job of selling to the community what became known as 'The Nursing Home Policy'. At the end of twelve months, when she was unable to sell the policy, she was dismissed as the minister and replaced by a man, and we were confidently advised that he would be able to sell 'The Nursing Home Policy'. After a very short period of time, during which he was harangued by little old ladies on national television, the policy was changed. The man was not sacked.

Before the 1996 federal election a woman politician, Ros Kelly (who was the Minister for Youth, Sport and Recreation), was accused of pork-barrelling. She may well have pork-barrelled in the sense that it was said certain grants went in greater numbers to electorates that favoured her political party than other electorates. Ros Kelly's career was destroyed. Politicians and journalists alike behaved as though this woman had invented pork-barrelling.

I am not prepared to be specific in my complaints about the way in which I was treated. I will save that until I retire. I will say, however, that I consider that it was very serious indeed. I further consider that I did nothing that could even remotely be said to have caused it.

When I was under siege some women gave me support. Unhappily, though, many women in the legal profession considered this siege was a sign of my stupidity and unsuitability for the work. The truth was that part of the reason I was treated in this manner was to prevent their advancement. Some of them even joined in. Had they been aware of the true purpose of the siege and stood against it they would have advanced more quickly. By joining in they assisted the stagnation of their own advancement.

The first woman attorney-general in Western Australia fared no better. Mrs Cheryl Edwardes was appointed Attorney-General of the Liberal Coalition Government in 1993, the party having been out of power for ten years. All the new ministers had teething problems but it was only in Mrs Edwardes' case that this was regarded as a reason for her to be pilloried. Everything she did was denigrated. She was finally forced out of the position into a lesser portfolio. This was done with the active assistance of sections of the media in Western Australia. In fact, in her time as attorney-general, Mrs Edwardes did an enormous amount of good work which has largely gone unremarked.

In the law the advancement of women is bedevilled to a great extent by attitudes to the concept of 'merit'. Every time the appointment of a woman is mooted, and it is feared that a woman will get that appointment, the men in the profession start to talk about 'merit'. On the face of it that sounds very reasonable. In reality, however, 'merit' is a very slippery term. Really, in the law, what is meant by merit is lots of Anglo-Saxon male values which are indefinable. But the only women who have this ephemeral quality are those who are absolutely outstanding, whereas very average men have merit. Merit really means people who are 'like us'.

Apparently, the message is that middle-class women should measure themselves against their less-favoured sisters and be content with their lot. Of course, such contentment is not called for from middle-class men.

Nevertheless, it is the case that poor women have worse problems. In the law we have particular problems with attitudes in relation to the needs of women. In the provision of legal aid, much more money is spent on men than on women. We are expected to understand that because men are charged with more crime they need more money to defend themselves. Again, substantially more money is spent on male prisons than on female prisons. And again, we are told to understand that there are more men. In actual fact many lay people would consider that women with domestic problems have a greater right to legal aid than male accused and male offenders. It is necessary for women to keep saying that they should not be denied adequate facilities just because their numbers do not match up to male numbers. It appears there is always a reason why women should come second. Women should regard such thinking with suspicion. Indeed, we should regard it as wrong.

Even where women do have the numbers, as with schoolteachers, nurses, secretaries and shop assistants, we find women's rights still fall off the agenda. In the first two areas most of the managerial work goes to men, and in the other areas no career path is provided: junior male clerks and shop assistants need a career path, female secretaries and shop assistants do not.

The community's attitude to domestic violence against women and children and the sexual abuse of female children leaves much to be desired. While many citizens complain that they need to lock themselves into their homes because of the perceived dangers in the streets, thousands of women and children may well believe, on reasonable grounds, that they would be safer to lock themselves out of their homes. The high incidence of domestic violence in Australia is now well documented and as to homicides, 40 per cent of those in Western Australia in 1992–93 were domestic; there were twenty-three domestic homicides in Western Australia in this period and eighteen of the victims were women and children. Surveys in other States show that the risk of being killed by a partner in a heterosexual relationship is three or more times greater for women.

So far as the sexual abuse of children is concerned, the community takes great interest in the sexual abuse of male children, which is undoubtedly serious. But the reality is that there are vastly more female than male children who are the victims of sexual abuse (and mostly in their own homes). Further, while the community has no difficulty believing male children when they say they have been sexually abused, it continues to struggle to believe female children.

A cursory reading of the history of the struggle for women's rights shows that while the scenarios change, the arguments and the struggles are identical. History constantly repeats itself. This is because women's history is ignored, or at best, revised and downgraded. I had never heard of Edith Haynes until I happened upon her by accident in 1984. By then I had been in practice for fourteen years.

In my own case the initial trials by fire have ceased and I have been accepted. However, I now discover that my history is being rewritten so that the matters that I complain of did not happen, or alternatively, I have interpreted them incorrectly. A senior member of the legal profession, who had actually seen a relevant letter written by one of those attacking me, recently informed me that that person was such a nice human being he would not have done the things I allege he has done. I have also been accused of the most extraordinary behaviour, from throwing tantrums in public to swearing at a senior member of the legal profession. Of course, none of this is true. I am quite happy to put the past behind me, but I am not happy to have my history rewritten.

I hope I don't disappear, as Edith Haynes did.

Margaret Thornton[5] tells us that women frequently regard the struggles of themselves and other women as of no consequence. She says that the poignant rider to the Edith Haynes case is that the only subsequent reference to Edith Haynes she encountered was an obituary in a Sydney newspaper in 1966. This item described Haynes as 'niece of a former Prime Minister, William Morris Hughes'. She was also the niece of Dame Mary Hughes, the article went on, and the daughter of the late Richard Hughes, one of the two founders of the *Bulletin*. More significantly there is, as Thornton describes it, 'a veil of silence' surrounding Edith's unsuccessful struggle to enter the jurisprudential community.

Another example given by Thornton is the case of Mary Kitson. She was admitted to legal practice in South Australia in 1916 and was a partner in a law firm. The Supreme Court found that she did not qualify for 'personhood' under the *Public Notaries Act 1859* when she applied to be appointed as a notary public. The functions of a notary public are relatively minor. There was no question of Kitson's fitness to perform the relevant functions, but she was excluded on the basis of sex. Furthermore, she was subsequently forced to leave her partnership because she married. Despite this, she asserted in the later years of her life that she had 'personally never ... come up against sexual discrimination in any walk of life, although it definitely does exist'.[6]

What of the future for women who follow? Consciousness-raising must continue but the area of immediate practical concern will be child-bearing and rearing. We all know that if women wish to have children, that is a 'hobby' or a 'frolic' upon which they embark at their own peril. They cannot expect to engage in this frivolous pastime and not have their careers severely interrupted. Nor can they expect any allowances to be made for them. This, of course, is grossly unfair. It is a biological fact that women have children. But the fact that society benefits as a whole from the bearing of children is a social fact. If men and women are to be entitled to equal opportunity then steps must be taken to ensure that women alone bear neither the biological nor the social and economic cost of having children. At the present time women bear all these costs. Women often accept this as a necessary part of life, but it is the basis of men's advantage.[7]

This is plainly inequitable. It is only by women recognizing that fact and standing together on the issue that these problems can be resolved. Raising a family means daily selfless giving over an extended period of time, and dealing with a number of tasks at any one time. One of the things that women must insist upon is that their life experiences in rearing a family give them considerable skills which should be seen as credit in other areas of human endeavour.

There is little that I have written in this chapter that gives us a new view of women in the legal profession. But my experience is that the message cannot be repeated often enough: women can make an equal place for themselves and for each other by standing together. Where that happens we have not had to wait. We will not have to wait in the future for men to invite us in, providing we support each other. My dream is that each woman will have a power base made up of every other woman.

---

1   For a comprehensive coverage of the heated debates on this Bill see H.C.J. Phillips, *The Voice of Edith Cowan*, Edith Cowan University, Perth, 1996, pp. 60–70.
2   *Western Australian Parliamentary Debates*, Vol. 69, 7 November 1923, p. 1378.
3   ibid.
4   ibid., p. 1380.
5   Margaret Thornton, *Dissonance and Distrust: Women and the Legal Profession*, Oxford University Press, Melbourne, 1996.
6   ibid., p. 67.
7   See Joan Eveline, 'The Politics of Advantage', *Australian Feminist Studies*, 19, Autumn 1994, pp. 129–154.

JUGGLING ACTIVISM AND LEADERSHIP

DONELLA CASPERSZ

Donella was born in 1959 in Colombo, Sri Lanka. In 1965, she migrated with her parents to Perth where she attended Sacred Heart Primary School and High School, completing her secondary education at Servite College. Donella worked as a social worker for five years before becoming a policy officer in Multicultural and Ethnic Affairs. From the late 1980s she was Principal Private Secretary to the State Minister for Ethnic Affairs. She was a member of the WA Women's Advisory Council between 1983 and 1986. In 1993 Donella returned to university to work on her PhD. Married with a young son, Donella maintains an interest in policy development and advocacy for ethnic affairs.

I prefer to see myself as an 'activist' rather than a 'leader'. This better describes what I think is the crux of leadership: that is, leadership equals trying to change things for the better. Righting wrongs, making things better — however you would like to put it. If change occurs through an activity or through 'being involved', then this is leadership. Or in my terms activism. But what does activism involve? The first thing that springs to mind is that activism requires juggling. Effective activists are jugglers of people, of time, of money. Being a juggler also means acting as a lighthouse keeper, or rather someone who is always looking for the options to make sure that the beacon keeps shining. An activist is also a negotiator — again, of people, time and money. In negotiating, however, an activist seeks to establish a win-win outcome. Finally, an activist has to listen to people. This is because activism requires acting with others and being able to tap into the aspirations, emotions, intuitions as well as disappointments of others. In short, effective activism requires effective juggling which requires effective listening.

What has motivated my activism? Quite simply, my major motivation has been the experience of migration. I am a product of two worlds. I call myself an Australian, one who was born a Sri Lankan. I grew up in a Perth society with its own customs and mores, yet my family maintained Sri Lankan customs and mores. The effect of this double-headed experience was to highlight some of the difficulties in becoming an Australian. How many migrant kids have stories of not understanding play activity because we did not understand Australianisms? How many can tell the tale of hearing about faraway places like Mandurah to which our friends went on holiday, but which may as well have been in Europe because Mandurah was just as physically inaccessible? For some of us the question of where we belonged was even more stark. As Eva Cox wrote about her own experience, 'I was not allowed to belong: I was still defined as a reffo and a Jew and I wondered what it all meant as by now my main source of identity was as an outsider'.[1] At the same time these experiences acted to motivate migrant kids like me to become involved and change things so that the task of being Australian could become easier.

An added motivation stems from a professional interest, which I accidentally stumbled across in my early days as a student social worker. I was fortunate enough to gain a student placement in which I conducted a study on the status of migrant women in the clothing industry. My research was a mini-version of a much wider study that had been conducted in Victoria in the late 1970s. The report of the Victorian study, entitled *But I Wouldn't Want My Wife to Work Here*,[2] was one of the first to document how factors like the lack of English reading and writing skills, the lack of understanding of Australian cultural practices, and the financial imperative to work, combined to enhance the exploitation of migrant women in the clothing industry. Looking back, the study I conducted was quite significant in motivating me to become an activist. It gave me a first-hand experience of how exploitation arises not only because of ethnic-related factors like language and culture, but also because of gender-related factors.

It is not surprising, then, that my activism has been mainly in the areas of women's issues and ethnic affairs. With regard to women's issues, I was chosen as a member of the Women's Advisory Council (WAC) in the early 1980s. At this time WAC held a number of consultations with different groups of women. The aim of these forums was to clarify the issues of concern to diverse groups of women and to then channel their concerns to government. I helped organize WAC-sponsored consultations for women from an ethnic background as well as for young women. While holding consultations may seem like 'old hat' in today's world where communications take place via microtechnology, one of the most effective facets of these consultations was that they provided a forum in which women could air their views freely to others, without fear or favour. In the case of ethnic and young women, many barriers relating to language, culture and general accessibility had usually prevented these women from being able to do this in the past. A significant feature of our consultations, or 'speakouts' as they were called, was that they provided exactly this opportunity. We passed the recommendations from these speakouts onto the relevant government agencies, and then looked for ways to apply lobbying pressure to see they were implemented.

Although I have always been concerned about women's issues, my participation in ethnic affairs has been more extensive. These two areas actually dovetail in my activities supporting women from multicultural backgrounds. In this respect I served as a vice-president of the Ethnic Communities Council of WA when it sponsored the conference on ethnic women's issues in 1996. Many matters arose from this conference and I had some involvement in ensuring they were passed on to, and acted upon by, various government and non-government agencies. Another area of activism related to ethnic affairs has been in the employment area. While working as a social worker at the Fremantle Migrant Resource Centre I helped set up one of the first ethnic Joblink programs. Employment, or rather unemployment and underemployment, has always been a critical area affecting the ability of people from different cultural backgrounds to settle into our community. Our Joblink program was established to provide assistance to newly arrived migrants looking for employment. It played an advocacy and facilitation role, helping people to improve their skills and giving them assistance with getting their qualifications recognized. It is gratifying to see that this program still exists today, albeit in a revised form.

Language services is another area dear to my heart. Again, this is a field where inadequate service provision seriously affects the ability of newly arrived migrants to settle. The scope of language services covers not only improving the ability of the individual migrant to speak English, but also the provision of multilingual information and multilingual services. Coupling the two is designed to ensure that, as a community, we are able to properly fulfil a duty of care to those new to Australian shores. One initiative promoting these interests, into which I had input, was the establishment of a Language Services Policy Officer within the Western Australian Government. Though this position has since been abolished, some of the principles underlying service delivery have been maintained in different forms in the public service generally.

Community relations is another area in which I have been active, especially in the late 1980s. Following a series of incidents, the West Australian Labor Government passed an amendment to the *Criminal Code* making it illegal for racial vilification activities to be undertaken. At the time I was working for the Minister for Multicultural and Ethnic Affairs, so I was involved at the policy level as well as in community discussions. The passage of this legislation was particularly significant for many people in the West Australian community. This government action carried the significant signal that racist activities were not to be tolerated in the community.

How does one learn about activism? I first learnt about activism from my parents. I am the daughter of parents who chose to migrate to Australia from Sri Lanka with six children aged between six months and ten years, and with only £50 in their pockets. We arrived in Australia and settled in Highgate with many other new migrants before moving into a State Housing

Commission home in Balga. When I say I learnt about activism from my parents I mean they did everything to make the world around us better for their kids. On top of his regular job my Dad played music in clubs and shows and both parents cleaned office blocks so they could give their six children the start in life for which they had migrated. It is from my parents that I learnt the first principle about being an activist: creating change means being fully committed. To fulfil their commitment, my parents sometimes woke at 4 a.m. to clean those office blocks before coming home to wake us for school and starting their second job for the day. Dad would drop us off at school before going to work outside the home and Mum would continue working on the domestic front. The fact that such hard work stemmed from a deep commitment is without doubt. My parents did all the things I have mentioned about being an activist: they juggled, they negotiated, they listened.

How can activism be evaluated? Activism is evaluated on the basis of the change that can be produced. My parents produced change because among their children today there is a speech therapist, a doctor, a lawyer, two teachers, and me, a social worker turned postgraduate. Has my activism produced change? On the surface some might answer 'yes'. But sometimes I have my doubts. I am thinking of a woman I knew, who I worry I was unable to help when she most needed it, despite my grounding in activism.

My friend was Asian-born, in her mid-fifties and she had lived in Perth for fifteen years. She spoke English but did not read or write it. However, she became adept at catching the bus, filling in forms, and even writing birthday cards. My friend had been having headaches for quite some time and had seen a few doctors who had diagnosed it as depressed migrant women's syndrome. Her weight dropped to 35 kilograms before she was hospitalized, but even then this was diagosed as a suspected eating disorder. It was only after she tripped over in hospital during her third period of hospitalization that a CAT scan was done and a brain tumour discovered. My friend was operated on and some of the tumour removed. But I was there when a young resident told her, 'Dear, you have a terminal brain tumour and you will die. Because of this, when the tumour grows back we will not do anything else for you'.

I was sickened and mortified at my friend's treatment. I knew that this offhand approach stemmed in part from the fact that she was female, migrant, not well off and did not have any close family to advocate for her. My friend's death caused me to reflect a great deal, particularly about the merits of my activism. I have been involved for most of my adult life in various activities aimed at trying to prevent incidents like this from happening. Sadly, my friend's death could not be prevented. Her treatment by those who were supposed to care for her, however, could well have been more humane.

After a lot of soul searching I believe that my friend's case highlights that activism can produce humility. Humility, that is, about ourselves and our capabilities. I learned early on that juggling, negotiating and listening are paramount in activism. But being an activist or being a leader also requires an ability to keep learning. To lead, to be involved, to be an activist or a leader requires continuous learning of 'how to do'. My friend's case taught me this. So too have some of the people I met during my years as a social worker. I have met people who have risked life and limb to migrate to Australia. Yet because their qualifications as surgeons, engineers, teachers, lawyers and a host of other professions were not recognized in Australia, they had to take jobs that did not utilize their professional expertise. Although these people did mind very much that they weren't able to do what they were qualified to do, they acquiesced in their new, lower status because of their motivations for migrating. Like my parents, a lot of them gave up their professions, jobs, homes and countries to give their children a better opportunity. That is a very special form of activism.

In summary, I have tried to outline what activism is to me, why we should undertake it and how to evaluate it. In other words, I have tried to present a job description of sorts. But is there really a job description for activism? Thinking about my own life, I suggest not. At the end of the day I think that activists are people who just become involved. While there are usually clear motivations to do so, becoming involved is often quite unconscious. On reflection, perhaps that is the crux of activism. One just becomes involved because there is a job to be done.

1. Eva Cox, 'What Ethnic Identity?', in K. Hearne, J. Travaglia and E. Weiss (eds), *Who Do You Think You Are? Second Generation Immigrant Women in Australia*, Women's Redress Press Inc., Broadway, 1992, p. 63.
2. Centre for Urban Research and Action, *But I Wouldn't Want My Wife to Work Here: A Study of Migrant Women in Melbourne Industry*. Melbourne Industry, Research Report for International Women's Year, Centre for Urban Research and Action, Fitzroy, 1976.

SCIENCE, BOOKS AND ME

ANN GHISALBERTI

Chief Executive Officer of the Scitech Discovery Centre, Ann was born in Perth in 1950. Apart from three stints living in Italy, Switzerland and the United States, Perth has always been home. She studied Science at The University of Western Australia and, after gaining a PhD in Biochemistry, Ann taught medical students and undertook medical research there, as well as at the Centre for Women's Health, Princess Margaret Hospital and the QEII Medical Centre. She has worked at Scitech since 1987 with a four-year break in the middle to run her own consulting business in training, employment and women's issues. She has been active in many community groups including the Women's Advisory Council, the Women's Electoral Lobby, the Women's Economic Development Organisation and the Family Planning Association. She has also been involved in many committees for science in Western Australia including the Australian Science Communicators Network and the Women in Science Enquiry Network. She thinks of herself as an activist.

I decided I was going to be a scientist over thirty years ago. Since then, and indeed even as a little girl, books have been vital to how I live my life. Scientists use books and scientific journals to gather information which they then use to design their own experiments to add to the world's knowledge of their topic. We all accept that books are a resource and a fountain of useful information we can use now or later in our professional or personal lives. For me books have always been so much more. 'We read to keep from feeling alone' is a phrase from 'Shadowlands', a movie about the life of the author C.S. Lewis. That phrase hit me so forcefully I decided to write about the books that I'd read during my life that made me who I am both as a professional and as a woman and along the way have stopped me feeling alone. To be called a bookworm is the greatest compliment I can be paid and I am truly one.

Being a Girl: Strong, Independent and Caring[1]

In fact as a kid I did read a lot of C.S. Lewis. I remember *The Lion, the Witch and the Wardrobe*. It was exciting and enchanting. Reading it did help me. I was unhappy as a kid and books of fantasy took me away from my life. But even then I loved books written by women and about women. I read all the *What Katie Did* books by Susan Coolidge. Katie was great, she got into lots of trouble by being strong and independent. What a great role model for an Australian girl growing up in the restrictive 1950s. I remember Anne of Green Gables who was a girl who did well in school, had romances and showed me that it was okay to be smart — you'd still have boyfriends. I read *Little Women, Little Men, Jo's Boys* — you name it, I read it. Jo was strong, independent and wild whilst the older sister Meg was caring, nurturing and married young. I never could decide who I wanted to be but I did know that Louisa May Alcott described happy families that I never knew existed. I can still remember those books and when I see the movie *Little Women* in any version I still cry. My Mum worked in the library at my primary school just like her grandmother who ran the library at the Mechanics' Institute in Geraldton. Consequently Mum didn't consider *The Famous Five* and *The Secret Seven* series by Enid Blyton as great literature. But I didn't care. I identified with the girl called George in one of the gangs and so I always had a model of women and girls who were strong, capable and outspoken . . . and often in trouble!

Being Educated[2]

I loved science in school. I grew 'curiouser and curiouser', so curious that I loved finding out about things. In fact when I give talks to girls about careers in science I always say that women make the best scientists because we are inordinately curious and we show attention to detail. The boys don't agree with this, needless to say.

In my job as Chief Executive Officer of the Scitech Discovery Centre, a hands-on science centre with about seventy staff, most of the books and journals I've been reading are about management. Many years ago I realized I could never be a good manager — I was too radical, too much an activist, I wanted things to change. I didn't want a job where all my energies went in making the status quo run efficiently. As a scientist I was always searching for answers to 'How does the body work?' or 'What can we discover about this disease so we can treat it?' As feminist activists we asked: 'How can we make changes to the world so it is fairer for women?' or 'What can we do to right this injustice?' No wonder leading is more my style and managing seems very pedestrian and very boring. I'm really trying to come to grips with what it means to be a leader with my values. How can I do things differently and still be a feminist in my workplace?

I remember when I was about seven I was a Brownie and I did a project about Marie Curie. I can still remember how it started off — 'Marie Sklodowska was born in Warsaw ...' I was really interested in her as a woman and as a scientist even when I was a kid. I thought she had it made: two Nobel prizes, smart healthy children, a wonderful marriage and then a lover when Pierre died. I never paid much attention to the fact that she died a lingering death from cancer due to her work on radioactivity. I recently had a letter from a Polish woman who berated me quite rightly for having described Marie Curie as a French scientist. Now I am careful to refer to her as a Polish scientist.

The one book I remember reading and re-reading many times as a teenager was a volume by Pearl S. Buck called *Command the Morning*. Although it didn't win her the Nobel Prize like *The Good Earth* it did make a big impact on a teenager looking for ways to be a scientist and a woman. The book described the Americans who were working on the nuclear bomb on the mesa in Nevada during the Second World War. One of the scientists was a woman who was smart and good looking. I read it over and over again, that woman scientist was a really good role model for me.

I don't remember much about what I read at university apart from my course books and *The Female Eunuch*. Germaine

Greer's book was published in 1968 when I was a very unfeminist first-year student studying very traditional male-oriented science in a class with almost all boys and certainly with all male teachers. *The Female Eunuch* made an impression on me but it didn't call me to action. I read it, I thought about my life, I thought about the things that needed to be done for women in the world but I was so busy making it in the man's world of science that I didn't take on any of it personally. In fact, I recall believing that as long as I studied and worked very hard anything was possible.

A Changing Life: Sex and Destiny[3]

Interestingly, many years later I met Germaine Greer and made a complete idiot of myself. A friend gave me Greer's book *Sex and Destiny: The Politics of Human Fertility* just before I attended a talk she gave in Perth. I was sitting at the table next to Dr Greer, so I thought I'd get it signed. I plucked up courage, and said 'Hello' to this icon of the feminist movement who was wearing, as I recall, green sneakers. I introduced myself and said, 'You live in Italy now, how is your Italian?' She enquired smilingly, 'Which one?' That quite surprised me because she'd just written that she no longer identified with women who were sexually active. I burbled on about how *The Female Eunuch* changed my life, she signed my book graciously and I slunk back to my seat. Later I read the introduction to *Sex and Destiny* where Greer states, 'Astonishingly people still write to some hapless authors accusing them of super human achievement. Your book changed my life. No! no! replied the author in despair. You changed your life, nobody else should or can'. Oh well, I can't help it, I am a hopeless fan.

When I finished my PhD I went to live in Italy for a year. It was a very tough year — my first time overseas, first time living in a non-English-speaking country, first time pregnant — working in a hospital department where I had to speak my feeble Italian. Unlike Germaine Greer, I had no doubt about my Italian whom I had married before we left Australia. In Italy we lived in a tiny little flat and the way I saved my sanity that year was to read every Australian book I could possibly find. We would go to the Australian Consulate just so I could speak and read English. I read all of Xavier Herbert's *Poor Fellow My Country*, every Patrick White, even Colleen McCullough's *The Thorn Birds*. Those books really helped me overcome homesickness for Australia. I remember once seeing a Qantas plane fly overhead and wishing somehow I could highjack it so I'd get back home. That year left me with enormous compassion for women who migrate to countries where everyone speaks a different language; every day becomes a nightmare, especially when you are pregnant and giving birth for the first time.

Trying to remember the books I read in the early days of being a mother is difficult. I was always tired and very depressed. I remember reading any book I could find to help me 'do it better'. Nothing I ever found told me to relax and trust my instincts. I was into breastfeeding and was a keen, even rabid, member of the Nursing Mothers' Association where I reorganized our branch library (books again!) and purchased lots of radical volumes like *Our Bodies, Our Selves* by the Boston Women's Collective. One book I really loved was *Babies Need Books* by Helen Butler, a New Zealand grandmother who wrote a book about her grand-daughter, Kushla. Kushla seemed to have lots of developmental problems and her mum reads her all these books and Kushla turned out to be a great little kid. So I figured that even though my kids were totally healthy and normal and bright, I would just read and read and read to them. Books helped me and made me feel that I was not alone, that other mothers were looking for the same things.

Becoming a Feminist[4]

It really wasn't until 1989 that I guess I 'came out' as a feminist. I was nominated for the Women's Advisory Council to the Premier, who at that time was Peter Dowding. It was two wonderful years and I learnt so much from the other women. I became radicalized and my eyes were opened to the injustices in Western Australia. I was incensed seeing women in Bandyup Prison for drug offences or social security fraud when the reason they defrauded the system was because they couldn't support their kids on the small amounts of money they were given. One author who took my fancy at that time was Ann Oakley. Ann is a British writer and she did her PhD on housework. I remember devouring *Sociology of Housework* when I was just married and hating housework as much as I do now. Her feminist analysis of housework was mind blowing: I didn't know you could criticize such 'institutions'. I read other books by her and one that made a big impression was *Taking It Like a Woman*. It's about a woman who survives cancer of the tongue and lots of difficult situations in her life. For the first time I wrote a fan letter to an author, but never got a reply. I wrote that my favourite book until this time had been Simone de Beauvoir's *The Mandarins* and I had read it once a year for the last ten years. By comparison, I wrote, I have read *Taking It Like a Woman* ten times in one year. It really did make a big impression on me. My copy is very tatty.

I have come to the belated conclusion that even though I can't be a 'pure' feminist at work I can make changes that improve the lives of all the women and men working with me. Staff having flexibility to look after their children, part-time work after maternity leave, salary and promotion based on merit, a staff that is at least 52 per cent women, women comprising over half the management team — these are important to me as a leader.

Revealingly, the book that has made the biggest professional impact on me is by a man: *Maverick* by Ricardo Semler. I love his style of leading which was totally casual. He involved staff in decision-making and made working in a factory in Brazil a fulfilling job for his employees. I've copied lots of his ideas with great success. He's the kind of leader I want to be. I find it hard to lead men and women when the men want me to be tougher and make decisions quickly, and the women want much more consultation and a collaborative style of leadership. With so many years in the women's movement I would love the idea of running a business as a collective, but I certainly can't achieve that with my current skills.

Being[5]

When I was young I was reading adventure books, books about courageous young women. Later on I read about being a mother and when I became a feminist I gobbled up all the important books on feminism. Books are still really important to me; I read all the time. One joy has been to be a council member of the National Library in Canberra. I love being there. I love the fact that it is the repository of Australia's written history. I am in awe seeing the originals of diaries by Cook and Bligh and David Williamson's plays written in pencil in a kid's exercise book. Being on the National Library Council seems to have completed the circle. I started as a little girl who read books about strong women in order to escape, then became a woman scientist trying to find her place in a man's world reading feminism. Now I'm trying to integrate it all and become a different kind of leader, a woman who tries to live her feminist principles in the workplace. Books have supported and strengthened me at all stages of my life, living in many parts of the world, doing many different jobs. I no longer need books as a refuge or an escape from reality — in fact I quite like the reality of my life now. That was not the case a few years ago.

In 1992 I went to California with my daughter for my sister's wedding. My sister Jade was born two years after me and she'd been living in America for about twelve years so I hadn't seen much of her. When we arrived in Los Angeles I found out my sister had been diagnosed with ovarian cancer. The wedding was bittersweet as she had a radical hysterectomy two days afterwards so she couldn't even eat any of her own wedding cake.

For the next eighteen months my sister underwent all kinds of treatments but she never recovered. I went over to be with her in November 1993 and for the last month of her life the book that I read with her, and by myself, was the *Tibetan Book of Living and Dying*. It became important for both of us to understand about the death process and for both of us to believe in life after death. I haven't read the book since and I don't know if I'll be strong enough to read it again. But it really helped me then.

I know books will continue to enthral, enthuse and enrapture me as I move through my life. I know that *When I Am an Old Woman I Shall Wear Purple* will become a new favourite as I get older. Reading, delving into, exploring and devouring all types of books will always be important for me. Books are my passion. Perhaps, who knows, I may even write my own one day.

1. Louisa May Alcott, *Little Women*, J.M. Dent and Sons, London, 1948; *Little Men and Jo's Boys*, Puffin Classics, Penguin, 1983; Enid Blyton, *The Famous Five*, Knight Books, Hodder & Stoughton, 1951; *The Secret Seven*, Knight Books, Hodder & Stoughton, 1949; Susan Coolidge, *What Katy Did*, Shakespeare Head, London, 1955; C.S. Lewis, *The Lion, the Witch and the Wardrobe*, Collins Publishing, London, 1960; Lucy Montgomery, *Anne of Green Gables*, Nimbus Publishing Ltd, Chelsea Green, 1955.
2. Pearl S. Buck, *Command the Morning*, Methuen, London, 1959; *The Good Earth*, Methuen, London, 1953; Germaine Greer, *The Female Eunuch*, Paladin, London, 1977.
3. Boston Women's Collective, *Our Bodies, Our Selves*, Simon & Schuster, New York, 1996; Helen Butler, *Babies Need Books*, Bodley Head, London, 1979; Germaine Greer, *Sex and Destiny: The Politics of Human Fertility*, Cox & Wyman Ltd., Reading, 1984; Xavier Herbert, *Poor Fellow My Country*, Fontana/Collins, London, 1975; Colleen McCullough, *The Thorn Birds*, Harper & Row, New York, 1977.
4. Simone De Beauvoir, *The Mandarins*, Collins, London, 1957; Ann Oakley, *Sociology of Housework*, Robertson, London, 1974; *Taking It Like a Woman*, Cape, London; Ricardo Semler, *Maverick: The Success Story behind the World's Most Unusual Work Place*, Century Business, London, 1993.
5. Sandra Martz (ed.), *When I Am an Old Woman I Shall Wear Purple*, Papier-Mache Press, Watsonville, 1991; Sogyal Rinpoche (edited by P. Gaffney and A. Harvey), *The Tibetan Book of Living and Dying*, Rider, London, 1992.

NOT AN IVORY TOWER:
LEARNING AND TEACHING IN A UNIVERSITY

PATRICIA CRAWFORD

Professor of History at The University of Western Australia, Patricia was born in Sydney in 1941. She attended the Methodist Ladies' College in Elsternwick and Hawthorn and later studied at the University of Melbourne, where a first-year course inspired her passion for seventeenth-century English history. Marrying in 1962 she moved to Perth and combined rearing a child with continuing studies. One of Patricia's greatest joys was gaining a PhD, yet not until she received a fellowship from the Australian National University in 1986 did she feel that she was at university because someone wanted her there. In 1995 she received a Nuffield Fellowship to study for a year in England. Her parents and husband continue to support her academic contributions and more recently there are also dear friends, colleagues and students who sustain her with their interest and enthusiasm.

As a historian of sixteenth- and seventeenth-century England, a university is where I believe I belong. Yet for much of the twentieth century, universities in Australia have not accepted that married women should have any place at all as students or staff.

Universities are in some ways different from other workplaces. The people in them, staff and students, voice a rhetoric of dreams and ideals, aspiring to 'truth' through the pursuit of knowledge. I too share the dream, the ideal, of the pursuit of learning and understanding, the belief that things of the mind and spirit do matter.

However, universities are not ivory towers, separate from the world. They are social institutions, workplaces, and for roughly 800 of their 900-year existence, they have been open to men only. Over the last century, women have been admitted to study and to teach, but individual universities have responded only reluctantly, slowly and conservatively to their presence.

In Australia, the idea of women seeking an intellectual life seems to be a bit of a joke. The women who pursued careers in universities were initially expected to be unmarried, which in itself was generally deemed a less than ideal state. It was widely believed in the late nineteenth and early twentieth centuries that women belonged in the private sphere of the family, and ideally were devoted to the welfare of husbands and children. Among the middle class, the domestic support of wives was necessary so that men were free to pursue their chosen careers. However, from the late nineteenth century a few wealthier women enrolled in universities; of those, some became university teachers. Most saw their decision as one made at the expense of marriage and family life. I recollect that even in the 1950s, when I was a student, we were shown that women could not expect both marriage and a career. In a mini-drama at the union theatre, a woman in academic robes debated her choice of career against the arguments of a wife and mother.

I became a historian by a series of accidents; I did not consciously choose at all. No-one in my family had attended a university, so it was not something I knew about. I can remember when I was about ten years old hearing at school for the first time about 'university': that sounded just the place for me. What I decided I wanted to do was 'go to the university'.

In many ways I was lucky because my parents (unlike some of their contemporaries) believed in education for girls. Although both had left school themselves at around fifteen, they made sacrifices to send me to a girls' private school. At the Methodist Ladies' College in Melbourne women teachers encouraged hard work and learning, and a teachers' college bursary took me to the University of Melbourne where I enrolled in honours in History and English. (This was largely an accident. The teachers' college wanted me to enrol in Geography and Geology because there were shortages of teachers in those areas. As neither of these subjects appealed, a sub-dean in Arts suggested my results were good enough to permit me to enrol in honours.) I was taught by impressive women (as well as by men). By my fourth year, I realized that I was doing well enough to think of a higher degree. I also wanted to marry. Under the terms of the teachers' college bursary, women were not permitted to marry before completing their degrees and serving for a year, so my bond was broken, and repayments of tuition fees and the living allowance were due. In 1962, I married and moved to Western Australia where I embarked on a master's degree at The University of Western Australia (UWA).

In 1962 I was grateful to be given a scholarship and permitted to study. However, at UWA I was told that my achievements would be limited: it was men who had the broad, meaningful ideas in history; female historians simply did the detailed work on which the generalizations were based. I was not sure about this at the age of twenty-one. It seemed to me that I might still make a contribution. Besides, I found that my imagination was fired by the history of seventeenth-century England: I wanted to keep working. The idea of a 'career' was still vague and no-one at UWA seemed to think that married women could have one. I kept going because I wanted to write history.

While I was working on my master's degree I took some first-year classes, which I enjoyed. My degree conferred, I sought full-time employment as a tutor, but I found myself employed as a part-time casual teacher. My tutoring load was the near equivalent of a full-time member of staff but the pay was about one-third of the full-time pay. I saw that the men who were employed in full-time tutorships were less qualified. I was told they had been given the jobs (they did not bother to advertise tutorships in the mid-1960s) because they had wives and children to support. I, with a husband to support me, was aberrant in not being at home and having children, and was clearly simply working for 'pin money'. Thus I found myself employed as a temporary member of staff in one year when there was a need, but unemployed the next.

By the mid-1960s I realized that UWA enforced a policy — which the Vice-Chancellor deemed 'an administrative rule' — that no married women would be employed on the permanent staff. Employment was on an annual basis, the assumption being that when a suitable man was found, the make-do woman would no longer be needed. I do not wish to labour this early unhappy history, which I have recounted in more general terms in a book entitled *The Missing Chapters*. But since I am a historian, I believe that the past matters. I want to explain something of the university culture, the context, in which women struggled to fulfil their intellectual aspirations.

Belatedly, I realized that a doctorate was necessary for a woman aspiring to be a historian. Finding a subject was difficult, for although I wanted to work on the seventeenth century, the general wisdom was that study for three years in England was essential. Airfares in 1965 were comparatively high in relation to wages, and microfilms were limited. Nevertheless, my husband and I decided that if I travelled to England to search for source material, I might find a topic which I could pursue from Western Australia. With most of the family savings, I embarked on a three-month research trip, and returned with the decision to write a doctorate about the political career of a seventeenth-century Civil War politician, Denzil Holles.

I find it strange, looking back, that the history I studied as a student, and the two theses I wrote for my higher degrees, were all about men. I spent six years on the political career of Holles, and it was another six before I found a publisher for my book. There was nothing there that I identified with as a woman. Only later did I come to see how the histories I was learning were part of a system in which the ideas, perceptions, experiences of women were not deemed important. In those years, I think my story was simply one of being accepted as a serious historian. Taking on the nature of the discipline was another matter altogether.

Work and family can no more easily be separated for academic women than for any others. By 1970 I had a PhD thesis to finish and a child. Still I wanted to teach at the university, but there were different obstacles. There was no maternity leave, and no child care. Like other middle-class mothers, I struggled against the stereotype of the 'neglectful mother'. Yet all academic women confronted negative stereotypes. In the 1970s, single women who had 'failed' to marry were regarded as profoundly frustrated — a veiled reference to what was assumed to be sexual deprivation — and unbalanced. We could only conclude that all women, irrespective of their marital and maternal status, were 'wrong' in some way. In the intellectual space of the university, women were out of place. Initially, I worked as a half-time temporary lecturer; in 1976, twelve years after I started teaching, I obtained my first tenurable position.

Meanwhile, universities themselves had changed. The abolition of fees allowed many mature-age women students an opportunity to study which earlier they had been denied. Tertiary education for women was generally more acceptable.

Mature-age women students, who entered the universities in the 1970s when there were no fees, spoke of husbands who permitted them to study 'provided nothing changed'; of men who always needed the company of their wives when essays were due, or who even burnt books and essays when severely provoked. Essays provoked contention, as women argued new ideas about work and sexuality with their partners. Classes could be emotionally charged when issues such as 'domestic violence' were discussed. There were times I longed for the calmer waters of Tudor history, and a standard tutorial topic of the 1960s, such as 'the foreign policy of Cardinal Wolsey'.

During the 1970s and 1980s, there were struggles to develop courses which reflected the experiences of women; courses which would help women understand that the problems they faced in studying were not due to their own personal inadequacies but were caused by structural barriers. A group of women in the Arts Faculty at UWA argued that we needed a course in Women's Studies. Our proposal for a master's degree by coursework was initially unacceptable to the overseeing committee. 'We think it's too Messianic', I was told. In the end, with help from some skilful male support, we were successful. Women's Studies has blossomed under wonderful teaching, but like many other such courses around the country, has not been well funded, and has unfortunately remained small.

Research and teaching in the humanities are, I believe, inextricably linked. My research about women led me to teach in different courses, which I found appealed to different kinds of students. Feminist activity and teaching led me to new subjects for research. Like many other women, I sought a new agenda for discussion. We argued that history itself might look different if women were viewed seriously as historical agents. Wonderfully exciting topics for research opened up, exploring the lives of women through the ages: as citizens, poets, reformers, convicts, police, miners, mothers, wives, mistresses, and aunts.

Crucial for me has been the freedom to choose a subject for research; or more, perhaps, of allowing a puzzle in the sources to choose me. This happened for me in 1975 when I received a Nuffield Fellowship, a year in England for research on the history of the family in sixteenth- and seventeenth-century England. I was working in the British Library, reading a seventeenth-century sermon about the uselessness of good works in effecting salvation, when I came upon the sentence, 'All our righteousness is but menstruous clouts'. I felt outraged. What intellectual system lay behind such an idea? Why was this the image of disgust which the preacher had chosen? I had the freedom then, with a doctorate and job, to choose to pursue my questions further, to try to understand something of how ideas about women's bodily processes so pervaded our culture both in the past and now. I went home that night and started drafting up the questions which formed the core of an article I later published about attitudes to menstruation in seventeenth-century England. The seminars I gave on the subject, while I was thinking it through, aroused a certain negativity: I suppose people were embarrassed. 'They'll be writing a history of nose picking next', I heard. The article itself was singled out as a sign of the 'mindless trendiness' demonstrated in the journal *Past & Present*, according to a critical reviewer. (At a dinner party recently, one of my critic's friends recounted his tearoom witticism: 'That article just shows you should work on problems, not periods'.) But younger women scholars have since told me they found that my article opened up a space for a different history which might include this history of the body.

At the present time (1999) about half the undergraduate students are women, and in Arts, where I teach, they are two-thirds of the student population. Even at postgraduate level, women's numbers are increasing. But at the level of academic staff, women are very few: 23 per cent at UWA in 1998. I have estimated that women were 10 per cent of the academic staff in the 1920s, so the progress after a decade and more of legislation and agitation seems miserably slow. Despite the complacent arguments of some that everything is fine, and it's simply a matter of time before women are half the staff, I remain unconvinced.

My story about becoming a professor, then, I see as one of survival, of a career by accident, in which family life and work were linked. The pattern is not unusual for my generation of academic women. UWA was worse than many other universities, partly because of its isolation; not until 1975 was there a second university in the State. But women in other universities in Australia (and abroad) have similar tales to tell.

In reflecting upon feminist women's leadership in universities, the first thought is about ambivalence. Feminists seeking to work within academia need the approval of the professional groups whose conservative views they challenge and seek to change.

Currently, tertiary institutions across the country are unhappy places. The government has precipitated yet another crisis by reducing funding. In this climate, any changes to benefit women seem very threatening. In academic debates I hear the same arguments I have been hearing for years: 'I won't allow anything which disadvantages men'. (Does this mean that men who currently enjoy the advantage of having 77 per cent of the academic posts at UWA are entitled to those until the end of time?) Some of women's problems arise simply from being outnumbered and overworked. Overwork is universal in tertiary education, not specific to women, of course. But the collegiality which makes some tasks easier is not so readily available to women; while the number in each department is few, women are extra busy, because they are a valuable resource for women students. They serve on comparatively more committees. (For every woman who might have the skills and status, there are at least four men.) Currently women find themselves overburdened with committee work, which, because they are a minority on most committees, can be additionally stressful. In addition, most women have domestic responsibilities.

My own ambivalence is such that on bad days I wonder why I stayed, why I did not just give up. Several things have helped me to stay. The presence of women as models has helped, even if the models themselves have ambivalent meanings for me today. At the University of Melbourne, Associate Professor Kathleen Fitzpatrick was one of my teachers. Fitzpatrick was an outstanding woman who inspired generations of students, and I was no exception. Yet later I read in an autobiographical piece which she contributed to *The Half Open Door*[1] that she had never applied to be a full professor. She insisted on the belief 'that no one should be appointed to the highest academic rank unless he or she is either a profound and original thinker or a truly erudite person ... I did not meet my own criterion for a Chair [a professorship]'.

The friendship and support of other women has made an immeasurable difference. Since 1966, I've been involved with groups of feminist women. There was a study group of women graduates who worked on retraining for women, and designs for better cities. We even spent time discussing how to manage the household tasks while working full time. I've been part of groups which have worked for the establishment of a child-care centre at UWA, for the appointment of an equity officer, and for trying to translate policies into practice. The campus women's group has tried to cut across barriers between academic and general staff, to work cooperatively. Even so, many women on campus are concerned about other issues, and we need to work harder at listening to what these may be. Aboriginal rights issues and racism are more significant for some women than the general feminist constellation of concerns.

Much of my research in recent years has been in collaboration with other women: putting together edited collections, writing books, working as part of a team. Working collaboratively offers insights into problems, so that the process may be more important than the end product. Collaborative research is common in the sciences, but is comparatively new in the humanities, committed as people are to the model of the individual scholar burning the midnight oil. Feminist collaborative research takes time and emotional energy, but the process matters. We are seeking to find ways by which research funding can be used to support individuals in doing their own work, as part of a group.

Humour and laughter have helped us to survive. While women colleagues have been few in number, they have been significant. They have shared in the analysis of systemic injustices. I have enjoyed, too, the intellectual company of students who enrolled in courses, and contributed to discussions. There have been friendships based on the sharing of experiences, mutual respect, affection.

Thinking about ways forward, how can we create a better professional environment, a world in which women and men can work together? How can we change universities? At the moment, the challenges seem the basic ones of survival, ensuring that all the younger people who do not have tenure are not the victims of the Federal Government's funding cuts. Not that there are so very many younger women: 75 per cent of the staff of history departments around Australia were appointed before 1975.

How do we reshape leadership so it becomes less about individuals who can star and more about everyone contributing, so that leading is something that everyone does?

On good days, I can see that by being there I've suggested a different way of proceeding, that my teaching has helped someone to rethink an issue, and that I've contributed a different way of understanding; research, teaching, life, have all come together. My presence has made a difference.

1   K. Fitzpatrick, in Patricia Grimshaw and Lynne Strahan (eds), *The Half Open Door*, Hale and Iremonger, Sydney, 1982.

DOING IT DIFFERENTLY

VAL MARSDEN

Val is Senior Policy Officer, Human Resource Policy and Planning, within the Education Department of Western Australia. Born in Geelong, Victoria in 1938, she moved to Perth in 1978. A prominent member of the Women's Electoral Lobby, Val was Coordinator of the National Council of Women in 1990. From 1984 to 1986 she worked as the inaugural Coordinator of the Women's Information and Referral Exchange, and completed a degree in Social Sciences during that time. Val loves reading, and passionately admires writers for their ability to create worlds for their readers. Her present-day 'heroes' are people who speak out against inequality, oppression and the erosion of human rights: people like Aung Sung Suu Kyi and Nelson Mandela, and in Australia, Sister Veronica Brady, Justice Elizabeth Evatt, Susan Ryan, Eva Cox, Pat Giles, Jennie George and others, who have worked hard to change things for women in this country.

My schooling was the rudimentary three R's considered sufficient for girls in the 1940s and 1950s who were going to marry and live happily ever after. Even so, I admired independent women who had a career — mostly my teachers at the girls' school I attended. But it wasn't lost on me that in order to have an independent career women had to forego marriage and children. No-one let me know that this was official policy in government employment at the time, but I was aware of the way in which women who never married were viewed by others: as 'old maids', and to be pitied. This made them ambiguous role models.

Although strong women figured prominently in my life, from my teachers to my paternal grandmother, I spent much of my teenage years reading of the exploits of adventurous men. Despite spending lots of my time with my nose buried in a book I was always physically fit and active. I played tennis, badminton and squash at various times, and cycled a lot. I did none of those things very well, I should hasten to point out, and although I admired the tennis and cycling stars of the time (all men) the chance of emulating any of them was so remote as to not even figure in my daydreams.

My passion for reading is the one lasting influence on my life. I find myself reaching for a book or a journal or an article whenever I'm puzzled or upset or feel ignorant about something. I enjoy study for that reason: I am able to make sense of my world through my reading.

In 1978, two years after the death of my husband, I brought my two young children to Perth to start afresh. I came to Western Australia at a crossroads in my life. I knew few people, but I soon found friendship and support from women I met through the Women's Electoral Lobby (WEL). My involvement in WEL not only brought new friends, it also led me to fulfil my ambition to gain a tertiary qualification and embark on a career change.

In the later 1970s access to information was one of the big gaps for West Australian women. For many years Perth women had lobbied the State Government for a women's information service. They had seen the establishment of one in Adelaide — the Women's Information Switchboard, which provided an ideal model — and they had tried to establish one themselves. Women's Liberation operated a telephone information service on a shoestring out of a room in the old Padbury Buildings (in what is now Forrest Place in the centre of Perth), and the WEL phone number was accessed by hundreds of women seeking information on a wide range of topics.

Another source of information was the Commonwealth Bank, but this was mainly for banking information. Women who couldn't access other information became allies of those lobbying for the establishment of a specialized women's information service. By the early 1980s lobbyists included a broad cross-section of individual women, women from both major political parties, and women's groups including WEL, the Young Women's Christian Association, and the National Council of Women. It was these women who later formed the nucleus of the Friends of WIRE group which was established by the Women's Information and Referral Exchange (WIRE) as a support group to keep a motherly eye on the service.

However, it wasn't until a Labor Government triumphed in the election of 1983, and a number of women sympathetic to women's issues were elected to parliament, that support for a properly funded information service for women was forthcoming. The introduction of programs for women at that time meant governments needed the expertise and understanding of women's issues that feminists brought to the job. To those of us with a feminist perspective, it seemed that we were about to enter a new era where the value of doing things differently would become evident once we had a few examples.

When WIRE was established in mid-1984 I became coordinator of the service and remained in that capacity until March 1986. I was thrilled to be part of this new service, not least because it gave me an opportunity to give back to women something of what I had received. We had a staff of five information officers, the coordinator and a part-time librarian, on loan from the Alexander Library's information service, Infolink.

In the climate of the time a representative bureaucracy had political currency. The idea that all sections of the community needed to be represented in the public service was given a shot in the arm in the early 1980s with the election of Labor governments around Australia. For West Australian services, and particularly for WIRE, this meant that the operating principles were developed from a feminist analysis of the position of women. Formal public service qualifications were not as essential as the ability to use one's own life experiences as the basis for knowledge and expertise when helping other women.

Management of the service was to be modelled on the 1970s-style collective: jobs would be shared and decision-making would be inclusive and participatory. The title of 'Manager' was replaced by 'Coordinator' which both demonstrated and emphasized the different ways in which this organization would work. This was an exciting time. We were given the chance to build a working environment where some new, different and feminist ideas about leadership could be put into practice.

I came to liken this new approach to that of the conductor of an orchestra made up of expert players in their own right, rather than a general in charge of the troops. It is a model of 'supported leadership',[1] which means in practice a sharing of the load, especially important in a stressful atmosphere such as existed in WIRE.

Yet although we were feminists, and the service was run on feminist principles, we were nonetheless public servants working in a government-funded service. We were aware that this was an unusual situation, and the difficulties it presented were formidable. But we had high hopes that we would succeed in building a new form of organization. In our heart of hearts we knew this was a formula which would work for women. All we wanted was a chance to prove it. By the same token, we were sensitive to the fact that we would be jumped on if we stepped out of line.

The week before we opened our doors we spent several days in planning and training. On the first day we were asked to depict how we felt about the service. Our ideas were drawn on a large whiteboard; the final drawing showed a boat, filled with information and WIRE staff, sailing off to women on an island across a sea filled with circling sharks.

Contrary to our hopes and expectations this different way of working did not fit easily within a bureaucratic structure. Some of our early wishes had to go. For example, it quickly became clear that the ideal of everybody sharing all tasks was not feasible in such a busy and stressful setting. After lobbying the department repeatedly for some time, we were eventually provided with some much-needed clerical assistance.

We also had to contend with those within the bureaucracy who had a great deal of difficulty coming to terms with our flatter structure. There were some who never did. They were the sort of people who simply had to speak to 'the person in charge' because, for them, there would always be someone 'in charge'. Despite this, little distinction was made between the various roles we played in the day-to-day running of the service. As Coordinator I was ultimately responsible to the Director, Office of Women's Interests, but decisions on a day-to-day basis were made collectively.

Women responded well to a service staffed by women to whom they could relate because of shared experiences. The friendly, unbureaucratic atmosphere inspired confidence that their concerns would be taken seriously and many found it difficult to believe the service belonged to government.

For many years WIRE provided a much needed space and service for women. However, its community-inspired focus was seen as increasingly suspect. WIRE always had its detractors, but these became particularly vocal during the economic climate of the 1990s in which 'economic rationalism' gained ascendancy. I had moved on from the position of coordinator by that time. As a member of the Friends of WIRE, however, I felt the subsequent changes at a deep and personal level.

Internal reports and reviews, carried out in 1991–92, suggested 'streamlining' was necessary in order to elicit greater 'efficiency' in dealing with the workload. This 'streamlining' was minimal and cosmetic. It consisted of introducing a reception desk, partitioning off some staff, and generally introducing a more formal and structured environment. However, the change in ambience from these minimal reshapings had enormous ramifications for the way in which WIRE now worked. From an open, inviting, shared space, there were now discrete, closed-off cubicles, secretive corners in which women spoke in whispers as if they had something to hide. It was no longer a woman's space. Feminist posters were removed from the walls and the Coordinator, now redesignated as 'Manager', was shifted upstairs, away from the day-to-day operation of the service. Women in the community felt that here was a hard-won women's service being reduced to just another government department.

However, the final nail in the coffin for WIRE was the 'Western Women affair'. Western Women was a financial advisory service established by a woman called Robin Greenburg. Later, as her business grew, she moved into investment advice and planning. When she began offering information to women from WIRE it was simply assistance with budgeting and bill paying. At that time WIRE staff were referring women to other agencies for this kind of support but we were keen to offer as many services as possible within WIRE. We were already offering free basic legal advice via volunteer women lawyers who came in for a couple of hours a week. So Robin Greenburg's services were added to the list. At least in the beginning, the advice and assistance she offered was sound. The women we canvassed appreciated being taken seriously and not being made to feel foolish and stupid if they didn't understand financial matters.

In 1993, Robin Greenburg pleaded guilty to fifty-five offences relating to the theft of more than $4 million from her failed Western Women group of companies. Because of her association with WIRE, staff were accused of referring clients to her and of therefore being implicated in their subsequent financial losses. The Labor Government was accused of giving support to Western Women, through WIRE and, by inference, also being implicated in the fraud. Greenburg received a seventeen-year goal sentence for her fraudulent handling of clients' money. Carrie Smith led the campaign for those who suffered financially from Greenburg's mismanagement. Interestingly, Smith later became the Personal Private Secretary to Attorney-General Peter Foss, who led the attack on the Labor Government over the so-called 'Western Women affair'. Greenburg's behaviour was shocking and reprehensible, but no more so than that of many male 'entrepreneurs' of the 1980s who fell from grace. Their sentences, however, were considerably less than Greenburg's — sometimes only months.[2] The question arises: why? Because she is a woman and bad women are more wicked than bad men? Whatever the reason, her criminal activities put the spotlight on WIRE in a very hostile and negative way.

During the Greenburg debacle the press not only exhibited a total lack of understanding of, or sympathy for, the aims and philosophy of WIRE, but also an obvious disregard for the demonstrated effectiveness of the service. During the inquiries and press reports that followed the revelations of Greenburg's fraudulent activities, no attempt was made to evaluate WIRE's worth or even to understand its reason for being. It was enough that the service was run by women for it to be viewed with suspicion and for decision-makers and media to assume that it was run badly.

Any other service which had had such success at meeting the needs of a large segment of the population in such a cost-effective way (WIRE's budget was comparatively small — in 1990–91 it was allocated $339,000: $248,000 for salaries and $91,000 for operational items) would have had powerful supporters and would surely have survived the crisis. Yet WIRE's closure came about despite the fact that it was needed and welcomed by women in the community.

The attacks on WIRE and its staff were damaging to those of us who had been involved in administering it. For me personally they caused agonies of self-doubt and enormous anger at what seemed to be a deliberate misunderstanding of what we had been trying to achieve. The media treatment made us all feel like pariahs, as if the dedication and commitment with which we had established WIRE had been for nothing. Perhaps that was our undoing. We did care, passionately; we were committed and dedicated, but those qualities make bureaucrats feel uncomfortable.

As public servants we were unable to speak out in our own defence. When the attack came, WIRE had few powerful supporters to speak on its behalf. The Friends of WIRE group was unable to assist, largely because the enemies of WIRE were not restricted to one side of the political spectrum. The women WIRE had served, who had the most to lose if the service closed, came mostly from the least powerful, and least organized sectors of the community. But perhaps our decision to deliberately keep the service low-key — partly from necessity as the budget was very small, and partly out of an unspoken fear that if we became too visible to the powerful we would be in danger — contributed to our isolation when trouble came.

This uneasiness about public exposure is, I believe, a (not irrational) fear held by many women. We have seen what can happen to women who become public figures, women who try to 'do it differently' or even try to do it the same as men. They become targets of derision by the media who seem unable to rest until they've publicly destroyed them. There is an eager anticipation associated with the fall of women who fly too high — look at what happened to Carmen Lawrence, Joan Kirner, Ros Kelly, Bronwyn Bishop and even Diana, Princess of Wales — that has much to do with the selling of newspapers, but has even more to do with a deep-seated hatred, in our society, of women.

Whilst Robin Greenburg was the instrument, she was not the architect of WIRE's demise. The fact that WIRE was closed down altogether indicates that the service was neither seen as essential nor desirable. Framed within the rhetoric of the 'level playing field', women's specific needs are seen at best as being transitory, requiring 'special' services for only a short period of time. Permanent programs directed at women are viewed as suspect, as a demonstration of 'special treatment' and evidence of 'positive discrimination'. Embedded in the anger and outrage expressed at the criminal activities of Robin Greenburg, who professed to be a committed feminist, was much antipathy to women and especially to feminists and feminism.

In a male-dominated society it is patriarchal power we experience. For women this is disempowering. Patriarchal leadership relies on a pecking order which has nothing to do with merit and everything to do with status and power over others. It demeans, belittles and disempowers followers; it does not foster independence, willingness to take responsibility, creative thinking, loyalty or respect. A different view of leadership brings a different view of power.

Feminism helped me recognize that it is the collective efforts of a number of people which results in the goal being achieved or the job getting done, or even my getting there in the first place. Very rarely is it due solely to the efforts of one individual even though our society rewards individual effort ahead of anything else.

One of the best things that has happened over the twenty or so years I have been involved in the women's movement has been the increase in the numbers of women in previously male-dominated areas, such as the law or economics, and the establishment of women's groups in these areas. These changes are proof that a critical mass of women can begin to make a difference, even if it is only to initially support an alternative point of view. I feel I have been privileged to have been able to work with supportive women so that at least at the micro-level I have not had to battle prejudice and stereotyping alone.

With the influence of the second wave of feminism from the late 1960s, and in the more 'experimental' climate of the late 1970s and 1980s, women had the opportunity to put into practice their theories about different ways of working in a variety of organizations which were established by and for women.

I think we proved our case, but a depressed economy and the move politically to the right, not just in Australia but in all western nations following the collapse of European communism, has resulted in a perceived triumph for traditional structures and the marginalization of alternative points of view.

Will the pendulum swing back again? I certainly hope so, but I fear not in my working lifetime.

1   Eva Cox, *Leading Women*, Random House, Sydney, 1996, p. 249.
2   Editor's note: On appeal in 1993, Robin Greenburg's sentence was reduced to fourteen years. In late January 1999, she was released. See J. Pratley, 'Western Women Swindler Leaves Prison', *West Australian*, 6 February 1999, p. 3.

Heart Dreaming

A LETTER TO LILLIAN

JOAN WINCH

Born Marie Joan Heath at King Edward Memorial Hospital for Women, Perth in 1935, Joan spent her childhood in Fremantle and schooling at Palmyra Primary School. Her mother was taken from her desert family and brought up on various missions, while her father, who was descended from a Cornish stonemason and an Aboriginal woman of Portuguese extraction, came from the South-West region of Western Australia. At sixteen Joan travelled Australia, working in factories, hotels, farms and hospitals. Returning to Perth four years later she worked as a nursing assistant, where she met the greatest influence of her life, Mother Gabrielle of St Joseph's Hospital. After obtaining a degree in Nursing at the Western Australian Institute of Technology (now Curtin University) in the 1970s, Joan became identified with community nursing and developed the Marr Mooditj Health Education Program. Married with one daughter, Joan is now the Director of the Centre for Aboriginal Studies at Curtin University in Perth.

Dear Lillian,

I've been asked to write about myself as a leader in the Aboriginal health field. I'm writing that story for you, my daughter, because you have always supported and motivated me. It is also for all the young ones coming along.

Having people recognize me as a leader would certainly come as a surprise to your grandfather, Lillian. Dad thought I would never amount to much, other than cleaning floors for a living. He told me so quite often. His badgering had a reverse effect on me though. Out of sheer determination I decided: 'I've got news for you Dad, cleaning floors is not for me'. Admittedly, there were few role models in the Aboriginal community at that time, especially female role models. If the white population gave us jobs at all they expected us to do the drudge work.

I was a swift runner when I was a child. One time when the family attended an annual work picnic, I entered in the open race and won. I raced over to my parents and shouted, 'I won! I won!' The prize was an electroplated nickel silver sugar bowl, the 'ants pants' in those days. Just then I heard that the race was to be rerun. So I lined up again and won by an even larger margin. The sugar basin was mine and remains so five decades later. Nothing before or since could more graphically signify the uphill road that an Aboriginal person has competing in Australian society.

Over the years I have been acknowledged as a role model, as a spokesperson, as someone who works for change. Behind the recognition I have been given, however, lay the deeds of the many invisible people who prepared the path for me, just as I am trying to do for those who follow me.

Of the tributes I have received, it could be expected that the greatest accolade came when I was awarded the Sasakawa World Health Prize in 1987. I spoke to 150 countries at the League of Nations Building on that day. It was awesome. People were seeking my advice on drugs, alcohol abuse, leadership skills for youth, and on the hows and whys of education. This was a very heady time in my life. Some would say the pinnacle. However, John McKay of the West Australia Week Council reminded me that it was my State of Western Australia that first recognized 'a future leader' in me. In 1986 I was named Citizen of the Year. Yet in my eyes the greatest of my achievements has been the recognition I received from my own people.

My heart was bursting with pride when I was named State and National Aboriginal of the Year in 1987. These awards are still among my most prized possessions. My own ilk had come forward to acknowledge me. Receiving the Pioneer Award was another of my greatest thrills. It was presented to me by the local Aboriginal people for paving the way in the health field and for giving our people the opportunities to work in that area. These people were not among the chosen few working in white organizations, but rather were pioneers working in their own community.

I learned to stand alone when I was quite young. My first major crisis came at thirteen when my mother died. This was a sad time for me and quite a shock to the system. I was the only girl with two brothers, one a year older and one a year younger. I was expected to take over the whole running of the house including the shopping, cooking, housework and the washing. My father worked at the gasworks, so his clothes were very dirty and gritty. No such thing as a washing machine in those days. I had to learn in a hurry. Learning on my feet stood me in good stead for later life.

One day, I was busy making the eternal watery stew when an inquisitive kid from down the street said, 'What are ya doing?' 'Just making a stew for tea', was my reply. 'Why don't ya put some flour and water in to make it thick?' 'Why don't you?' I said. Away he went and made a stew just like my mother used to make. I learned a lesson on that day which I never forgot. When someone knows what they are talking about, listen.

Aboriginal people do a lot of listening. Traditionally, we have a system where we spend a lot of time waiting and watching others to see what we must do. This could possibly stem from our being dependent on tracking skills where any noise would disturb the prey. A comprehensive sign language was used prior to contact with white man and remnants of this language are still in use in the metropolitan area. This is in evidence whenever groups of Aboriginal people meet. Our conversation is interlaced with a series of hand movements which have specific meanings. This is one way Aboriginal people can pinpoint whether a fellow Aboriginal has been brought up in white society or in the Aboriginal community and this creates a common link. Having knowledge of this sign language enhances the prospects of role modelling. It puts us onside because it says, 'She talks the same language as me'.

I learned to listen a lot before I learned to speak up, which may be why I have never thought of myself as a leader but just someone trying to improve the lot of some of my people. Others gave me that title. When I was a young child it was not fashionable for children to speak up and put their point across like it is in the 1990s. This also applied to me. Your grandfather, my dad, was a forceful disciplinarian, Lillian. His father came from Cornwall and his mother was Aboriginal and Portuguese (a result of the sealers' presence in the Albany area). Coming from this background, I had to deliberate for some time before I brought any of my ideas up to the surface. On most occasions I would be wiped aside without so much as an acknowledgement. This treatment of trial by fire, whether by good management or chance, did a lot to keep me together when the going got tough in the outside world.

In many ways I have been pushed into speaking up for others, firing bullets made in the back ranks. As a trainee nurse I found I was speaking up about unfair treatment of my fellow workers; I lost a lot of jobs over that. One time when I was eighteen, the whole of the Goodna Mental Hospital went out on a rolling strike because I was being treated unfairly on the wards. I didn't know then that Aborigines were not allowed to take strike action, especially in Queensland in the 1950s.

Self-discipline, like determination, is one of the mainstays of life. As a hospital worker I was expected to face up bright and enthusiastic every day, no matter what happened 'out of hours'. If I was less than enthusiastic after a very hectic party, I was soon convinced otherwise by the dour matron on the ward rounds where I worked as an aide. The discipline practised in hospitals inspired the adage 'shape up or ship out'.

To be a leader there must be followers; there must be a certain amount of charisma to attract others to your ideas. I did not set out to be put up front, but it seemed I fitted the bill for the unpopular jobs. I stepped into the role of union representative at a Catholic hospital, a job nobody wanted because it meant fronting up to the mother superior with complaints from the staff. This was another signpost in my life, Lillian.

The same mother superior taught me one of the most effective rules of leadership: 'Don't ask anyone to do something you are not prepared to do yourself'. One of the greatest tests I had of this advice was a stop-work meeting at Fremantle. I was the only one who fronted up and asked for time out for union business;

no other staff member joined me. I was told that if I was the union representative then it was my job to attend the meeting regardless of who else attended. I was standing alone. I left the building a one-man band. It is one thing to be firm and resolute, it's a lot harder when you are standing alone.

Although it was not clear to me at the time, all these lessons of self-reliance, believing in myself and my convictions, listening to others, determination and self-discipline, prepared me for the next difficult turning point in my life.

I was thirty and very keen to have another child, a playmate for you Lillian. Unfortunately I had a miscarriage and ended up in hospital. Though this was a sad time, it was also most fortunate for me. A pap smear revealed that I had changing cell patterns on my cervix. As this could lead to cancer further down the track, I eventually had to have an operation. This life-threatening event made me change my direction and focus on others instead of myself. I had always felt close to my dead mother and found myself turning to her then to discuss my deepest thoughts, hopes and fears. I asked, 'As I have been shown this and it has saved my life, I must be here for a reason. Now show me what it is and what direction I must take'. It took a few more years before I realized that I would not have been able to accomplish what I did if I had had another child.

Although I was always interested in education it seemed impossible until 1972 when Aboriginal study grants were introduced into the education system. Lillian, you showed me the way into the field of education. I was not conversant with the system and you encouraged me to enrol for the university entrance course. It was very difficult for me at first. My life consisted of working during the day and learning at night school, with the housework fitted into the time remaining. Luckily, I had you to help me.

The new nursing program at the Western Australian Institute of Technology (WAIT) was just what I wanted. I had always been interested in nursing and had worked in the field as a nursing assistant. When I was a child during the war years there had been a strong focus on the Red Cross and how we could help in the war effort. The thing which grabbed my fancy most was the hit song 'Nursie Come Over Here and Hold My Hand'. I put a tea towel on my head and became that nurse who held the hand of those in need. So these tertiary studies fulfilled another point of my self-actualization. Feeling good about what you do, being able to keep your goals in sight and identifying your special ability helps set down a solid foundation. These are important survival skills to develop because there will be plenty of deviations from the set target and readjustments will have to be made to get back on line. I learned this while attempting to complete my formal education.

Studying did not come easy to me. I had injured my back lifting when I was twenty-one and spent many years chasing a cure or relief from chronic pain. After five years, I finished my training of general nursing, midwifery and child health. Battling the pain of sitting for many hours studying, my back took a turn for the worse. I was in tears. I had put in my best effort and, just when I was poised to be effective, I feared that I would not be able to fulfil my life's work. I was very depressed. Was this my fault because I read it wrong? Or was it that fate was handing me a bitter pill?

Talking to my lifelong friend, Loueeze, I said, 'I have spent all this time studying for nothing. Here I am and my back is too painful for me to carry out the work I felt I was called to do'. The next day was Saturday, I was lying on the bed and felt I was touched on the back by something superhuman. I had instant relief. It was like nothing I had ever experienced in my life before. I felt an inner strength. At that same time you told me you had an overwhelming urge to see me, Lillian. When I told you about the experience you said, 'Well?' I said, 'Well what?' You said, 'Can you walk?' I got up. No pain. That was in 1978 and it has been a permanent cure ever since.

I joined the Perth Aboriginal Medical Service in 1980, but felt like I was caught up in a time warp. Back when I was a child, while I was still dreaming about being a nurse, I remember your grandmother had trouble coping with the health problems of us kids. School sores, scabies and head lice were things she did not learn about on the mission where she was brought up. We combed our hair with kerosene and a fine-toothed comb; zinc cream was the panacea for everything else. Thirty-five years down the track some of our people still did not know simple rules of good health, nor what measures could be taken to help prevent school sores, scabies and dehydration in infants.

As the first Aboriginal nurse at the centre, I soon found that in a lot of ways my role changed from being a second-class citizen to being a second-class nurse. When I approached the doctor with my ideas of training Aboriginal health workers and explained how they would fit into the system, I was met with a derisive: 'Who's going to train and supervise them — you?'

At that time the State Health Department had been trying to set up a program for health workers that would make them understudies for nursing aides. These health workers would be advocates for our people. Nobody had a vision for a totally new branch of Aboriginal decision-makers in the health field. I felt deflated and alone. However, I worked night after night on a program which would give our people their first contact with issues of health and wellbeing. Eventually a new doctor at the Perth Aboriginal Service, Dr David Paul, and the secretary, Pat Haynes, joined me in my vision for the future.

At this time I was probably the most highly trained Aboriginal person in the medical field in Perth. Yet when I applied for the vacant position of Director of the Aboriginal Medical Service I was 'out run' by a footballer and 'bowled out' by a cricketer, neither of whom had a background in health. A series of directors followed, and all were Aboriginal males without qualifications.

Obviously these administrators did not have faith in me as a leader. Later, when teaching in the classroom, I found that the women often had a lot more knowledge than the men, but the men were always delegated as spokespersons. Why couldn't the women speak up as equals in the classroom? The Aboriginal women were certainly lacking role models in leadership. Women were placed as followers of men. Over the last decade or so this has gradually changed as our people graduate from higher education and take up their rightful places in society. Now, of course, we are very proud to have our own Dr Eades at the Aboriginal Medical Service. Luckily, my disciplined childhood stood me in good stead against all the knock-backs and disappointments I faced trying to improve the health and wellbeing of our people.

Growing up in this country stunts a lot of growth. If an Aboriginal person succeeds, he or she is told that they are different from the others. I experienced this type of discrimination from a doctor who was working for the Health Department. He looked behind me one day and asked where my snotty-nosed kids were. I treated him with the disdain he deserved. I set out to enhance people, make them feel good about themselves. To be an Aboriginal is generally a negative experience and until we can identify and understand this situation we are unable to change it for the better. I was in conflict with many lecturers who let students through the net saying, 'They are Aboriginals', implying it was acceptable to have second-rate results because they were Aboriginals.

Don't set yourself apart and make things look too hard, Lillian. There will be plenty of times when the going seems tough and problems appear insurmountable. For any one achievement, there are a hundred knockers. Don't run with the knockers. There is a little voice inside the head that feeds us all the negatives that are voiced from outside. 'You can't do it', 'It won't work', 'You'll never get the money', and so on. This conversation within has to be counteracted with a positive approach, so have plans B, C and D ready to hand.

I have learned to listen to my spiritual guides or conscience when planning for the future. When a project has a series of blocks to success, I leave it until things settle down and then probably take a new approach. I had some excellent advice when I was a student which was, 'Always speak the truth because if you ever reach the top, as well you may, someone will remember that lie'.

Why persist when the system is biased against women at the top and Aborigines in the work force? I often asked myself this question. I also wondered about how a young person in today's world can achieve excellence of performance. A successful person, I believe, is one who makes their job their life's work. This is also a good preventative for ulcers and burnout and a counterbalance for the million frustrations we find when trying to fulfil a dream for our people. But there are also words of appreciation such as those from an audience member who once wrote to me saying: 'You gave me hope and confidence in myself after I heard you give a public speech on leadership'.

Times have changed since the 1970s. A clear statement for the twenty-first century is being made by Aboriginal women who are showing the way in tertiary education. They will be a powerful force to draw upon in the future. The road is now open for young women (like yourself Lillian), who have full knowledge of the political scene and managerial skills, to go forward and take their rightful place in our society.

I don't believe most people set out to be leaders. Others put them in that role. As for me, I feel the awards bestowed upon me reflect the work done by other Aboriginal women. My actions simply made the way possible for others to achieve their dreams, and hopefully to continue to work for change.

PUBLIC BISNIS, PRIVATE BISNIS

BARBARA BUICK

Born in Adelaide in 1924 Barbara attended Rose Park Primary School and Girton Girls' School (now Pembroke). Her work as researcher and advocate for children's literature took her to Brisbane, Canberra, Chicago, Port Moresby and London. While in Papua New Guinea Barbara worked on her book *Squatter Settlements in Developing Countries*. This research sparked a lifelong interest in issues concerning indigenous peoples. In 1973 Barbara moved to Perth, where she became involved in the push for the introduction of anti-discrimination legislation. Later she served on the Equal Opportunity Tribunal from 1985 until her retirement in 1995. People who have most influenced Barbara's life are her mother, Madge Laughton, her husband George, work colleagues in libraries and universities, and her many friends in the Women's Electoral Lobby. Barbara is currently on the board of Fremantle Arts Centre Press.

There are many thousands of women like me who have worked through voluntary and/or professional organizations for most of their lives. Sometimes this leads to positions of responsibility, occasionally to a more prominent role. More often than not our names are unknown. Mostly the work is unpaid, although some of the skills we use derive from our work in a wide range of professional or semi-professional occupations. For us, agitation for improving the world around us is, in the vernacular of my friends in Papua New Guinea, more like 'private bisnis'.

Rather than personal prominence, we prefer the give and take of ideas. Group effort is used to devise strategies and to achieve results, with the group rather than individuals receiving recognition. Is this more of a female characteristic than male? My experience is that women on the whole don't think of their community work as an avenue of self-advancement. Certainly it has been so with women of my generation even though blockages to advancement were endemic, ingenious sometimes, but systematic: men had *droit de seigneur*.

Working in the library world, for example, I constantly saw able and highly qualified women passed over for promotion throughout the country as lesser men reached positions beyond their competencies with consequent waste of public money. In Australia it took until the 1980s and the passage of anti-discrimination legislation before this was slowly rectified. Despite the bias against women, library work and the world of books and publishing has been my inspiration and delight.

Growing up in Adelaide during the Depression of the 1930s affected me greatly. Although my family did not suffer much in a material way, we were touched by the desperation and despair around us. Perhaps because of this I was a diffident child. The person I adored and respected most was my mother. She was gentle and charming, warm and loving, married to a much older man with Victorian attitudes. My father made it difficult for her to lead a life outside marriage, but she nonetheless helped establish the mother and baby clinics in South Australia.

In her widowhood my mother blossomed, intellectually and politically. She joined the League of Women Voters and the Peace Movement, and read widely. Mother particularly enjoyed my 'subversive' books like Bertrand Russell's *Marriage and Morals*, and Winifred Holtby's *Women: A History and Evaluation of the Suffrage Movement in Britain*. She had a profound effect on shaping my personal philosophy and my future activities.

Libraries and Literature
In 1942, when I was seventeen, my mother used her network to gain me a position in the State Library of South Australia. I studied at night for library qualifications, specializing in school libraries and children's literature. This specialization was to be the centre of my life's work for thirty-five years. For the first time in

my life I revelled in work, made friendships with bright colleagues, read omnivorously, discovered art and music, and became passionately imbued with the social role of public libraries in a democratic community.

I was an active member of the Children's Book Council during those years, but the Library Association of Australia (LAA) became my chief interest through my capacity as Federal President of the School and Children's Library Section. While in Adelaide I wrote papers criticizing the dismal state of school libraries and the lack of children's books in public libraries. With others from the Children's Book Council I campaigned for a Bill supporting public libraries. When the autocratic Premier Playford banned librarians from the parliamentary public gallery, we fed information to sympathetic politicians like Don Dunstan. I spent a year in Britain working as a children's librarian and returned to work in Queensland.

The Private Nature of Voluntary Work
After my marriage in 1954 I moved back to Adelaide. My domestic life in the 1950s and 1960s was typical of married women of that time. Because of the notorious marriage bar, and with work as a librarian available only in the Public Service, I was excluded from paid employment. We had two children, Roger and Janet, who have always been at the centre of our lives.

With a move to Canberra in 1964 (where my husband worked at the Australian National University (ANU)), I became Children's Book Editor for Cheshires, and organized and wrote children's book reviews for the *Australian* newspaper. I could kick myself now, but I did this work for nothing, except for payment for book reviews. The cause of improving the quality, knowledge and reading of good children's books was the spur, but I was exploited. Yet I was not alone; I was surrounded by academics and librarians who did similar work without remuneration.

As a member of the LAA project designed to gain proper funding for Australian school libraries, I co-authored a series of articles on school libraries for the *Australian Book Review*. With school laboratories already receiving public funding, we decided the time was ripe for lobbying the Federal Government.

I approached the most informed senior officer in the Department of Education, J. McCusker. Happily for us, he turned out to be a supporter. The strategies we adopted and the report I wrote, plus careful lobbying, spurred John Gorton, then Minister of Education, and later Malcolm Fraser after Gorton became Prime Minister, to introduce a Bill to fund secondary school libraries. Thirty-five million dollars was allocated; a significant sum at the time.

This experience taught me that when the goal is to change government policy it is essential to be informed not only in the ways of parliaments, but also about the personalities involved, party political moves, prejudices and likely enthusiasms. I learnt to aim for what was achievable, and not to expect that you would gain everything you know is needed. It helped greatly to obtain the active support of well-regarded backbenchers seeking preferment, as well as the support of respected professional and community groups, and to have research evidence to support the case. Above all, we learnt to be aware of the permutations and sensitivity of Federal–State relations as each would try to take credit for any reform.

Living in Canberra was an education in itself. Contact with politicians was relatively accessible and news of political permutations was easily obtained. Our sources of information were also more 'private' than public. I chuckle now when I think of them: babysitting groups, weekly meetings at the tip, comradely dinner parties, and enthusiasts we met in the Bird Watching Society. We discovered who was the right person to approach, what were the personal attitudes and philosophy of a certain minister, and who was his most effective adviser. Our lobbying also showed what women's organizations later realized: to be influential and effective, it is necessary to have Canberra-based representatives.[1]

Bisnis in Papua New Guinea

In middle age I had a life-changing and mind-expanding experience. For six years from 1966 we lived in pre-Independence Papua New Guinea (PNG), where George was Foundation University Librarian at the University of Papua New Guinea. Our children attended multiracial schools, and I joined the New Guinea Research Unit of ANU.

My first project was as a research assistant on small business possibilities for indigenous people in villages and towns. Later I became the librarian which meant working with the international anthropologists, sociologists, economists, nutritionists and political scientists who came, usually for a year, to try to help solve political, social, land tenure, housing and other problems through their research and advice.

My second love was compiling a book on squatter settlements in developing countries, an endemic crisis in PNG. The Dick Whittington syndrome had caused thousands of tribesmen to leave their subsistence life. Followed by their families, they flocked to the bloated and unprepared towns seeking employment and prosperity. Instead, they usually found frustration and uncertainty. As ANU's representative on the Council of Social Services, which highlighted indigenous problems in health, housing, tribal and cultural differences, I wrote a report on 'Post Mortems and Human Rights', then a subject of controversy due to cultural misunderstanding in expatriate-run hospitals.

George and I were members of the multiracial Papua and New Guinea Society, where for the first time issues of social and political importance were publicly discussed and dissected. I became editor of the society's journal, and developed close friendships with PNG women and students. These friendships were helped by my membership of the Contact Club, established to bring expatriate and PNG women together.

In PNG the Young Women's Christian Association (YWCA) was a lively place where I gave simple talks and practical sessions to village and Port Moresby girls for whom there were no places in secondary schools. The object was to help skill them in the tools of living in a big town, such as how to understand a telephone book and ring up on a public phone, and how to find and borrow books from a public or school library. With embarrassment and bitterness on my part I shared the humiliation of young women when their legitimate applications to join the public library in Port Moresby were refused by the unqualified ex-planters wife who 'ran' the library. Some young women lived in squatter settlements or on lakatoi boats at Koki Market and were accused of 'not having an address' — a crime of omission which did not extend to foreigners living on yachts or in transit. There were no postal deliveries in Port Moresby. The only way to get mail was to pay for a post office box. This was far too expensive for locals who earned a fraction of expatriate wages, even when doing the same job.

Missions then and now provide education, health, work and other services.[2] The country was divided up between various denominations, usually drawn with a line on a map and sometimes with tension-building results. For example, a village in the Central District was divided arbitrarily with Catholics on one side of the central road and Methodists on the other. Most of the missions were mainstream denominations, but increasingly well-funded Christian Fundamentalists have now become the largest growing group. Their patriarchal beliefs and practices do not auger well for the long overdue rise in the status of women.

In the early 1970s there were 700 women's clubs across the country, then organized by local government, the National Council of Women, or missions. Women learned how to sew and make clothes, and to cook food from the trade stores. They also discussed nutrition and village affairs. It was women who supplied most of the food, cultivated the gardens, grew and collected the basic staple foods such as taro, yams or sago, and carried those home with other vegetables as well as wood for cooking and water. They also looked after the pigs and poultry. Men's work included clearing land, building houses, hunting, fishing and managing reciprocal exchanges, as well as rituals and village affairs. This gender division of labour could lead to awkward situations, such as when the didiman or agricultural adviser came to demonstrate how to make chooks, pigs and crops grow better. In some villages men would refuse to allow women to listen; they would attend the talks themselves and would not pass on the information to the women who did the work.[3]

Like their sisters in other countries, women in PNG have learned the political process the hard way. For instance, in l988 a group of top women public servants prepared a National Plan for

Women for Cabinet. Over a period of two years it was rejected and rewritten several times before it was finally endorsed. One of the women remarked, 'We got what we wanted. Things Cabinet threw out, we changed the words and inserted them somewhere else'.[4] Sounds familiar?

Public Bisnis in Perth

In l973 we became West Australians when George took the job of Foundation Librarian at Murdoch University. In the mid-l970s I joined the most obvious organization that fulfilled my belief in social reform and the advancement of women in society. This was the Women's Electoral Lobby (WEL) which works cooperatively in a non-hierarchical mode, outside party politics, but keeping ears to the ground.

The cause that fired me most was the need for legislation to promote fair treatment for women, at work and in institutions. This had always been one of WEL's major goals, since its inception in l972. When I became Co-Convenor in 1980, we started a new campaign to persuade two successive West Australian Liberal premiers to follow their peers in other States and appoint a Women's Adviser to assist in framing anti-discrimination legislation. In spite of support within all parties, and the vigorous help of a range of women's organizations, the conservative premiers would not be persuaded.

In the lead up to the l983 election, women both within the Labor Party and outside it lobbied extensively. WEL held successful public meetings, canvassed marginal seats, talked to women's groups, and generally blitzed the media with information, press releases and interviews. After the election the Liberal leader, Bill Hassell, admitted it was the women's vote that lost him the election.

The day after Labor's win, we urged the new premier to become the Minister of Women's Interests, thereby giving the power and prestige of his position to achieve change quickly. Deborah McCulloch (who had been Don Dunstan's adviser in South Australia) was appointed Women's Adviser for a year. She was followed by lawyer Liza Newby who helped frame the *Equal Opportunity Act 1984*. A committee was set up on which I served with other WEL women, as well as with women from other organizations, such as Business and Professional Women, Country Women's Association (CWA) and the YWCA. Our aim was to lobby members of the Legislative Council where, because of a gerrymander, Labor has never had a majority. In the event, the Equal Opportunity Bill gained support across the political spectrum, with several Liberal and National Party women putting pressure on members from their side of the House.

Long-standing WEL member Yvonne Henderson, although not then a minister, introduced the Bill in the Lower House. The balconies thronged with clapping and cheering women, and for once we were not reprimanded by the Speaker. The writing was on the wall, and the coalition parties supported the Bill with some amendments. In spite of some ludicrous speeches from opponents, it passed through the Legislative Assembly and the Upper House in 1984.

After the Act was proclaimed the Equal Opportunity Commission was established, with June Williams (formerly of the Anti-Discrimination Board in New South Wales) as Commissioner. I was approached to join the Equal Opportunity Tribunal and was appointed as one of the two full members because of my experience in women's affairs and race relations. The first President, Justice Henry Wallwork, was followed by Nicholas Hasluck, QC. Barrister Kate O'Brien and Len Roberts Smith, QC were both appointed Deputy President. Three of us heard each case. A number of supporting members were appointed to make up the panel of three, if Professor Patricia Harris or I were not available. All tribunal members have expertise in at least one area of discrimination covered by the Act. These include disability, age, marital status, family responsibility, sex, pregnancy, religious or political conviction, race, or sexual harassment in employment, education and accommodation.

During my nine years on the tribunal I sat on many different cases. Initially most of the complainants were men. This changed after two years, once women gained the support and confidence to face not only the legal system but also the hostility that complaints often brought out in their colleagues.

The Act has its 'private' and its 'public' forms of dispute resolution. All legitimate complaints are conciliated initially and about 95 per cent resolved by mutual agreement. Only those where this process is unsuccessful come up for public hearing before the tribunal.

Every judgement profoundly affects the lives of participants, so members of the tribunal carry a heavy burden of responsibility. Cases of sexual harassment are always traumatic for participants. It takes a great deal of courage to bring any act of discrimination to public attention. Both complainants and respondents are deeply affected by the decision of the tribunal which has the powers of a royal commission. The tribunal attempts to promote a non-adversarial atmosphere. Sanctions imposed include the payment of damages or restitution of lost wages, and rulings to change employment policies and practices.

The work was intensely interesting. It stretched my mind, analytical powers and understanding of human nature and social structures. Discrimination against women teachers was a continuing problem. There were several cases against the Department of Education over unfair access by women teachers to promotion, the continuing problems for relief teachers through in-built barriers to permanent employment, and compulsory rural service.

I believe the equal opportunity legislation has improved the lives of many West Australians who erroneously believe they are untouched by it. It has made many workplaces more fair, more civil, and will eventually help to bring more understanding of the difficulties of those affected adversely by the stain of racial prejudice. There are still areas of reform necessary. The Act needs a provision to cover discrimination because of sexual preference. Many believe racial vilification should be covered also.

I am wary about awarding costs against unsuccessful complainants, unless it is clearly proved that the complaint was malicious. I have not sat on any case where a complaint could be so categorized. Should a pattern of awarding costs to the opposite party emerge, this could drastically affect a number of legitimate complaints being lodged. Large companies and governments — both State and local — often employ Queen's Counsel supported by lawyers. Complainants can rarely afford such powerful legal advocates.

In retrospect, I notice that the socialization of boys has not changed much over the years. Prejudice against women is still apparent, as is contempt for intellectual effort. Sporting prowess is valued above education, and racial intolerance is becoming more obvious on the right of the political spectrum, even though more Australians are taking up an anti-racist stance. As a librarian I observed how boys avoided books written by women, even when the subject involved both boys and girls. Recent surveys show these views are still held by boys, often more strongly in single-sex schools.

But I remain hopeful. My son and his male friends on the whole are different people in outlook and practice than was my brother, and he was unlike his father. I was unusually lucky in marrying the right man. Our temperaments were different, but we both compromised. Our world view was similar, although our personal enthusiasms were not always the same. We shared a love of books and an interest in libraries, and many other activities; we were both driven by curiosity.

About the future, I am a restrained optimist. As long as younger people have the time and energy to put effort into reform, and are not too stressed, anxious or alienated by increased competition and insecurity, I believe that with collaborative community effort, improvements will occur. My experience has been that a fertile blending of minds, opinions and energies brings better-devised policy and actions. Among the wonderful women I work with, lobby with and relate to, that cooperative approach remains happily constant.

---

1 Don Smart, *Federal Aid to Australian Schools*, University of Queensland Press, Brisbane, 1978, pp. 81–96.
2 Charles Rowley, *The New Guinea Villager*, Cheshire, Melbourne, 1965, pp. 35, 42, 43.
3 ibid., p. 40
4 Rachel Cleland, *Grassroots to Independence and Beyond: The Contribution by Women in Papua New Guinea*, Dame Rachel Cleland, Claremont, 1996, pp. 279–395.

FREEDOM AND LOSS: AN IRANIAN STORY

MALI VALAMANESH

Mali was born in Iran in 1953 and came to Australia in 1985. She gained a degree in Sociology from the University of Shiraz and an MA in Management from the University of Manchester, England. In Australia she studied Social Work at Monash University and is currently employed as a counsellor in the health sector. Mali has been particularly active within the Iranian community, with projects such as ethnic radio and the establishment of a cultural centre in Perth, as well as the foundation and coordination of the Women's Health Centre in Gosnells. Mali has lived in Perth with her husband and daughter since 1990 where she continues to work for change in women's lives.

I was born in a small village called Bardsir in the central Iranian province of Kerman, where my father was posted as the Governor. Though he had escaped possible death and loss of livelihood in the aftermath of the Azarbaijan uprisings of the 1940s, the political repercussions for his actions meant that he had to serve in the most remote areas of Iran, mainly the Central and Eastern States.

From Bardsir we moved to a remote arid town in Baluchistan, Khash. Here we had hot sunny days all year round. The tiny stream at the back of the garden kept my three brothers and me busy all through the summer. I remember how overjoyed we all were when the air finally turned cool and suddenly we felt tender raindrops fall from the sky. The most amazing event to take place during our time in Khash occurred in our front garden. A well was sunk. The sight of huge machinery drilling into the hard, dry earth day after day caused great excitement in the town, as did the sight of all the water that covered our garden. The increased water supply would not only serve our household but the rest of the neighbourhood as well. This action sent a very powerful message to me. It made me believe that change was possible.

The happiest adult I can remember in my early years was Shahbibi, my favourite Baluchi woman. She was intelligent, beautiful, cheeky, happy and a free soul, with big dark eyes and blue stones in her shiny hair. Her laughter was a wonderful gift to a child whose own mother was filled with sadness and loss. We loved to be around Shahbibi whenever she managed to escape my grandmother's teachings of cleanliness and housework.

My father was an influential man in these communities. I clearly remember a case that came before him in those early years. A man had beaten up his wife and the family was referred to Dad for judgement. I remember him being very angry with the man. 'How dare you touch a woman like that?' he demanded.

My father was a key support for me. He encouraged my independence in thought and deed, clearly ignoring many of the traditional and religious customs of the day. Ironically, I was the one to severely challenge him for the erratic and impatient behaviour he sometimes demonstrated toward my mother.

We moved to Teheran in 1961. We considered it to be 'the centre of the world'. Life for my mother became more difficult. Although we were relatively well off and enjoyed a reasonable lifestyle, Mum had to manage four young children in a very different and new social environment without the support of my father who had to return to his rural post. I was gradually becoming conscious of the hardships in my mother's life. I remember swearing to God and telling her that I would not lead my life like hers and other women. I did not want to live my life in the kitchen.

My mother was a religious woman, who preferred to bring me up in her own way. In response to her concern about appropriate behaviour for a woman, I would think 'I don't mind if my bare legs burn in hell's fire, so long as I can show them off in my short skirts in this world'. I didn't want to learn how to cook sholeh zard (yellow rice) in the grieving month of Moharram and sit down quietly under my chador while the mullah was lecturing us on the tragedies of an imam's death, clearly enticing the women to cry for him.

Girls my own age seemed to mature much sooner than me. They all came from deeply religious families and by the end of primary school they were beginning to think of marriage. This was the most common and safest practice for the majority of young girls and they seemed willing to swap their individual freedom for the jewellery, wedding dress and dowry associated with marriage. I have to admit I also shared a few joyous moments with the other girls whispering about young boys, but I was not eager to give up a chance at further education and the opportunities associated with that. For me 'womanhood' was like a damp, dark and scary basement where you would hang your underwear to dry. Away from sight, not even the sun could have a glimpse of it. I still sense the damp smell of that basement where I hung my underwear.

In the poorest part of our neighbourhood in Teheran, in an area known as Kuche Khordad, lived a high school friend of mine, Manijeh. After I left Teheran to begin university in Shiraz, I wrote to Manijeh sharing my excitement over university studies and the recent news of my engagement. I received a letter back which I read in despair. Manijeh wrote that she didn't deserve my friendship as she was no longer a 'pure' and untouched woman. Her life had totally changed and she was now dependent on the money she received from prostitution. I was reminded of my childhood image of a successful journey through life: a girl is climbing a high, straight wall while anxiously gathering her skirt with her hands so that nobody can peek underneath her dress. This was a very real image for me. I wished I had shared it with Manijeh, so she too could have held on tight to her skirt.

Now I understand more fully why I felt threatened and fearful of my own sexuality. On the one hand at such a young age I was expected to be sexually mature, while on the other I knew my safety and success as a woman greatly depended on my sexuality being unexplored and untouched. One woman in particular made me feel I was not alone and affirmed my feelings. Forough Farrokh-Zad was the first Iranian woman poet to write poetry from a woman's perspective. My brother bought me her book of poems. It opened a window of light into the otherwise curious and dark room of my womanhood. In her most famous poem, 'Wind-up Doll', she wrote:

> One can with bent head
> Kneel for a lifetime before a cold shrine ...
>
> One can hide with shame the beauty of a moment
> At the bottom of a chest
> Like a funny black-and-white snapshot.[1]

Living and Breathing the Fear

I felt that going to university would give me the knowledge I needed to understand and change Iranian society and my position in it as a woman. I associate my first sense of dictatorship with a young dark boy my brother knew. He would often come to our door to leave messages and illegal pamphlets. Later this boy was taken away by the SAVAK.[2] This was frightening but also strongly motivating. It made me want to know more and aspire for change. For me, change also meant rejecting many of the values that were embedded in Iranian culture, religion, music and customs, particularly those relating to women's position in society. This rejection was as strongly felt as the rejection I experienced as a woman.

My independent life at university proved to be short lived. I had only just begun to explore life, and was starting to get to know my future husband when the whole family turned up in Shiraz. Before long I was back home fending off unwanted inquiries about marriage plans. It wasn't that I didn't feel deeply for my husband-to-be, nor that I felt marriage would impose impossible constraints on me. It was more that I was reluctant to go directly from the care of my parents into the care of my husband. I wanted to be able to care for myself first and know myself as an independent woman. Eventually I conceded and committed myself to a long-term relationship.

Much of our early married life was spent in separation. My husband moved to another university to complete his degree, then to Manchester to commence a postgraduate degree. As I still had nine months remaining of my degree, I stayed behind. During this time the increasing tension between agitating students and the Shah's regime made life at university an ordeal.

I now had to be extremely careful about how I framed my written assignments, which we knew were being scrutinized by the security forces. Our lives became very tenuous indeed. One day while undergoing an exam, police pulled two students out of the examination room; one of the men was a close friend of mine. Later when I met up with him again, he cautiously showed me the marks of torture on his body. Fear became a tangible part of our lives. It sank into our bones and became a part of our every action. Despite this we could sense the time for social change was coming.

The Fight for Freedom

As soon as I was able, I left for Manchester. I was looking forward to my own postgraduate studies there and the experience of living in England, the 'cradle of civilization' as it was known in Iran. I was looking forward to breathing in the fresh air of democracy, but mostly I was looking forward to being alone with my husband.

Through our involvement with the Confederation of Iranian Students we got to know many people interested in meeting to read and examine strategies of past revolutions. This was something I could connect with and it gave me a sense of purpose. Back in Iran political agitation was escalating. We wanted to be able to participate in the push for social change and being in England meant that we were in a position to bring the struggles in Iran to world attention. We held demonstrations, actively publicizing the Iranian cause. We also formed a singing group that travelled all over England and produced a tape which was widely distributed back in Iran. A lot of these actions were also used to raise funds for the cause. It wasn't until I was actively involved in the fight for democratic rights in Iran that my ingrained fear gradually began to dissipate.

Of course there was talk about women's rights. There was a women's movement in Iran, but we had been told time and again that our fight was tied to the bigger fight for democracy.

Once that was achieved all else would automatically follow in its path. In this respect the lessons of history were ignored. We really felt that this time it would be different. Iran was a different place for women. Despite the constraints I felt about being a woman in Iran, the woman's position in England presented no real alternative. In many ways women were more respected in Iran than in England, the supposed seat of democracy.

I looked to the revolution to bring in radical change. I remember how I felt in 1979 when I saw pictures of women on top of tanks heading into the city to crush the last of the Shah's regime. These were confident, courageous women who played an equal role in the success of the revolution. They were the visible symbol of the many other active women who also strove to secure a democratic way of life. For International Women's Day that year thousands upon thousands of women from all walks of life, some veiled, others not, gathered to walk through the streets of Teheran. They gathered to send a message to those taking up the reins of political power that the time had finally come for women to reap the rewards of their commitment and their courage.

As we were able to move freely in and out of Iran we never viewed our time in England as living in exile. If anything our involvement with the Iranian people's push for democracy deepened our bond with home. So despite the reports about the rapid erosion of democratic principles under the new regime, we felt that our country now needed our expertise and so we returned. We hoped that the emerging difficulties would dissolve once things settled down. However, the revolutionary moment known in Iranian history as 'the spring of freedom' proved to be transitory and the grim reality of the situation hit us as soon as we arrived home.

Although I had no personal affiliation with the religious practice of wearing the veil, I decided to cover my head with a scarf for the journey home. This was meant to be an expression of solidarity with the many active women in the revolution who complied with this practice. The bitter irony of this gesture became apparent as soon as I entered the airport terminal. I was greeted by official signs which proclaimed that women not wearing the veil were considered enemies of the revolution. My symbolic gesture of solidarity could only be understood in an Iran free of all forms of political and religious persecution. Instead it symbolized a future of more fervent repression, especially for women.

With each new day in Teheran our hopes faded for an Iran that belonged to its people. I volunteered my services as a teacher, but was rejected after an investigation of my past history revealed that I was not sufficiently 'righteous' for this politically sensitive occupation. In the meantime my husband got employment which took him to the Iran–Iraq border. Four weeks later war erupted.

It may seem strange that in such violent and uncertain times I decided to have a child. In this desolate place, which eroded the senses and left me virtually no space to realize myself, I needed something which would give me hope. Even before our daughter was born, I knew that we must leave Iran. But giving birth to a girl set my conviction. Her life as a growing woman would be different from mine, of that I was determined. Golnar was to be my oasis. From her sprung both my motivation and my hope that things would change.

The Price of Freedom
Australia was to be our new home. It took nearly two years of waiting and planning before we were able to secure passports and visas. The day we left Iran we were full of trepidation. Only after we changed planes in Tokyo did we dare breathe a sigh of relief. For the first time, we allowed ourselves to contemplate what the future might bring.

It took us a few years to settle in Australia. After some months in Melbourne my husband found work and we were happy to just watch our daughter grow away from war and political persecution. However, the strong emotional connection we felt to Iran remained.

My recent experiences in Iran made me realize that the politicization of women called for attention to their life experience. This led me to shift my political focus from mainstream political activism to 'grass roots' politics. I became interested in community work and on my daughter's first day of school, I began a two-year degree in Social Work at Monash University. At times I couldn't help but sigh with grief when I compared the discussions about clients and human rights in Australia with the violation of human rights back in my country.

After I graduated in 1989 we moved to Perth. I found employment as a community worker, providing support services and advocacy for Iranian migrants and refugees. Given my professional skills and my personal passion, this sounded like an ideal job. However, being effective in this work environment presented some challenges. Although I was Iranian, I was also educated, a woman and a newcomer to Perth. I was considered a leftist, but I also wanted to be me. I left my country to escape the constraints on individual freedoms imposed by political and cultural ideologies that didn't allow me to freely express myself as a woman. Now I was being compelled to respect some of those cultural constraints, in order to function in my job.

I found myself wanting to give the Iranians here all those things that I thought they deserved back home. I threw myself into the work with my whole heart and soul. There was a pressing need for health programs such as stress management, building self-esteem, understanding issues like domestic violence, and generally getting settled in Australia.

During this time my husband and I were also active in the Iranian community. Many of us expressed a need to get to know ourselves as Iranians. The years and years of repression back home meant that we never had the opportunity to openly examine ourselves. So a group of us came up with the idea of establishing a library. We called it a cultural centre because we wanted it to be more than simply a place where people borrowed books. We also wanted to be able to meet and talk in our own language and get the news from home. We wanted to model the centre on democratic principles, where regardless of political affiliations everyone would be given the chance to talk and express their views. It was a great idea. We received funds to buy books and together with personal donations of books from many families we created a proper library system. For several years the centre opened every Saturday at Mt Lawley Primary School.

Four years passed and to the outside world I was at the peak of my public achievement. The cultural festival I had just organized was a huge success. I received great feedback and many expressions of appreciation. Personally, however, there were many things left undone. Over the years I had put great effort into the wellbeing of others, but neglected my own needs. I see now that I was motivated by a tremendous sense of loss and guilt for abandoning the struggle at home. I felt that as I was now safe I should give something back. I was trying to rebuild my shattered dreams for Iran in Perth. I thought if I could give the community what had been missing in Iran they would be happy. I became everything for everybody – the good Iranian woman, the martyr and the saviour. My public self overtook my private self and I ignored my personal life.

By the time I arrived in Australia my sense of self was very vulnerable. My experiences in Perth as a community worker and subsequently as the Coordinator of Gosnells Women's Health Service, taught me a long hard lesson: if you want to do something good for somebody, you don't do it in their way, you do it on your own terms. Unless you look to yourself first, you run the risk of at best overextending or at worse totally neglecting yourself. Either way you end up losing. I started to conserve my thoughts and desires in order to survive.

I learnt a lot about myself working in the Iranian community. Among other things it gave me an opportunity to revisit my culture. I had almost totally ignored my Iranian culture until then and I found out that there was much I could embrace, aspects which were humane. Many cultural traditions which I had rejected in Iran had a different value here and I gave myself permission to enjoy them. Our motivation for coming to Australia was to create a better life for our daughter and I believe we have provided her with that opportunity, although I now know we cannot do it for her.

Currently I am working in the health sector counselling individuals and groups and I am enjoying it very much. I find that knowing my own boundaries is personally liberating. I'm not working to achieve recognition and power — I'm free.

I believe everybody's interest in politics initially stems from a basic thirst for freedom. You want to feel free as an individual to begin with, that's what pushes you. For some this journey of survival leads into mainstream political activism while others struggle on their own. Whatever route you take, the journey teaches you that unless you are free within yourself, you cannot free others. That's the experience I have had, and I know many Iranian women back home are continuing on this journey.

1 Forough Farrokh-Zad (1935–1967) began writing at sixteen and by twenty-five had written three volumes of poetry, *Prisoner*, *The Wall* and *Rebellion*, which established her as one of the most promising Persian poets of her time.
2 Iranian National Security and Intelligence Organisation at that time.

IT'S ALL IN THE UNFOLDING

VERONICA BRADY

Veronica Brady is a Roman Catholic nun, a member of the Loreto order. She taught for many years in the Department of English at The University of Western Australia. Since retiring, she has been an honorary Senior Research Fellow. As a member of a community of women she has always been interested in women's issues, seeing them as part of the wider concern for justice which in her view any intelligent and caring person in this country should entertain. She has been involved in public affairs as a member of the Appeals Tribunal of the Department of Social Security, the board of the ABC, the board of the Library and Information Service of Western Australia, and in other organizations, like Outcare. She has also published widely in the areas of Australian literature, culture and belief. Veronica believes passionately in the need for us all to learn more about Aboriginal people and their culture and history, and to work for justice and understanding between us all. Her most recent books are *Caught in the Draft*, *Shall These Bones Live*, and *South of My Days*.

One of my favourite poems is Rosemary Dobson's 'Folding the Sheets'.[1] Amongst other things it is about the way women know that existence is relational, that we need to play back to one another, cooperate rather than compete (to put it simply and a little crudely). We know — at least I have always thought we do — that living properly has to do with weaving and unweaving, a rhythmic to and fro, a dance, if you like, in which we are played upon as well as players.

    I don't see my life and my career so much as something I have consciously made and shaped as a kind of listening, following possibilities as they unfolded. These promptings sometimes coming from outside and sometimes from within. In a sense, I suppose, I have always been on the side of the poet rather than the historian (if you take Aristotle's distinction that the historian is concerned with what has happened and the poet with what may happen). Looking back over her life the historian would try to be objective and disinterested and try to make sense of it in that way. But the poet is involved in it still, she is part of what has happened, is happening and may yet happen. What is still unfolding.

The unfolding, for me, begins with the practical. Even as a child I wanted to be a teacher, and I have spent most of my life in that profession. But teaching, I believe, involves a kind of leadership which has to do with sharing, listening and empowering, enabling people to discover who they are, where they want to go and how they should get there. It is not, in my view anyway, really about ordering people about or telling them what to do. Indeed, my favourite image of the teacher is of a gardener: she finds the seed already there, plants, waters and manures it, and weeds and perhaps prunes the plant as it grows, but essentially her task is to liberate the life it already contains. I would like to think the kind of leadership I have given has been of that kind.

But I think there is also something more. The world view I happen to believe in is, I hope, rather different from the one which seems to govern most people in power in our society. I happen to believe that its preoccupation with what D.H. Lawrence called the 'business of money making, money-having and money-spending' is foolish and destructive, dangerous not only to people but the world we live in. As a human being, a teacher and a citizen, I have spent most of my life reflecting on this and trying to contest what I regard as this madness. That, too, is an aspect of leadership which is surely as much about ideas and values as about getting things done — leadership, after all, like beauty, is in the eye of the beholder. But how did I get like this?

In childhood I would go off by myself into the garden, climbing to the top of an old Norfolk pine and looking out across the roofs to Port Phillip Bay in the distance or up at the clouds or lying outside at night and looking up at the stars. I have always had a sense of mystery, unknown, of some reality beyond my own projections, which nevertheless leaves its trace on them, a reality that can be subversive and can interrupt my plans in a way that is both painful and pleasurable since it calls me to go further, to challenge the pain of things in the name of a love, justice and understanding which it is our responsibility to achieve. I was also fortunate to have parents who obviously got on well together and loved me and my sister, making me feel that I was the centre of their world, if not the world — that was a lot more problematic if you first came to consciousness, as I did, during the Great Depression and went to school during the Second World War.

They were also intelligent, educated Catholics, not in the slightest fanatical. But I grew up within a tradition of belief. Looking at the lemon tree in the backyard when I was very small, for example, after I had heard the story of God creating Adam from the 'dust of the earth', I wondered whether it would turn into a human being if I threw dust over it (the implicit assumption that I might be able to do what God could do is an interesting one!). The point is, however, that I had a place in a world of myth as well as of matter of fact. I was also fortunate enough to be intelligent and imaginative and to live in a house full of books where ideas were discussed. My father, who married late, had travelled before he settled down so I also had a sense of the larger world beyond Australia.

Someone who feels confident in herself and in her place in the world like this is, I suppose, fortunate, possibly unusual, and may affect others for this reason. I was lucky enough to be at the University of Melbourne just after the Second World War, when most of the students were men — I wasn't aware of any 'returned' women — who had survived the war, mature age students who knew where they were going and who were, many of them, concerned to make a better world. The teachers I had at that time, too, in particular Max Crawford, Ian Maxwell, MacMahon Ball and Norman Harper, taught me to think, to question and to take a larger view. But I also still had a sense of being called to 'follow the dream', to try to explore the mystery I was aware of from time to time, in my friendships as well as in what I was thinking and seeing around me.

Being a nun did not seem a very attractive thing to do but it was what I thought I ought to do. So I joined a teaching order founded by a remarkable seventeenth-century English woman, May Ward, who believed that women were not inferior to men and wanted her sisters to live according to the Jesuit rule: not enclosed, not wearing special uniform, but free to move about at the service of others as teachers and scholars — for which belief she spent some time in a prison of the Inquisition. But her community and her vision survived, even if it had to go underground for a time.

Then in the late 1960s I was sent to do my doctorate at the University of Toronto. On the way there I spent a week or so in Los Angeles, not long after the Watts riots. I found the racist mood pretty ugly but when I criticized the whites someone asked me what right I, an Australian, had to do so since we treated our Aboriginal peoples so badly. This gave me something to think about. So, too, did the Civil Rights movement, which I saw at first hand when I spent a semester at the University of Chicago, as well as opposition to the Vietnam War. Toronto brought that home to me personally since several of my fellow students were young Americans who had been allowed to defer their call-up to undertake graduate work. But they had to keep up a 'B' average. Three of them did not and were drafted; one of them, I know, was killed.

That kind of experience gave me a different view of the Vietnam War which many Australians supported. So, too, did watching the television news every night and seeing villages razed to the ground, women, children and old people killed or maimed, and farmlands and forests devastated.

When I came back to Australia, however, many people still supported the war, arguing that otherwise 'communism would take over the world'. But it seemed to me that one of the main reasons why people were turning to communism was poverty. The war was creating poverty and was hardly an advertisement for 'democracy', so in my view it was probably creating more Communists. If anything was 'taking over the world', it seemed to me to be American-style violence: high-tech and impersonal.

Just as important was my discovery one winter afternoon in the library of the University of Chicago of the writings of Dietrich

Bonhoeffer, a German theologian who had opposed Nazism from the start. Although he was a pacifist, Bonhoeffer had joined the group of army generals and others who had tried to assassinate Hitler in 1943, and after some time in a concentration camp was executed for treason. His insistence that being a Christian does not mean living on the fringes of society in some kind of religious enclose affected me powerfully. Faith did not just offer comfort and consolation, is not just a cosmic Linus blanket by which we try to cling to security or control all around us; it belongs to the centre of things and obliges one to act whenever human dignity, freedom and hope are threatened.

Not long after I returned to Australia I got a job as a tutor in English at The University of Western Australia where I have been ever since. Perhaps because of these experiences, or because of my beliefs, or even because my father had been something of a social critic, I found myself speaking out on a range of issues here in Western Australia: attacks on trade unions, uranium mining and the visits of nuclear-powered warships, the destruction of our native forests and, above all, the continuing oppression of Aboriginal Australians whose land we took from them by force and without compensation and whose culture we so profoundly misunderstand.

It seems to me part of the task of an academic is to ask questions, and part of the task of a Christian is to interrogate injustice. In our kind of society information is both the source and stuff of power. Yet by and large only a small group of people define and control what we mean by information, decide which 'facts' and opinions we will have access to and often suggest how we should react to them. This can be a form of tyranny as absolute as any in the past, perhaps more so since it involves control from within rather than merely from without. Moreover, some of these 'facts' may be fiction. One of Salman Rushdie's characters, the wonderfully named Alleluia Cone, described it this way, perhaps or perhaps not with a certain exaggeration:

> Information got abolished some time in the twentieth century ... Since then we have been living in a fairy story.

> Everything happens by magic. Us fairies haven't a fucking notion what's going on. So how do we know if it is right or wrong. We don't even know what 'it' is.[2]

Helping people question what they are told, especially by those who stand to gain by persuading them to accept it, and to find things out for themselves, seem to me an essential part of being a teacher, especially a teacher in a university. So, too, is interrogating the values which are generally accepted. This can be regarded as subversive, of course. But a society which does not ask questions about itself is likely to become repressive. It is also unlikely to be able to meet the challenges of the rapidly changing world in which we live. Being a leader, I think, means helping others make decisions which make their lives, the lives of others and the life of the planet richer, more just, compassionate, loving and hopeful.

That, I suppose, is why women have tried to do just this. True, I have not *done* much, but thinking, talking and writing matter too. The most potent force in the world is surely the power to imagine things differently, and for that we need to have some kind of vision of what the world is and what it might be, a vision which is in tune with what is actually the case. It seems to me that the hairy-chested individualism which believes it owes nothing to anyone or anything, the passion for money and possessions, the power which defines itself in terms of mere physical energy, the determination to satisfy one's desires at whatever cost, all of these things are out of touch with what is actually the case.

I believe that we need to recover a sense of the splendours and challenges of existence, the poetry of things. For me life is open, not closed; we are all mortal — something technology tends to ignore — vulnerable and surrounded by mystery, out of our depth in the ocean of being. That, I think, means, in the words of Conrad's Stein, we need to 'follow the dream, follow the dream, right to the end'. French feminist author Hélène Cixous puts it more romantically, so let us end with her words:

> I see above my head the meaning of my whole story. A single night separates me from it. I try to cross it. I hold

out my hands. I have it at my fingertips. My star that has no name! my secret is no bigger than a hazelnut of eternity.[3]

1 Rosemary Dobson, *The Three Fates*, Hale and Iremonger, Sydney, 1984, p. 23.
2 Salman Rushdie, *The Satanic Verses*, Viking, London, 1988, p. 313.
3 Graham Ward, 'Words of Life: Hustling Post-Modern Plenitude', *The Way*, Vol. 36, No. 3, July 1996, p. 231.

TRANSFORMATIVE MOMENTS

ANNIE GOLDFLAM

Annie is the Director of the Centre for Research for Women, a joint initiative of the four public universities in Western Australia. Born in 1955 in Melbourne, she moved to Perth as a young girl. Graduating from The University of Western Australia with an honours degree in Psychology in 1976, she worked as an Australian Volunteer Abroad in Papua New Guinea and Indonesia for five years before returning to Perth. Annie has worked in the public, community and private sectors in a variety of positions covering teaching, training, community development, research and project management. Much of her work has been cross-cultural with people of diverse backgrounds. Besides her paid work Annie is involved with a number of community groups which focus on women's issues, cultural diversity, global development and lesbian issues. The key influences and mentors of her adult life include Joan Carlin, Thea Mendelsohn, Pat Giles and Bev Thiele.

In the 1970s feminism was firmly based on subverting the patriarchy, dismantling hierarchies and working collectively. Now I have been asked to consider the ways in which I have been a 'leader'. For me, that term is most commonly imbued with connotations of 'power over' rather than 'power with'. I therefore look over my shoulder when I stand up, step forward and speak out. Will I be accused of emulating male power structures? Will my 'sisters' try to pull me down? When I act politically in the public arena I often feel as if I am walking a tightrope. Will radical women condemn me for being too conservative? Will conservative women condemn me for being too radical? And what will men think? I have always encouraged other women to walk alongside me, but that is not possible on a tightrope; someone has to take those first tentative steps.

When I was a public servant, I went abseiling as part of a team-building exercise. Two male colleagues were instructing and anchoring us. The call went up for the first person to descend. I was petrified. I looked at the women and saw my abject fear reflected in their faces. I was determined that a woman would lead the way. So, over the cliff I went, urging my sisters to follow. My passion for feminism was stronger than my fear of falling.

My feelings about the concept of leadership are ambivalent. As feminists, I believe we need to reclaim the term and use it in a way in which we feel comfortable. Management 'experts' are beginning to recognize the qualities of 'feminine leadership': leading within a participatory, flat structure; managing the personal as well as the professional; mentoring others; and operating from a holistic perspective. Too often, this rhetoric only restates traditional management approaches under a different name. In taking on genuinely feminist leadership roles, we are challenging the foundations of patriarchal structures.

For more than a decade I have found the space and means to work within a feminist framework. I feel very fortunate. By maintaining part-time jobs and a part-time consultancy for thirteen years, I can pick up work, paid and unpaid, which is consistent with my commitment to social justice. As a consultant and unpaid worker I can afford to be discerning about the work that I do. My greatest challenge is balancing my paid/unpaid, public/private and work/leisure commitments. Because I enjoy most of the work I do, I have a tendency to overcommit myself. As a woman with no children I sometimes feel guilty as I wonder at the ability and stamina of mothers who maintain multiple careers.

Whether I am working publicly or privately, I strive to operate from a community development approach. In working alongside people in the community, I aim to gain insight into their worlds, listen to their needs, link them with available resources and ensure that I do not take their power away in my boundless enthusiasm for everything to be put right. I am an avid networker. I keep my ear to the ground and revel in liberating resources which have been withheld from those most in need. This form of leadership is much more in tune with my politics than the 'malestream'[1] notion we have been conditioned to accept as 'normal'. I also strive to lead alongside the people I work with, by maintaining reciprocal relationships with my colleagues. Good 'leaders' share information and opportunities and listen and respond to people's needs, irrespective of their assigned status within an organization. I owe an enormous debt to the women who have acted as mentors to me over the years in various ways.

My journey towards becoming a feminist activist has been winding but determined. I was brought up in the 1950s, in a household with clearly defined domestic gender roles. My mother, however, had been a pioneering female science student at The University of Western Australia, so I thought that it was perfectly natural for me to study two mathematics and two science subjects for my matriculation. As a consequence, I spent much of my senior high school years in male-dominated classes. I have never lacked a voice and I started using it politically in high school, lobbying for the right for female students to have the choice of wearing trousers rather than pleated skirts. Reading *The Female Eunuch*[2] in my final year at high school was *naturally* a transformative moment, despite the fact that my understanding of feminist issues was patchy and somewhat inconsistent. I increased my awareness a little at university, although I was much more absorbed with studying, socializing and experimenting with my new-found freedoms.

After university, as an Australian Volunteer Abroad, I had some daunting experiences in dealing with gender and leadership issues in cross-cultural settings. In the early 1980s, as a secondary school teacher in the Papua New Guinean highlands, I was the form teacher of an all girls class. This was a unique experiment in a schooling system where only 10 per cent of secondary students were female. Being in my early twenties and unenlightened about feminist research, I was opposed to the idea of single-sex classes. I believed that Papua New Guinean women would have to learn how to be with men as adults and that these lessons should start in school. Furthermore, I worried that my class would lack the spark and imagination of the boys, whom I had found so much more active and engaging to teach.

As I had no choice my thirty-eight students and I set off together. We had fabulous times. These young women found their voices and discussed wide-ranging issues with me, including how they were torn between the relatively western environment of school and the traditional setting of their villages. My students invariably won awards for classroom inspections. They put fresh flowers in old jars and kept our battered weatherboard haven immaculate. Then an English male colleague suggested that we have a debating competition. The young women from my class thrashed the male opposition. We experienced a backlash less subtle than Susan Faludi's version. Our classroom was trashed. The assailants smashed our makeshift vases, tore up all the work on the walls and defecated on the furniture. We were shocked and humiliated, but we persisted in our journey together. I sometimes wonder what has become of those thirty-eight young women. Are they fulfilling leadership roles as adult women?

The biggest dilemma that I faced in writing this chapter was whether to be open about my sexual preference. As women, we learn to censor ourselves in many ways to protect our safety and avoid embarrassment and rejection. As lesbians, we learn to be doubly watchful. My lesbianism is not just 'what I do in bed'. It is a crucial aspect of my identity, an aspect which many people would prefer that I hid. I receive subtle, and sometimes not so subtle, messages that I will be acceptable only as long as I refrain from mentioning 'that stuff'.

Although few people knew the term forty years ago, 'lesbian' is now too often a word of abuse, one that immature boys hurl at girls in the school yard, and immature men hurl at feminists of all kinds. Hughes et al. write: 'Women who are independent, assertive, articulate — regardless of their actual, social, emotional or sexual lives — have, at some point in their lives, been called lesbians'.[3] Considering the power of this weapon when it is used against feminists, imagine how it makes actual lesbians feel, especially those who maintain 'closeted' lifestyles. Consequently, much of the crucial work that lesbians do in a range of social justice organizations is not acknowledged as such.

The enforced closet is a pernicious oppression. So few lesbians feel safe to be open — with their family, in their workplace, to their neighbours, with their heterosexual friends or *especially* within publications such as this! Enforced invisibility eats away at our self-esteem, confidence and sense of safety. The biggest oppression for me would be the 'glass closet', desperately trying to hide my identity all the time, wondering whether anyone suspected, whilst others perhaps knew about my lesbianism, but did not dare to broach the issue.

So much progress would flow from lesbians having the space to be seen and heard as we really are, in our full numbers. I have chosen the path of being an activist, feminist lesbian and I encourage other lesbians to walk proudly alongside me. I do not judge women who choose to remain closeted, however. Each of us needs to weigh the risks and benefits of being 'out'. My journey has taken me on some fascinating adventures.

On my return from Papua New Guinea, I shared house with a woman who was known as a 'radical feminist', a term which I later realized had been used as a euphemism for lesbian. After being in denial for some months I had to acknowledge that I was, indeed, sharing house with a lesbian. As time progressed I gradually recognized that I preferred women as sexual partners. It was an exciting time for me. In rejecting the heterosexual conditioning I had been subjected to, I became increasingly politically aware of a range of social justice issues.

Leadership, for me, is about standing up for what I believe in. I learnt about community activism through my active participation in groups such as Community Aid Abroad, the Women's Electoral Lobby, the Australian Association of Adult and Community Education, West Australians for Racial Equality, the Migrant Women's Interest Group, the Multicultural Women's Health Centre, the Jewish Lesbian group, and collectives organizing International Women's Day, Reclaim the Night,[4] Burning Down the House[5] and lesbian dances. I will relate some of my experiences involving leadership issues. They illustrate transformative moments, for myself and/or the broader community.

In the late 1980s, I took on the task of liaising with authorities for the organization of a Reclaim the Night rally. I dutifully wrote to Perth City Council and the Police Department for permission to hold the Reclaim the Night march through the streets of Northbridge, the main centre of Perth's nightlife and a particularly dangerous place for women. This was the route we had followed for several years. Receiving no reply from the police, I phoned the relevant officer. He tried to convince me to hold the Reclaim the Night march during the *day*. A night march, he maintained, would not be safe for women and children! He also urged me to relocate the rally to the Esplanade, a 'safe' place on the other side of the city. I reiterated the rationale for the march in a non-confrontationist and patient way, thereby gradually reclaiming our right to march when and where we wanted to. After forty-five minutes, he reluctantly agreed. I think the police were becoming nervous as our rallies were attracting increasing numbers of women and children from a range of backgrounds. The police would have preferred to portray us as passive and vulnerable, locked away in our homes, rather than as powerful women who were confronting the issue of violence by coming out en masse, on the streets at night. This incident was a transformative moment for me as I realized I had the power to stand firm against a police officer's prejudiced and faulty understanding, thereby keeping the Reclaim the Night march on track.

In 1991 I was invited to facilitate a workshop, 'Women Combating Racism', at the Derby Women's Conference. Derby, a town in the Kimberley region of Western Australia, has a high percentage of Aboriginal people. I planned to run a sixty-minute simulation activity. When I checked the schedule for my workshop venue I discovered it was to be held under a tree. Clasping butcher's paper, pens and other paraphernalia, I went to wait in the shade. To my excitement I saw droves of tribal Aboriginal and non-Aboriginal women converging upon the tree. Until that time I had observed that the Aboriginal and non-Aboriginal women were not really mixing in workshop sessions. I quickly reassessed my plan to use the simulation activity as it required advanced literacy skills in English. I chose instead to assign the women to mixed groups to discuss their experiences and understandings of racism. Several of the rich stories the women told were recorded by a local radio station. The strength, openness and courage of the women at that workshop resulted in a powerful learning experience and a transformative moment for us all.

I was recently at a party where the guest of honour was a prominent African feminist. She heard someone refer to me as a lesbian, sat bolt upright and asked incredulously whether I actually was one. She had only had one (negative) encounter with lesbians and harboured many prejudiced myths, which she proceeded to voice: 'Why do you all try to look like men? Are you ashamed of being women? How can you possibly be religious, with what the bible says about lesbians? What's wrong with you? Have men been rough with you? Why do you only want to be with other lesbians? It's so divisive for the women's movement. What about your maternal instincts? Don't you want to be a mother?'

I felt shocked and dismayed by these questions, partly because I knew that this woman was actually voicing the covert attitudes of many Australians. I understood how important it was to deal with her prejudices assertively. I braced myself and thought keenly about how best to deal with the situation.

This was the ideal environment in which to attempt to shift this highly influential woman's views. She was in a safe place and keen to discuss lesbianism. She acknowledged that her questions were 'basic'. Half-a-dozen of us talked with her for two hours, striving to be frank, assertive and non-confrontationist. I perceived her attitudes softening gradually as she connected with the two lesbians in the group and began to see us as feminists and allies, as well as lesbians, but not in the stereotypical mould. We would *never* have been able to gain a formal audience with this woman to lobby her on lesbian issues. Transformative moments often depend on synchronicity and timely activism.

In 1995 I stood on the steps of the Western Australian Parliament House, speaking at a demonstration for lesbian and gay rights. We were lobbying the State Government to amend the *Equal Opportunity Act 1984* to include protection on the grounds of sexual preference. Holding onto the microphone, I felt euphoric but nervous. The crowd cheered as I called to the politicians inside Parliament House, urging them to front up. The atmosphere was charged with energy and determination and I was right in there. My rights as a lesbian had been denied, but I could still demonstrate.

I look back now on the extended campaign we ran on the *Equal Opportunity Act 1984*. Many people would say that we lost because the Act remains unchanged. We did make gains, however. Our campaign attracted mainstream media attention which largely portrayed the anti-lesbian/gay stance as irrational and judgemental. We changed the minds of some right-wing politicians and chipped away at community resistance to lesbians, gays and transsexuals gaining equal rights. We have not given up. Political activism requires perseverance and strength and the lesbian/gay community has both. As with many transformative moments, this one needs to be seen within a broader temporal and political context. We need to monitor the ebb and flow of attitudes towards lesbians and deal with issues promptly, assertively and persistently.

It is crucial that we, as women, avoid the trap of believing that we are powerless and cannot effect change. Our actions, large and small, have consequences. When we realize that we can be agents of social change then we unleash an abundance of creativity and power. As the black women of South Africa say: 'You strike the woman — you strike the rock'.

---

1   Mary O'Brien coined this term to suggest the normalization of male-centred thought in *The Politics of Reproduction*, Routledge and Kegan Paul, Boston, 1984.
2   Germaine Greer, *The Female Eunuch*, Paladin, London, 1971.
3   Nym Hughes, Yvonne Johnson and Yvette Perreault, *Stepping Out of Line: A Workbook on Lesbianism and Feminism*, Press Gang Publishers, Canada, 1984, p. 139.
4   An annual rally designed to protest against rape and violence perpetrated against women and children.
5   A feminist talk show on RTR FM, a Perth community radio station.

SUGGESTIONS FOR FURTHER READING

If you have enjoyed the stories in our collection, the following is a guide to some other works which have traced women's contributions to Australian life during recent decades.

Bulbeck, Chilla, *Australian Women in Papua New Guinea*, Cambridge University Press, Cambridge, 1992.
> An evocative and compelling account of the experiences of white women in Papua New Guinea between the 1920s and the 1960s. Based on oral reminiscences and the written records of nineteen women whose lives are situated against a backdrop of official colonial affairs.

Bulbeck, Chilla, *Living Feminism: Impact of the Women's Movement on Three Generations of Australian Women*, Cambridge University Press, Cambridge, 1997.
> Three generations of women from various ethnic backgrounds, from cities and the country, tell their stories. Partly a history of feminism, the book also unflinchingly considers whether feminism is only relevant to white, university-educated, middle-class women.

Cleland, Rachel, *Grass Roots to Independence and Beyond: The Contribution by Women in Papua New Guinea*, Dame Rachel Cleland, Claremont, 1996.
> An entertaining insight into the life and times of women in a developing territory on Australia's doorstep. Looks at the role of individuals and community organizations during a time of social, economic and cultural upheaval in Papua New Guinea. Details the contribution of many notable women working for future generations in independent PNG.

Cope, Bill and Mary Kalantzis, *Productive Diversity: A New Australian Model for Work and Management*, Pluto Press Australia Ltd, Annandale, 1997.
> Emphasizes a collaborative approach to Australia's diverse and multicultural workforce. Provides a new model for managing local and international work practices and business relations.

Cox, Eva, *Leading Women*, Random House Australia, Sydney, 1996.
> Based on Eva's considerable experience in the workforce and as observer and participant in many key debates about social policy, feminism and power. The narrative covers much more than the problems inherent in masculine leadership models. It also takes a look at the attitudes and behaviour of women and challenges all those unhappy with their present leaders, women and men alike, to initiate change and become leaders themselves.

Eisenstein, Hester, *Inside Agitators*, Allen & Unwin, Sydney, 1990.
> A former 'femocrat', Hester Eisenstein tells the story of a group of Australian feminists who set out to create a woman-friendly state. Drawing on first-hand accounts she shows how women used state power as an instrument for social change. Analysing the unique achievements of Australian femocrats, as well as the obstacles they faced, she reviews how the reforms these women agitated for have fared in the face of the recent conservative backlash.

Gale, Fay (ed.), *We Are Bosses Ourselves: The Status and Role of Aboriginal Women Today*, Australian Institute of Aboriginal Studies, Canberra, 1983.
> Traditionally, white society looks on Aboriginal women as victims of a patriarchal culture. What this book shows is the power of Aboriginal women, and the powerful positions they hold in their traditional communities. Contributors include: Catherine Berndt, Marlene Chesson, Helen Boyle, Annie Isaac and Doreen Kartinyeri.

Gardiner, Jane (ed), *Here We Come Ready or Not!* Women into Politics, Sydney, 1998.
> As a consequence of women's under-representation at all levels of decision-making in Australian public life, contributors in this book propose that women change the thrust of their political lobbying for social, health and educational services from relying on the good will of powerful men to working for legally guaranteed social, economic and political rights. Women such as Sue Walpole, Elizabeth Evatt and Marian Sawer present us with a vision for the future and provide a proactive platform for the present.

Grimshaw, Patricia and Lynne Strahan (eds), *The Half Open Door*, Hale and Iremonger Pty Ltd, Sydney, 1982.
> At a time when personal histories generally reflected men's lives, Patricia Grimshaw and Lynne Strahan asked women at the University of Melbourne who read art, law, literature, music, teaching and medicine to write about their lives and their formative experiences between the 1920s and 1940s. Contributors talk about the pressure exerted by religion, education, sexuality and domestic life and about the men who helped and hindered them.

Hearne, Karen, Joanne Travaglia and Elizabeth Weiss (eds), *Who Do You Think You Are? Second Generation Immigrant Women in Australia*, Women's Redress Press Inc, Broadway, 1992.
> Contributors, including Eva Cox, recount their stories of growing up in Australia as the children of immigrants and what that experience of being in a social minority, as women, has meant for their social lives, customs and social conditions.

Huggins, Rita and Jackie Huggins, *Aunty Rita*, Aboriginal Studies Press, Canberra, 1994.
> 'Auntie' is a term of respect for older Aboriginal women. It stands for an expression of kinship which does not rely on blood ties, and a sense of community which ensures that no-one is ever truly alone, that there will always be someone to turn to. Stolen from her country as a child in the 1920s, Rita Huggins relates her memories to her daughter Jackie. We witness their intimacy, their similarities and their differences, the 'fighting with their tongues'. Two voices, two views on a shared life.

Mitchell, Susan, *Tall Poppies*, Penguin Books Australia Ltd, Ringwood, 1984.
> Mitchell explores how women become successful. She talks to nine women from diverse backgrounds in business, media, community and policy-forming organizations. Their personal and professional accounts about the narrow rocky road to success reveal the secrets behind their public lives and the many painful and difficult choices they had to make along the way.

Mitchell, Susan, *Icons, Saints and Divas*, Harper Collins, Sydney, 1997.
> The women in this book are the scribes, the catalysts and pioneers of a social revolution which generated the most dramatic and long-lasting changes to our lives that we have witnessed in the latter part of this century. Intimate conversations with a number of great postwar feminist writers, including Susan Faludi, Erica Jong, Kate Millett and Gloria Steinem, reveal the frank accounts of these wives, mothers, lovers and trail blazers and their undaunting belief in the power of words which has inspired us all to stretch the boundaries of possibility.

MumShirl, with the assistance of Bobbi Sykes, *MumShirl*, Heinemann Publishers Australia Pty Ltd, Richmond, 1981.
> An inspiring story of hope, love, spirit and struggle set in the outer suburbs of Sydney and rural New South Wales. Issues of survival in Aboriginal social welfare and social justice.

Sawer, Marian, *Sisters in Suits: Women and Public Policy*, Angus & Robertson, Sydney, 1985.
> Draws on extensive interviews with women who 'went into government' to describe how Australian feminists took advantage of opportunities presented in the 1970s and 1980s to make inroads into the bureaucracy.

Sawer analyses the bureaucratic and gender politics involved, as well as the relationship between the 'femocrats' and the women's movement outside.

Scutt, Jocelynne A., *Growing Up Feminist: The New Generation of Australian Women*, Penguin Books Australia Ltd, Ringwood, 1984.
> Ten young women aged between sixteen and twenty-four talk about their upbringing and experiences and how they evolved their own feminist doctrines in sometimes hostile and obstructive, sometimes supportive, environments. The views, ideals and goals they express give a very personal insight into the lives of contemporary women.

Scutt, Jocelynne A., *Living Generously: Women Mentoring Women*, Artemis Publishing Pty Ltd, Melbourne, 1996.
> Twenty-five personal accounts of women who have been encouraged by the generous support of other women. For some this support marked a turning point in their lives. For others, having a network of supportive women meant survival both in their public and private lives. Contributors include Joan Kirner, Natasha Stott Despoja, Val Marsden, Mary Owen, Kay Saunders and Carmel Guerra.

Sinclair, Amanda, *Doing Leadership Differently: Gender, Power and Sexuality in a Changing Business Culture*, Melbourne University Press, Carlton South, Victoria, 1998.
> Argues that Australian organizations are clinging to an outdated concept of leadership. Draws on interviews with senior executives, male and female, to show why our faith in this traditional style is so strong — and so misplaced. Offers a challenging and original analysis of why the traditional style of leadership has failed and details how men and women can benefit from understanding how gender shapes leadership styles.

Sykes, Roberta B., *Murawina*, Doubleday, Moorebank, 1993.
> A collection of very powerful life stories. They give us an insight into how life has been, and is now, for Australian women in general and Aboriginal or Torres Strait Islander women in particular. Contributors include Mary Ann Bin-Sallik, Joan Winch, Pat O'Shane, Tracey Moffatt, Oodgeroo Noonuccal, Marcia Langton, Andrea Collins.

Watson, Judyth, *We Hold Up Half the Sky*, Australian Labor Party (WA Branch), Perth, 1994.
> Demonstrates the need for equal representation of men and women in Federal Parliament and State parliaments throughout Australia, using the medium of Hansard recorded speeches of West Australian female parliamentarians. Starts with May Holman (1925) and ends with women MPs elected in 1993. Insight into the passions and focus of female politicians, the impact they have had on the political system and the response they have elicited from their male contemporaries.

Williams, Justina, *White River*, Fremantle Arts Centre Press, Fremantle, 1979.
> This collection of short stories is drawn from a wide range of experience in journalism, local government, politics and women's interests.

Williams, Justina, *Anger & Love*, Fremantle Arts Centre Press, Fremantle, 1993.
> Against a background of national and international events a turbulent and eventful life struggles for social justice and women's equality. This life of few regrets is told with compassion and hope for the future.